PICASSO'S WOMEN

ROY MAC GREGOR-HASTIE

Lennard Publishing
1988

This book is dedicated to the memory of
Tristan Tzara (1895–1964)

poet, trouble-maker, founder of Dadaism
and inspiration of much else, who was
my guide, philosopher and friend. He encouraged
me to translate his and other
Romanian poetry and condemned me to a
quarter of a century wrestling with UNESCO.
He was an almost bottomless pit from which
I mined Picasso tales, long before I thought
of writing this book.

Lennard Publishing
a division of Lennard Books Ltd

Lennard House
92 Hastings Street
Luton, Beds LU1 5BH

British Library in Publication Data

MacGregor-Hastie, Roy
    Picasso's women.
    1. Women associated with Picasso, Pablo,
    1881–1973
    I. Title
    759.6

    ISBN 1–82591–013–5

First published 1988
© Roy MacGregor-Hastie 1988

Phototypeset in Linotron Garamond
by Input Typesetting Ltd, London

Cover design by Pocknell and Co.

Reproduced, printed and bound in Great Britain by
Butler and Tanner Ltd.,
Frome and London

Contents

Introduction

'There were five factors that determined his way of life and likewise his style: the woman with whom he was in love; the poet, or poets, who served as a catalyst; the place where he lived; the circle of friends who provided the admiration and understanding of which he never had enough; and the dog who was his inseparable companion and sometimes figured in the iconography of his work. On occasion these factors overlapped . . . . . . [but] as a rule, when the wife or mistress changed, everything else changed.'

(Dora Maar to John Richardson,
from *New York Review of Books*
17 July, 1980)

On Friday, 17 October, 1986, I went to the rather depressing funeral of Picasso's widow, Jacqueline, at the Château de Vauvenargues. Picasso himself had taken a dislike to the place a decade before his death in 1973, but he had willed his burial there and had asked that a place be left for Jacqueline in his little mausoleum.

At the funeral, there were some friends, but not many local dignitaries—Picasso had offended the priest and mayor by removing the remains of Saint Séverin from the (ruined) castle chapel and walling it up as unsafe. The State was represented by the vultures who had fallen on the painter's effects and enriched lawyers for four years before a settlement of death duties was reached; they were led by Laudet (Conservateur des Musées de France), hoping perhaps to discover some undeclared works. The most sociable, and most moved, of all the mourners present was the Spanish caretaker, Ribero; he told me that Jacqueline had kept her promise not only never to sell anything, but also to buy back those of her late husband's pictures she felt had fallen into the wrong hands.

Sra Occana, curator of the Picasso Museum in Barcelona, was worried that her forthcoming exhibition (and one at Barcelona's sister city in Japan, Kobe) might not take place as the State had sealed up the rooms at the castle and those at the farmhouse at Mougins (ironically known as Notre Dame de la Vie) where Jacqueline had taken her life.

By chance, I was on my way to Avignon (to the International Eminescu Conference) and so I was able to look up two of the people who knew Picasso best towards the end of his life—Mario Atzinger, who had the exclusive right to photograph his last exhibitions (and who lives in two boxlike rooms next to a treasure house of negatives) and Nelly Ruaux of the Conseil Culturel, whose late husband had set up the posthumous exhibition of Picasso's works.

It would be wrong to call them 'friends'. For most of his life, Picasso had very few close friends. He treated most people abominably, male and female alike. He borrowed money freely when he was poor, at the beginning of the century, and refused to lend any when he was rich; for many years he dressed virtually in rags, even when he became a millionaire, to discourage approaches from the needy. One of his mistresses passed most of her pregnancy in a pair of his old grey flannel trousers because it never occurred to him that she ought to have the appropriate clothes (he later complained that she had put the trousers out of shape). He discarded people when he felt they could no longer be of use to him, and never listened to them when they sought comfort or advice. He was a well-known hypochondriac but lived long enough to celebrate the death of all his early critics. He also outlived all his rivals to fame except Marc Chagall and Salvador Dali, and managed to claim as his own new techniques and attitudes to art which should properly be credited to Van Gogh, Cézanne, Toulouse-

Lautrec, Munch, Matisse, Braque, Severini, Sassu, Mondrian, Modigliani and Klee. The Czech Nobel Prizewinner Jaroslav Seifert once told me that Picasso was a great admirer of the Czech-born Andy Warhol and would like to have made Pop Art all his own.

Mario Atzinger also reminded me that as an old man Picasso kept a parrot to abuse him (like a medieval Court Jester) and used to say (as sincerely as a medieval prince): 'Even that bird knows I must get on and paint better.' He was rich and famous for most of his long life but he was always sorry for himself. Jacqueline used to say: 'He awoke in me all my maternal instincts and often called me Mummy.' He was maudlin to the end of his days. He was also undoubtedly one of the half a dozen seminal figures in the history of art in the world.

Mario Atzinger and I fell to talking about biographies of Picasso. We agreed that the sharpest eye focussed on him in the early years was that of the lesbian writer Gertrude Stein. Braque was rather rude about her books (though he was not alone in this), and sneered in *Transition*: 'Miss Stein understood nothing of what went on around her. For one who poses as an authority on the epoch, it is safe to say that she never went beyond being a tourist.' But then Braque was peeved because he claimed that 'in the early days of Cubism, Pablo and I were engaged in what we felt was a search for the anonymous personality. . . . Thus it often happened that amateurs mistook Picasso's painting for mine and mine for Picasso's, as neither of us signed his canvasses until they were sold (in order to make them more difficult to steal)'. Among those 'amateurs', Gertrude Stein was one who never made that mistake. She was among the first to recognize Picasso's genius as something on a different plane from that of Braque. She collected his paintings, and urged others, especially Americans, to do the same; for forty years she could say that hers was the only house at which Picasso dined regularly, and, mean though he was, he often gave her paintings and other artifacts which pleased her.

The books by Fernande Olivier (Paris, 1933), Françoise Gilot (1964) and Jaime Sabartés (New York, 1948) are indispensable works by the people who shared his daily life for many years, but the many other biographies seem to have been either ingratiating or intended for the art student, connoisseur or collector and there is still much to be said about the man and his ambience.

It was in Avignon that I had an idea for a new approach to Picasso. This is perhaps not surprising because the city makes much of what is rather a slight connection. *Les Demoiselles d'Avignon* was Picasso's first internationally known painting, though the Avignon in the title was really Avinyo, a street of brothels in Barcelona. The city of the Papal schism also remembers Braque and Apollinaire, Gertrude Stein and Alice B Toklas and many of the cast of thousands who performed at the *Comédie Picasso*. But it was in Avignon that Picasso helped to set up his last exhibition, a few months before he died, and he always liked the place.

While I was there somebody remarked to me that all Latin men are hag-ridden, under the thumbs or skirts of their wives, mistresses, mothers, daughters, female cousins and even servants. Unable for this reason to enjoy women, they get what they can out of them in fleeting sexual satisfaction, dowries, mothering, exploitation of one sort or another (the fashion and cosmetics industries)—or, in the case of artists, what is called (loosely) 'inspiration'. An artist may be inspired by women, inspired in spite of women, inspired by love, hatred or contempt for women; there is even a sort of inspiration which grows against the background of unintellectual domesticity. Picasso's work seems to me to be divisible between these categories of inspiration. As woman succeeded woman in his life, the visible product of this inspiration changed, too; one of the few really intelligent mistresses he had, Dora Maar, told John Richardson that she had noticed this from her position of vantage, as it were. Each domestic interlude became a chapter in his artistic as well as personal life. I think this natural division would have been accepted by Picasso himself, and, indeed, he dropped many a hint about it.

Picasso's mother *Maria* was much more important to him

than his father, even materially; she had a vineyard outside Málaga from which she supplemented the inadequate income of her husband, José Ruiz, an unsuccessful painter and art teacher. Notwithstanding her own disappointing experience, she encouraged her son Pablo in his love for art and crafts, in Málaga, La Coruña and Barcelona. She even closed a maternal eye when, as a teenager, he began to frequent *Els Quatre Gats* in Barcelona, a notorious haunt of painters, sculptors and whores. At this café, Picasso met the man who was probably the only intimate friend he ever had, Carlo Casagemas; after this unhappy man's suicide, he built his life around women of one sort or another, even rejecting his father's surname in favour of his mother's. From 1900 to 1904, he consoled himself, mostly in Paris, with whores, household pets, and work, and out of this industrious melancholy came the paintings of what came to be known as the Blue Period.

In the summer of 1904, he took a fancy to a young girl, *Fernande Olivier*, who had a room in the same block as his studio; she was an elementary schoolteacher, abandoned by her husband, earning a living as a washerwoman. They lived together at 13 Rue Ravignan, Montmartre, until 1909. At first, the domestic bliss (she tidied up his life and his ambience) produced the paintings of the Rose Period and many beautiful drawings. As he now had a socially ambitious hostess anxious to entertain, he turned the studio into a meeting place for writers and artists, critics and collectors, all of whom were used to advance his career. Occasional holidays were spent in Spain, in Tiana and Cadaques, or in the French countryside. The bliss began to grate on him, but he hid his frustration in a search for new art forms.

In 1906–7, having 'discovered' African and Caribbean art, he began to experiment with those techniques which led to Cubism; the most visible advance at that time was the ongoing painting, *Les Demoiselles d'Avignon*. He was full of new ideas and always hard at work. Money began to flow in as Gertrude Stein and others made his work known, and dealers (notably Vollard) 'bought' his *atelier*, but Fernande started to irritate him to the point where he began to abuse her. She left him, but returned when her money ran out. She became very pretentious, accused him of painting *blagues* and made much of a sort of papier-mâché plaque of snorting pigs which he had made for Gertrude Stein (who liked pigs). She forced a move to 'a better address' on the Boulevard Clichy, and bought an expensive dog; he kept the studio (the so-called *Bâteau-Lavoir*) on the Rue Ravignan as a storeroom for an immense quantity of saleable and unsaleable work, and for entertaining candidates for the now inevitable succession. In 1912, Fernande began to spend vast sums on hats and perfume. She pushed her luck too far, and was replaced by Marcelle Humbert, known as *Eva Gouel*, the mistress of his friend the sculptor Marcoussis; Marcoussis refused to accept Fernande in part exchange, so she had to earn a living giving French lessons to Americans.

Eva did not like Picasso's Spanish friends, the *Bâteau-Lavoir* (which he had to give up), the dog (which he kept), or his messy photography (he had dabbled in this a few years before and kept the necessary bric-à-brac handy in case it should ever interest him again). However, she had a wide acquaintance in the world of art and letters and introduced him to the Futurists, among others. She was fond of the theatre and took him to plays and the ballet as often as she could. She was also very good at public relations and entertained foreign dealers, collectors and critics, especially from Italy, Russia, the United States and Britain. She got on well with Gertrude Stein, and looked after her flat when she and Alice B Toklas went off to war as ambulance drivers.

She set up two homes for Picasso, in the Boulevard Raspail and the Rue Schoelcher, and entertained those who could be useful commercially, teaching Picasso to distinguish between them and the time wasters. She played on his natural meanness and tried to persuade him that beer was cheaper than wine for entertaining: Bass appears on some paintings and collages about this time. She also introduced him to the Ripolin paints used by decorators, and for a while he boasted that they were better than expensive 'artist's colours'. The influx of new ideas for which she was responsible laid the foundation for 'Synthetic Cubism'. She also introduced caged birds into the household. Unfortunately, she died in 1916, but her introduction of Picasso to the theatre led to an invitation by Jean Cocteau to Rome in 1917; Picasso was to design the sets and costumes, Satie to compose the score, and Massine to arrange the choreography for Diaghilev's *Ballets Russes*. The time he spent in Rome and Naples was to inspire the so-called Classical Period (1917–1924), though his next woman was to claim the credit for this.

In Rome in 1917, Picasso met *Olga Koklova*, a dancer with Diaghilev and daughter of an *émigré* Tsarist General, who had seen his paintings in the Moscow Shchukin collection. A greedy and ambitious girl with little talent (Diaghilev recruited half his company from among the socially well connected), she was impressed by everyone's admiration for this apparently rich artist. His admiration for her was transparent. However, she was determined to settle for nothing less than marriage, in Paris, at his expense—and this is what she got. After a splendid wedding at the Russian Orthodox Church on the Rue Daru, they set up house in a very chic apartment on the Rue de la Boétie. She left the stage immediately, though Picasso continued to work with Diaghilev until 1924, and she was certainly a practical and experienced adviser. She also gave her husband a son, named Paolo, the Italian version of his name, to commemorate their meeting in Rome.

They seem to have been happy at first, but slowly he began to tire of her 'Slav temperament' and the innumerable, impoverished Russian exiles at the door, all of whom seem to have been Counts or Generals, or both. Among the handful of non-Russians she welcomed was Tristan Tzara, the Romanian founder of Dadaism, whose part Picasso took in the dispute over who had made the greatest contribution to the birth of Surrealism. Picasso even tried his hand at verse (Olga thought poets members of a higher caste than painters because they were 'tragic' and 'cleaner'). By the end of the decade, however, Picasso had had enough of his wife's posturing, as it was interfering with his work. One morning, while out shopping for some 'real food' (Olga's cuisine was exquisitely Russian), he picked up a teenage model waiting for her friend outside the Galeries Lafayette. He bought a fortified house a short drive from Paris, the Château Boisgeloup, made a studio for himself and installed the girl nearby. Olga tolerated the *alliance* for a time, but eventually created so many scenes that a separation was inevitable. She helped herself to hundreds of paintings and drawings, took away their son and renamed him Ivan.

The beautiful model, *Marie-Thérèse Walter*, seemed to be a quiet, almost timid, little miss. She was just what Picasso was looking for—a girl who was silent, thought mostly about sex and cooking, and made no other demands on him. She brought calm and domesticity into his life, two new, large dogs, and a parrot. There were no more hysterical scenes, no questions about his movements, and he could work at his painting without fear of interruption. His work became as soft and sensual as his companion, although when harassed by Olga he had produced some marvellously vitriolic portraiture. Marie-Thérèse served meals at the proper hours on the proper plates, and insisted that he went to Mass every feast day. For a time he seemed to revel in this; he explained to friends that knowing he had to go to Mass at 11 am helped him to get out of bed and start the day. Driven by the chauffeur Marcel in the Hispano-Suiza, the happy couple travelled widely, even to Barcelona on the eve of the Spanish Civil War (to organize an exhibition). In 1935, Marie-Thérèse gave birth to their daughter Maria (Maia) and began to hint that he take steps to legitimize the child—he could apply for French nationality and so get a divorce from Olga. But Picasso had no intention of changing his nationality, which had kept him out of the First World War, and the long honeymoon was over. Into the sensual portraits of Marie-Thérèse, another more dramatic face began to insinuate itself.

During Marie-Thérèse's pregnancy, Paul Eluard had introduced Picasso to Dora Marcovitch, a professional photographer and photoreporter known as *Dora Maar*. Apart from her physical attractiveness, she fascinated Picasso because they had so many points of contact. She spoke Spanish (most of her childhood had been spent in Argentina), knew a lot about painting (she had studied at the Académies de Passy and Julien) and more than he did about photography (she was a graduate of the City of Paris School of Photography), was a good talker and a good listener. She had read Fernande Olivier's book *Picasso et Ses Amis*, and the excuse for their original meeting was to take photographs for a magazine article based on the book.

By the middle of 1936 their affair had begun and was certainly the most intellectually stimulating he ever had. Dora Maar had been on the fringes of the Surrealist circle ever since she had been introduced to it by Brassai, and so Breton, Eluard, Leiris and Man Ray were soon at Picasso's table, and Tzara banished from it. She was shrewd enough to refuse to live permanently with Picasso and kept up her own establishment in the Rue de Savoié (where she still lives) as well as making a home for them in the Rue des Grands Augustins round the corner. One of her reasons, she said was that she did not like birds or dogs, Picasso's habit of rising late, or the chauffeur Marcel (who seems to have been used indiscriminately by Olga and Marie-Thérèse).

Dora Maar, a fine photoportraitist herself, inspired a whole series of portraits over the years and these are generally considered to be among the best Picasso ever did. She was also allowed to take part in some of the major paintings, such as *Guernica* (1937) provoked by a German blitz in Spain. Picasso was ostensibly outraged by the Civil War but had turned down an invitation at the London Surrealist Exhibition in 1936 to go there and fight. When the Second World War broke out in 1939, Picasso was noticeably reluctant to take sides or flee from the advancing German Army. He was, in fact, protected after 1940 by the Nazi Ambassador to Occupied France, Otto Abetz, but seems to have stayed the right side of collaboration. There was some minor harassment by the Gestapo, but Abetz had been a teacher of drawing before the war so perhaps this inspired his declaration of the 'essential neutrality of artists'. Dora Maar was very shrewd as a guide through this particular minefield (she was the daughter of a Frenchwoman and a Yugoslav architect, but had herself classified neutral, too); during one month in 1942 she procured for Picasso some special Japanese paper from visiting emissaries of Hitler's Asian ally, and also negotiated with the Resistance to get some sculpture to a foundry under its control. She was a very good black marketeer and they never lacked good food or wine, though this did not endear them to their starving neighbours. Though devoted, she drew the line (with the other Surrealists led by Breton) when Picasso, scenting an indefinite Left-Wing hegemony in Europe, announced one day that he had decided to join the French Communist Party (1944).

Making use of the collection of daft periodicals Dora had put together ('Picasso, Jew painter', etc) and his Party card, he managed to stay out of trouble during the years of revenge (1944–46); there were ugly scenes at a special Picasso 'Liberation' Exhibition but he shrugged them off.

Those years were also lightened by his courtship of a young art student, *Françoise Gilot*, whom he met first in a restaurant in 1943. Though young enough to be Dora Maar's daughter, she was shrewd and talented enough to know that she had her age and his vanity on her side, and her admiration for his work was informed and sincere. She was particularly good at other new beginnings, and when she went to live with him in 1946 many of Picasso's cards were reshuffled. He became less dependent on his secretary, Sabartés. The Surrealists, with the exception of Éluard, went out of one door and men like Tzara came in again through another. His relations with Braque and Matisse improved, and she even managed to keep the Communist Party hacks in their place—they mistook an old lithograph of one of Matisse's pigeons for a dove and made it the emblem of their 'struggle for peace'. In quick succession Françoise bore Picasso a son, Claude, and a daughter, Paloma (named after the dove which was a pigeon), and slowly moved him away from Paris to spend most of the year in the South of France; after the humiliation of a holiday spent at Dora Maar's house at Menerbes, she got an establishment of her own, *La Galloise*, and made the fortune of the town of Vallauris by encouraging Picasso to interest himself in pottery. She found him an abandoned perfume factory to work in and gave him a new rhythm of life and work. We owe to her the best descriptions of Picasso at work, and of his slow decline. She saw the end of the affair coming, and used Picasso's dealer Kahnweiler to sell her own paintings and drawings; when the parting came it was without animosity on her side—he complained bitterly that she had betrayed him.

It came as a shock to Picasso to be dropped by a woman, any woman, and the more so by the mother of two of his children; he was especially angry to realize that all his other children looked to Françoise for guidance and friendship, even his son Paolo, who was older than she was. He sulked for a time, but soon recovered, solaced by sycophants who tut-tutted and drank his wine. He was determined to get his own back on Françoise, and when his wife Olga died of cancer he took up with a young divorcée and married her in 1961.

Jacqueline Roque could offer him little in the way of artistic or intellectual inspiration, but she was genuinely fond of him and was determined to give him a serene old age. She allowed back into his establishment the menagerie Françoise had eliminated (with the exception of a stinking goat) and was rewarded with a château of her own. The cats, who had been so important to Picasso before he met Fernande Olivier, came to the forefront of his life again and appeared in innumerable portraits. He also began to 'rework' the Old Masters (he turned *La Fête de Madame* by Dégas into a sort of *Demoiselles d'Avignon*) and made all sorts of extravagant artifacts knowing that his wife had not the slightest idea of what he was doing and thought it all a work of genius. His entourage reported that he became less mean, more hospitable and his work was certainly full of colour.

He died on 9 April, 1973. He was sprightly to the end, and

at the age of ninety said to a friend: 'Sex and smoking—age has forced me to give them both up but the desire remains.'

What did these women really do for Picasso, other than satisfy his sexual needs and (in the case of his second wife) make him give up smoking? I have tried to show in this book that the connection between the domestic Picasso and the artist is very strong. Of course, not all of his *amies* understood his work, or even what he was talking about when he discussed it with his colleagues. This did not matter. As John Addington Symonds said in another context: 'Providence deigns frequently to use for the most momentous purposes some pantaloon or puppet . . .' and some of Picasso's women, especially the many with whom he had ephemeral relationships, merely gave him an idea for a plate, a piece of sculpture, a patch of colour. His wives and mistresses, however, did more than that, even when they were unaware of what they were doing, and Picasso was shrewd enough to know this—this is one of the reasons why he was so reluctant to let any of them go. In this book I have tried to identify the nature of the contributions to his life and art made by the leading ladies in the lifelong Pablo *commedia dell'arte*.

Maria

'Que bueno es hacer nada, e despues descansar un poquitín.'
(How good it is to do nothing, and then rest a little)
(Andaluz proverb)

'The atmosphere in my house when I was born was like that at a funeral. The midwife thought I was stillborn and just dumped me on a table while she looked after my mother. Everybody was weeping and wailing. When he thought my mother was alright, my uncle Don Salvador, a doctor, lit a cigar and the smoke blew in my face. I coughed and came to life.'

Pablo Diego José Francesco di Paolo Juan Nepomuceno Maria de los Remedios Cipriano de la Santisima Trinidad Ruiz Picasso never earned a reputation for telling the truth, but to the end of his life he swore that he came into the world at midnight on 25 October, 1881, after his departure had already been announced. It is also typical of him that he used to add: 'It was a good cigar.'

Only after his death did it come out that the time of his birth was 23.15, throwing into confusion the thousands of astrologers who had cast his horoscope. The cigar was not a good one either, but a black local weed.

The 'house' where Picasso was born was a small flat in a white block on the east side of the Plaza de la Merced in Málaga, a square perched above the slums which straggled down to the port. The slums, inhabited by gypsies and whores, was known as the *barrio de chupa y tira*, the 'suck and chuck district', because its denizens were supposed to live on shellfish, throwing the shells into the streets in their thousands after sucking out the molluscs.

Jaime Sabartés, failed poet and Picasso's devoted secretary for forty years, made every possible effort to drum up distinguished forebears for his idol. This was especially difficult on the Ruiz side, where the first notable one was his grandfather Diego, who earned a place in police records when he was beaten up by Napoleon's troops (1811) for throwing stones at them. Diego's eldest son, also a Diego, became a minor civil servant, though his fourth child Pablo made a career for himself in the Church and became a Canon of the Cathedral. The Canon seems to have been the only Ruiz with any money. He also seems to have kept Pablo's father for years. José Ruiz had decided to become a professional painter at a very early age and, as his son said scathingly on many occasions, he was never much good at either painting or selling his work.

Picasso's mother's ancestry is just as obscure. The family had only been in Málaga for two generations. Pablo's maternal grandfather was born there and went to school in England. He was very probably Italian, a cousin of the painter Matteo Picasso from Recco near Genoa, a city with centuries of friendly commercial relations with England. Don Francisco Picasso seems to have had money, which he invested in vineyards outside Málaga and in a tobacco plantation in Cuba, where he died of yellow fever in 1883. He was very fond of his daughter, Maria Picasso Lopez, and when she announced her intention of marrying an unsuccessful painter he consulted the Canon and they agreed to take on, jointly, this financial burden. He had a large establishment on the Plaza de la Merced, and it was he who found the young couple a small flat on the same square so that he could keep an eye on them. He also gave them some Chippendale chairs, which travelled with Pablo until the end of his life and are still at Mougins.

José and Maria were delighted with their child and its rich godparents. Life in the little second floor flat was agreeable enough, though the bridegroom soon reappraised his diminutive wife ('The women in Andalusia only seem to be small. In

reality they are stronger than bulls and, of course, last longer.').
Like a good Andaluz, José would have been happy to dream
his life away, doing a bit of painting, fathering a few children,
sitting for hours at a café table gossiping and putting the world
to rights, going to bullfights and brothels in moderation, and
being entertained by his landlord, the rich Marques de Ignato,
a distant relative of his wife who would often take a painting
in lieu of rent.

Maria, however, was ambitious, both for her husband and
her child. She put pressure on her husband to take a job as a
teacher at the San Telmo School of Fine Arts and Crafts. The
Marques procured for him a political appointment as curator
of Málaga Museum of Fine Arts, housed in the Town Hall, but
it was typical of José's bad luck that shortly afterwards the
Marques' party lost power and, though José held on to the
curatorship, he lost the salary attached to it (this was the
traditional way of dismissing unwanted protégés of rival
parties).

Disaster struck regularly in the life of the Ruiz Picassos, but
just as regularly something turned up, Micawberlike, to make
life seem less tragic. On the evening of 13 December, Don José,
as he called himself, was gossiping with the local pharmacist
when he felt the tremors of an earthquake. He ran home, threw
a cape dramatically over his shoulders, enfolded his son in it
and dragged his wife to the house of a friend in the lee of the old
Moorish fortress of Gibralfaro. There, the friend, the painter
Antonio Munoz Degrain, helped with the birth of the Ruiz
Picasso's second child, Lola.

Fortunately, the earthquake was a minor one and the family
was able to return to the flat in the Plaza de la Merced. Pablo
always said he could remember those days, when he was only
three years old. He was slow to speak, and his first word was
'piss'. He had a weak bladder and his first gesture to his father
on being taken to the studio in the Museum where he painted
was to relieve himself on his father's paint brushes.

Maria used to say later that it only sounded like 'piss' and
was really the child's imperfect pronunciation of the word

'lapiz' or pencil, a sort of precociousness one would expect from a great artist. Maternal pride apart, there is no doubt that Pablo showed as much delight as any small child in scribbling, even drawing in the sand which was all that was left of the poor soil in parts of the Plaza. It is also true that the episode in his father's studio presaged his contempt for his father's work. This contempt was not entirely unmerited. José was a workmanlike painter who produced scenes of the chase to hang on dining room walls (pheasants and partridges a speciality), and, to please the Canon, decorated plaster heads for the Cathedral (golden tears on the Madonna were a hallmark). What he was really good at, and never exploited, was paper sculpture and this did impress his son. He used to tell Sabartés that his father and his mother's sister Eloisa taught him this art of sculpture, though he was once thrashed for using Eloisa's embroidery scissors without permission.

Lionel Prejger (*L'Oeil*, **82**, Paris, October 1961) notes that by the time Pablo was seven years old he could cut out animals, flowers, birds and all sorts of mysterious figures to order. 'His cousins Concha and Maria would tell him to cut out things for them: 'Make us one of Doña Tola Calderón's Newfoundland dog.' 'Where would you like me to start?' 'Start with the feet', the girls would say, and he was as happy to start at the top or the bottom of any figure they wanted cut out.'

John Richardson (*New York Review of Books*, 17 July 1980) wrote that when Picasso moved the contents of his last Paris studio to Cannes in 1964, he had seventy portfolios among the trunks full of household bric-à-brac, including several envelopes full of paper sculptures dating back to this time. Lionel Prejger, who had a factory making steel tubes, was told by him: 'I am fulfilling an ambition I have had for a long time, to give a permanent shape to all these bits of paper.' It was Prejger's factory which was commissioned to turn them into steel *objets d'art*.

The first ten years of Picasso's life in Málaga seem to have been happy enough, in spite of a certain amount of bickering between his father and mother. Maria was not too subtle in her remarks that without the income from the vineyard which had been put in her name, and other handouts from 'her side', life would be rather grim. Pablo seems to have gravitated to his mother, attracted as he was all his life by the smell of money, and had spent nearly all his time with her, with Lola and a new sister Concepción (b. 1887) and the girls in Aunt Eloisa's family. He seems to have had no boy friends. He took a feminine interest in clothes; his favourite outfit was a white sailor suit with black boots and stockings, and a navy blue topcoat and blue beret for winter, but he also remembered a gaudy outfit worn at the age of four—a red jacket and green kilt, bronze coloured boots and a shirt with white collar and bow tie. He liked handling the girls' clothes, too, though this was often misinterpreted by his mother and her sister, who threatened to confiscate his biscuits (he had a passion for Olibet and swore he learnt to walk pushing a tin around) if he did not leave them alone.

The one activity he seems to have shared with his father was the weekly *corrida* during the summer months. The bullring in Málaga is close to the citadel, Alcazaba, so it is possible to get a free view of the fight by just sitting on the hillside (when Pablo was not with his father, this is what he used to do). All Málaga turned out to welcome the actors in this barbaric drama, whether they were paying or not, and the bullfight to come was the topic of conversation from Wednesday to Saturday when the inquest on Sunday's *corrida* had been dealt with on Monday and Tuesday. The boy seems never to have been bored by it all, and their lack of interest was the only thing for which he reproved the girls. When autumn came, however, he forgave them, and out of school they all went into the family's vineyards to pick the grapes. For nearly a month, the children virtually lived in the open air. Pablo's mother cooked for everybody, peasants and proprietors alike. Even some of the gypsies came out from their *barrio* to work for a few days and told marvellous tales round the fires at night. The old men went on exhuming earlier bullfights and matadors.

The debate about the 'morality' of bloodsports had not yet

begun, either in Andalusia or the English countryside; bored peasants, like bored English squires, found the colour and the noise a welcome relief from the tedium of life, and in the case of the peasants, from poverty. Throughout Andalusia bulls were bred for the *corrida*, and it probably struck Pablo that they were rather better fed than most of the spectators whose thin sinewy arms he saw at close quarters in the vineyards. It was certainly among the blood and sand of the local arena, and the glow of the autumn colours of the vine-covered hills, that he began to draw and paint.

The years 1889 and 1890 brought about a dramatic change in the fortunes of the family. As elsewhere in Western Europe, phylloxera blighted the vineyards around Málaga. All the local proprietors, including his mother, had to root up the sick vines and leave the ground fallow for a couple of years before they could plant *uva americana* (a resistant strain from California, taken out there by Franciscan friars in the sixteenth century) and graft traditional strains onto it. The family's income dropped, and for the first time José found himself in the position of principal breadwinner. This was good for his morale and prestige in the family, but it posed a number of problems. The swing of the political pendulum had left him without a salary for his curatorship again. There was the additional problem of finding a larger flat now that Concepción was no longer a small baby. José solved his financial problems by accepting a well-paid post as Art Master at the Instituto da Guarda in Coruña. He celebrated by arranging a sea voyage to take them all there.

As usual, things did not go according to plan. The voyage, although it was in September (1891), was rough. Maria and all the children were so seasick that he had to cut short the 'cruise' at Vigo and finish the journey by land. When they got to Coruña it was raining, and this was followed by three days of fog. Worst of all, Concepción caught diphtheria and died. José was blamed for it all.

As Sir John Moore had found to his cost, Galicia is a bleak region in the North-west of the Iberian peninsular which takes its tone from the inhospitable granite of Cape Finisterre. It is inhabited by hardy peasants and fishermen, and is a prized source of recruits for Spain's armed forces; one of the twentieth century's better known soldiers, Franciso Franco, was growing up there as the Ruiz family moved into a flat in the Calle Payo Gomez.

The ten-year-old Pablo seems to have been indifferent to the move from Málaga. In a way he was relieved that his father had a senior post at the Instituto because he was an educationally backward child. He could barely read or write and he copied down his arithmetical tables much as he drew the plaster models of arms, legs, heads, animals and birds in the art room. Some of his drawings survive and show that he used numbers as the skeletons for portraits of men and women (especially sevens and eights), but his most impressive portraits were those of Lola and her friend. The portrait of this young friend, a girl from a poor family who lived nearby, is a very mature work for a boy, and was obviously important to him (he kept it with him all his life). She is sitting on the sea wall, dressed in a ragged shawl, with bare feet. The feet and ankles are swollen, and reappear again many times a score of years later in a series of paintings done after the First World War. The sad symmetry of her face, with its large, staring black eyes, was to become another constant in his work. The drawings of Lola are happier, perhaps because she was always a happy child, and are a record of almost any happy child at play or helping her mother in the house. There is also a portrait, unfinished, of Don Ramon Perez Costales, a friend of his father, who was to be a member of the first Republican Government.

José Ruiz seems to have been very unhappy in Coruña. He had a good job, and was able to protect his son from the consequences of his general backwardness (fortunately there were no formal examinations) but he never got over the death of Concepción, the only child who looked like him. Pablo and Lola were both short, black eyed, meridional. José was tall and thin, with reddish hair, and did not look as if he were part of the same family. In fact, he became more and more an outsider, as his son's talent became greater, far greater than his own. One day, in desperation, he threw his brushes and palette at Pablo and said: 'There, take them. I shall paint no more'. The boy replied: 'You do well. You were never able to paint very well. I can do better.'

Left without any desire to paint, for years José Ruiz spent his time, when he was not teaching, just walking up and down the Alameda, talking to his few friends. In Málaga the Ruizs and the Picassos had known everybody in their introverted middle-class society, and the outward forms of respect were everywhere. The *gallegos* were in general rougher, if not less kind. La Coruña was slightly smaller than Málaga but there was a great coming and going of the British, French and Portuguese which gave it the air of a metropolis, intolerant of poverty and good manners. It was not the sort of place for a failure who hoped for 'respect' as a consolation for lack of any real ability. His few friends said that he seemed to grow taller and stringier and, out walking with his short, stocky wife and children, had the air of a Don Quixote with three Sancho Panzas.

Fortunately, relief came in 1895. A nun from Málaga, Sra Josefa Gonzales, had been moved to Barcelona, and she offered Don José a post teaching art to the young ladies in the Convent of St Vincent de Paul. She had also heard that an old teacher at the Barcelona School of Fine Arts, a native of La Coruña, wanted to go home and was looking for an exchange post there. With the help of Ramon Perez Costales, the exchange was authorized. Now José Ruiz was off to a new life with two salaries; he could live like a señor and look forward to a substantial pension from the state and a lifetime retainer from the Order of St Vincent de Paul.

Pablo was rather impressed by his father's new status and treated him with slightly more courtesy as they packed to leave. He may also have been taken down a peg by the failure of his first exhibition, in a local junk shop which sometimes put on 'artistic events'. As the journey to Barcelona was to be a very long one, by land this time, via Madrid and a holiday in Málaga, he felt it was worth cultivating the man who had his immediate destiny in his hands. Both father and son enjoyed the few days in Madrid, in the Prado where for the first time Pablo saw the works of the great Spanish masters, Goya, Velazquez and Zubaran; Lola and her mother went shopping. The triumphant return to Málaga was, however, more to the teenage boy's liking. There, he was made much of by all the women (he was still the only male child on both sides of the family) and even by the local notables. Unable to write more than a few misspelt words (to the end of his life he could never recite the alphabet), he had sent back to Málaga from La Coruña a series of what would now be called comics, with titles like *The Blue and White* or *Coruña News*, and these were resurrected and admired. His uncle Don Salvador gave him five pesetas a day and a room in the Department of Public Health to paint in, and an old sailor as a model. His father's eccentric elder sister Josefa also posed for him (these two paintings survive in the Museu Picasso in Barcelona). Everybody admired his flashing black eyes and his small, strong hands ('How like his mother, so *capable*'). Far from resenting all this attention given to his son, José seemed to be relieved that he could renew all his old male acquaintances, the *aficionados* of the *corrida* and the cronies in the cafés, and spend the summer 'doing nothing, then resting a little'.

At the beginning of October, the idyll was over and the family set out for Barcelona. Sra Josefa had found a flat for them in the Calle Cristina, a hundred yards from the School of Fine Arts; they were near the old port and the sea, as they had been in La Coruña, but this time it was the Mediterranean, warm, colourful, bustling with people and small boats earning a precarious living fishing or freighting down the coast. The school had the top floors of La Lonja, the Exchange, and there were good views from the roof, too.

Though he was only fourteen, Pablo was accepted as a student, on the strength of his portfolio and his father's position. The school had no formal entrance examination, and the Rector encouraged the sons of artists because he said that at least they knew what went on in a studio. Each applicant was given a series of subjects to draw and was allowed a month to complete his portfolio. Pablo Ruiz Picasso was given his 'themes' at nine o'clock one morning, and by sunset he had completed his set of drawings so brilliantly that he was immediately given a small scholarship. The Rector wrote a complimentary letter to Don José, which the boy intercepted and destroyed.

Before the onset of winter, Don José found a larger flat not far away, in the Calle de la Merced (the address reminded him of home) and found a small studio for Pablo nearby in the Calle de la Plata. There and at the school Pablo worked hard, was more or less disciplined, and was admitted to the Life Class.

Several important paintings date from this period, *The Bayonet Attack* (lost), *First Communion* and *The Choirboy* (in the Museu Picasso), and the controversial *Science and Charity*. Though it was sent to the National Exhibition in Madrid in 1897, received an honourable mention, and later won a gold medal in Málaga, *Science and Charity* became the object of some rude doggerel by a critic who resented the boy's growing reputation. The critic wrote that the scene was very moving— a doctor and a nun on each side of the sickbed of a woman— but the woman's hand—long, limp and graceful—was surely wearing a glove?

> I'm sorry that I titter
> At so much care and love
> But I've never seen a doctor
> Take the pulse now of a glove.

Pablo was furious and blamed himself for listening to his mother and using his father as a model. He moved out of the studio in the Calle de la Plata and would not tell anyone where he was now painting. In fact, he had met a fisherman, during one of the family's periodical sea trips in small boats, who had fixed him up with a room above a bar.

During the summer of 1897, the family went for a long holiday to Málaga. The two children stayed with their grandmother, so that José and Maria could enjoy a second honeymoon. It was during this stay that Don Salvador had a number of serious talks with Pablo, pointing out that the way was now open for him to become a successful painter. The El Liceo Club was to hold a fête in his honour, and he should welcome the support of local artists and pay more attention to 'tradition'. Perhaps he should go to Madrid, to the Royal Academy of San Fernando where he would make 'useful contacts'?

Everybody was so sure that the boy, now a strapping youth going on sixteen, would become a respected and respectable member of society that the elders of the family, men and women, began to talk of arranging a suitable marriage. Pablo was inveigled into taking walks in the evening with his cousin Carmen Blasco, a very good-looking girl. They made a handsome couple, though she was taller than he.

Pablo wore a new suit, a black bohemian's hat and carried a walking cane, and seems to have had his sexual instincts aroused by the girl. She was heavily protected by an aunt, however, who acted as duenna, and never left them alone, always keeping just in sight. It was a frustrating experience, only relieved by the emotional safety valve of the regular bullfights. By the time the holiday came to an end he had decided never to return to Málaga, with its provincial smugness, arranged marriages, and respectability. He wanted a woman, a real woman, freedom from his relatives, and a life of his own.

When he got back to Barcelona, he had the usual interview with his tutors. They had watched his talent flourish, with admiration and a touch of envy. He was, however, self-assured to the point of arrogance, and they were determined to get rid of him. Realizing that the boy was susceptible to flattery, to say the least of it, they put it to him that genius such as his should not be wasted outside the metropolis. The San Fernando in Madrid, the most famous in the country, would certainly welcome him with open arms; he owed it to himself and art to apply for admission. They would recommend him with all their hearts. The strategem worked, and Pablo presented himself for the admission tests in Madrid. He passed with flying colours and was congratulated personally by the Rector.

Before he left Barcelona, he found a way to lose his virginity. Even before the holiday, he had had his eye on a young girl who drew the wine in the bar above which he had his secret studio. She was a tall thin girl, unlike the voluptuous women most male virgins are attracted to, but she had a ribald sense of humour and made him laugh. She said later that one day, while she was laughing with him, he got her up against a barrel and 'made himself a man'. Looking at her spare body and red hair, he said to a friend that it had been 'like fucking his father'.

The move to Madrid was one of the few mistakes in Picasso's career. Barcelona was certainly more of a metropolis, open to influences from the rest of Europe which never reached the Spanish capital. A great many of the unemployed in Barcelona eventually went to Britain to work and brought back new political ideas. The proximity of France had attracted Symbolists and Impressionists, and there was even some Russian revolutionary ferment and a whiff of Wagnerian German Romanticism. Madrid, in contrast, lived in the past, in the *Siglo de Oro* and the Government often behaved as if the South American colonies had not been lost and the Armada was rebuilding. The Academy was old-fashioned in its approach to teaching and its only attraction for Pablo lay in its vast store of great paintings by his dead predecessors. Pablo did what he was asked to do by his teachers, who did not seem to appreciate the young genius, filing away his drawings and paintings as if they were invoices (a brilliant portrait of a girl, which won an internal third prize in 1899, was discovered sixty years later in one of the general storerooms). For most of the time, Pablo squatted— first at a pension in the Calle San Pedro Martin and then in rooms belonging to other provincials as short of funds as he was. He became even worse off when his uncle Don Salvador stopped his allowance after a report that he did not show respect to the institution or attend its social gatherings. He was accused of being a 'Bohemian'.

This was an unfair accusation. Young Picasso did not have the money (he was reduced to a small allowance from his father) to lead a Bohemian life in the capital, even if he knew how a Bohemian was supposed to live (of that he was uncertain). He was invited to tutors' homes, where he talked too much, but his gaucheness was put down to his tender years. He was especially embarrassed by the girls, the young daughters or nieces of his tutors, who had a visiting English professor to teach them watercolour painting on the periphery of the Academy's activities. The girls all seemed to be tall and to carry themselves like famous actresses with who knew what experience of life. He was too young to know that they were probably as timid and frightened of him as he was of them, but knew better how to disguise it. He joined a boxing club in the hope that regular workouts would help him to grow taller, but in the end they only made him stronger and stockier; he acquired that characteristic half-crouching stance which made him look like a young bull, no matter how much he tried to give himself a distinguished air in several self-portraits (1897, 1898).

He was more at ease with the down-and-outs, with whom he shared what food he could afford and in whose doss-houses he often passed the night. He really got to know the slums, especially those around the Plaza del Progresso, and some of the emaciated men and women he knew and drew then reappeared in his work for years. He made one last appearance at an Academy function, at the St Anthony's Gala on 12 June, 1898, when he got drunk and fell into the river, to be saved by a gypsy.

Shortly after this unfortunate evening, he went down with scarlet fever and staggered home more dead than alive. When he could walk and eat again, he fled from the moralising of his father to the village of Horta de Ebro (now Horta de San Juan) to stay with a young painter friend, Manuel Pallares. Manuel, a year older than Pablo, had been a student at the Barcelona School of Fine Arts and had seen the meteoric rise of his contemporary. Like him, he had left the school because he felt he could learn no more and resented the formality of the teaching and the ambience. The two young men spent most of the summer living in a cave above the village, sketching and talking the days and nights away. When they ran short of money they would do a day's work on a nearby farm and take payment in food and wine. Many of these sketches survive, and among the gypsies singing and dancing there are scenes of everyday life on the farm showing Pablo yoking and driving oxen.

When the time came for the grape harvest, something Pablo really knew about, the young men left the cave, went down to work and earn a few pesetas. In the vineyards he met a second girl with whom he seems to have had a physically violent affair, though it grew into a tender liaison and has left behind a beautiful portrait, given to her when he left for Barcelona in November. This girl, Joceta Sebastia Mendra, was fascinated by the way Pablo and Manuel lived, let them sleep in her father's barn, and joined Pablo whenever she could steal away. The attachment seems to have been one of the usual *vintage* passions, inflamed by the new wine, and Pablo was back in Horta de Ebro for Christmas; he stayed until the spring and did several more sketches of the girl.

Picasso used to say that he only went back to Barcelona because he ran out of paper. This, of course, was not true. The love affair had run its course and he was anxious to get back to work in the city where people did all the innumerable, even bizarre, things he found fascinating. Jaime Sabartés met him on his return, when Picasso was sharing a flat with the sculptor Cadona. Cadona, to make ends meet, let out most of the rooms to the rag trade and Sabartés noticed Picasso one day playing with a machine which put eyelets into corsets. There were paintings everywhere, including *Science and Charity* and the canvasses he had covered in Horta.

Maria Picasso visited the flat once a week, brought some food and tidied up her son's room as best she could. For a few hours after she left it looked like a model student's study bedroom; *Science and Charity* hung above the bed, which was neatly arranged. A 'painting area' was clearly delineated, with brushes displayed in jam jars and tubes of paint laid out like sausages on a butcher's slab. The crockery from home was simple kitchen stuff, but unchipped and with the occasional decoration. There were glasses and—a touch of refinement—a silver fruit knife. There were photographs everywhere, many taken on the roof where Picasso used to drink when the sewing machines were going full blast below.

Maria did not like Sabartés, whom she suspected of leading her son astray into the whorehouses of the Calle d'Avinyo and to *Els Quatre Gats*. The seventeen-year-old genius was certainly learning 'the Bohemian life'. Though he never lost a personal preference for cleanliness—he was always well washed and as well shaven as he could be—he wore the right clothes, including the black velvet trousers, black jacket and waistcoat, string tie or choker and broad-brimmed black hat, like an anarchist lacking only the smoking globe with the word *bomb* on it. A more influential friend was Carlo Casagemas, a patron of *Els Quatre Gats* since it had been opened by Romeu (Père Romeu) in 1897. He was said by Sabartés to be an expert on the girls and could tell you who had the pox and who was clean. This reputation turned out to be undeserved, but Casagemas did introduce Picasso to the male habitués—Miguel Utrillo (Maurice was his adopted son) the playwright, the painters Isdro Nonell and Ramon Casas, and later the mad Basque Zuloaga. And it was Casagemas who helped to organize Picasso's first one-man show at *Els Quatre Gats*, in February, 1900. The original intention was to show only pencil and charcoal drawings (in competition with Casas who had shown a hundred drawings of local notables at the Sala Peres the previous year) but Maria, who liked Casagemas and invited him home to discuss the exhibition, insisted on some paintings. If he did not want to hang *Science and Charity* he should at least show a deathbed scene he had painted recently, of a priest standing reading comfortable words to a young woman breathing her last. The choice was not unwise. Manuel Rodriguez Cocola, writing in *La Vanguardia* (3 February, 1900), saw the attempt to parody Casas in the drawings and disapproved, but he liked the painting. Four days later, Sebastia Trullo i Plana in *El Diario de Barcelona* resented in the drawings the presence of 'melancholy, bored and taciturn characters'. To draw only Bohemians instead of local dignitaries was thought to be evidence of *modernismo* and anyway disturbed the nice equilibrium between painter and patron, with the critic eating at both their tables. However, an anonymous visitor wrote in the book: 'In each stroke of the pencil or charcoal there is a kind of inspired fever, reminiscent of the best works of El Greco and Goya'.

For a nineteen-year-old, the show was as great a success as he could hope for, and brought an invitation to hang a painting at the Paris Exposition Universelle later that year.

Maria was overjoyed, even though she knew at heart that her son was starting down a road which would separate them forever. At first she toyed with the idea of going with 'the two boys' (Casagemas had decided to go, too) to make sure they were properly looked after in a foreign capital and did not make unsuitable (female) friends, but Lola was at that age 'when girls have to be protected from themselves'. She contented herself with buying him a new suit of Bohemian clothes. Her husband tried to reassure her, though he suspected that their son would seek out the most 'unsuitable' women immediately on arrival; Pablo's sketchbooks were already full of local cabmen, dockers, gypsies, beggars, whores and bars, and these drawings had started to appear in *Juventud* and *Cataluña Artistica*.

The *Els Quatre Gats* gave Picasso and Casagemas a great send-off. Mateo Fernandez de Soto (in whose flat Pablo was living) made a long speech, then fell asleep. The poet Joan Olivia Bridgman read *The Call of the Virgins*. The whores wept. At dawn, the whole party accompanied the two 'heroes of Catalonia' to the French Station and laid them out on the seats in a third class compartment.

Picasso's first short stay in Paris was in many ways unremarkable. He was not homeless—Nonell had lent them his studio at 49 Rue Gabrielle in Montmartre. They were not short of money—Casagemas had substantial private means and shared what he had willingly. A certain amount of time was wasted: 'Some nights we go to café concerts or theatres but it usually ends up in a riot . . . *Quatre Gats* here would be a gold mine.' But in addition to the hours spent in the cafés and bars there was work. As Casagemas wrote home: 'Tomorrow I'll light the stove . . . painting for exhibitions in Barcelona and Madrid. Whenever there is light we are in the studio painting and drawing . . . there's room for everybody and money for whoever works . . . Here there are real teachers everywhere . . .'. They were lucky to be in Montmartre, where distractions were fewer than down on the Seine. The Butte was still not part of the city proper; the white monstrosity of the Sacré Coeur had only just been completed and there were still a few vineyards and stone quarries, slowly being overwhelmed by blocks of flats, hotels, brothels and cafés—the Exposition Universelle really marks the beginning of Paris's history as a tourist trap.

When they were not painting by day, the two young men toured the great museums and public galleries where they saw the works of artists who were to influence Picasso—Toulouse-Lautrec, Van Gogh, Gaugin—which both painters tried to copy during that first trip. Pablo had a stroke of luck a few days after he arrived. They were 'doing' the dealers and had stopped for coffee with Berthe Weil, a shrewd woman who later made a fortune out of Matisse. Talking together in Catalan they were approached by a man who turned out to be the Catalan industrialist Manach. Manach had started to collect drawings by young and promising artists and had invited himself to their studios, after giving them a very good lunch. There he saw Picasso's work and immediately offered him 150 francs a month for his whole output. When Berthe Weil heard of this, she assumed Manach must be on to something, and bought three of Picasso's bullfight scenes for 100 francs, reselling them the same day for 50 francs profit to the publisher Adolphe Brissen.

The Picasso entry in the Exposition Universelle was well received, too, and he found himself appraised by the critics who found 'a true sense of grief' in *Derniers Moments* (the deathbed scene he had painted for *Els Quatre Gats* show). Unfortunately his friends and acquaintances were so scathing about it that he painted over it, but he soon forgot even the painting in his joy at being in Paris, at having 'got a start' and 'being free'.

Casagemas' description of their home does not make it sound very attractive: the furniture consisted of one bed, with twelve blankets, an eiderdown and two pillows (which they rearranged to make two sleeping places, alternating with the mattress), a table, four chairs and a green armchair, a few pots and pans and 'a mysterious utensil for use by ladies. I don't know what it's called in Spanish but the idea is that it stops them having babies. They put their cunts in it and it has the opposite effect from putting their heads in the niche in the sanctuary at Nuria. . . . We can't get out much because the Moulin Rouge now costs 5 francs to get in some days.' That day the only food they had in the house was 'a tin of coffee and a can of peas'.

Being unable to get out very often, and unable to afford even the most modestly priced brothels (they were saving up for the winter in Spain), they picked up two girls, Odette and Germaine, and moved them in. Drawings of the two girls show them to be attractive and it is difficult to see what they got out of the relationship; Odette was a good deal taller than Pablo, and Germaine rather resented the fact that Carlo swore he was desperately in love with her but would not marry her. However, Casagemas wrote to a friend in Barcelona on 11 November 1900 that 'family life is heaven'.

Work had not been lost sight of and 'after a formal meeting with the ladies we agreed that we have been getting up too late and eating at irregular hours, not good for the digestion. On top of this, Odette has been getting drunk every night. . . . We arrived at a decision, that we will all go to sleep before midnight and lunch will end at one and not three. After lunch we will paint and they will do the housework, clean the place up, do a bit of sewing and be fucked as well. This is a kind of Eden, or dirty Arcadia'. (letter to Reventos.)

In December, the 'dirty Arcadia' closed down. Nonell was being paid a rent by Manach, so they do not seem to have been evicted. In later years, Picasso said he decided to get Casagemas out before he lost his head completely over Germaine, and he took his friend all the way to Málaga ('he could have got a train back to Paris too easily from Barcelona'). They arrived on 30 December, 1900 to anything but a heroes' welcome. The land-lord of the *Tres Naciones*, in spite of the cosmopolitan name of his establishment, said that he kept a respectable house and would not have these two unkempt, long-haired Bohemians in it. In the end, Picasso's aunt Pepa had to act as guarantor for the bill before they were allowed to stay.

The other members of the family were less obliging. His uncle Don Salvador disapproved of his looks and told him that he had been a great disappointment to them all. His father Don José harangued him to such an extent that Pablo stormed out of the house and never saw the old man again. Lola, of course, thought it was all a joke and promised to look after his pictures and take them with her to Barcelona. Maria's reactions were predictable. She did not like the looks of her son, nor the smell of Casagemas, formerly a favourite, who seemed to be always drunk. However, she apologized for the one by saying that all geniuses passed through 'difficult moments', that Pablo was only nineteen and look how well he had done in Paris, and excused Casagemas when she was told that he was the victim of a hopeless love affair. There was nothing she could do to clean them up or console the drunken lover, except let herself be taken out to lunch at restaurants where she could not be seen by too many of her friends. After a fortnight she advised them both to leave: Málaga did not want them any more.

On a cold day in mid-January, they arrived in Madrid. Picasso plunged into the deep end, reviving old acquaintance-ships and full of new projects. Casagemas was less enthusiastic and slipped away, to Barcelona and then Paris, without his friend making too much effort to persuade him to stay; perhaps he did not know he had gone. In Madrid, Pablo met Francisco de Assisi Soler, a poet from Barcelona hoping to make his name in the capital, and with the help of a friendly tutor from the Academy they started a magazine called *Arte Joven*. By some miracle, the first number was on sale on 10 March, 1901, but it was not clear whether it was to be a weekly or a monthly—the Spanish word *periodico* covered all eventualities. No accounts survive for the magazine, which lasted for five issues (until June); the unpaid printer refused to extend credit. Undaunted Picasso announced that he would soon launch another magazine, *Madrid Art Notes*, but this never appeared.

By mid-June Picasso was back in Paris. His friends in Barcelona had tried to detain him, with a one-man show at the Sala Pares, but he had had news which put him on the first train: Casagemas had shot himself in one of their favourite cafés. Apparently, Germaine had refused to see him again, much less reopen the 'dirty Arcadia', and the boy had got drunk, borrowed a pistol and blown a hole in his head as the bar was closing.

Picasso was never to have such a friend again. When Utrillo wrote from Barcelona and sent him the clippings from *Pel Y Ploma*, full of praise for the energetic if unsuccessful stay in Madrid ('did not sleep for a moment, studied in the galleries, ran around painting and drawing in the streets, founded two magazines . . .') and Barcelona ('Like fireworks, he lights us up'), he replied with one of his rare letters full of the sad news ('You can imagine the shock this has given me'). The news did not prevent him from 'fixing up' Germaine with a fellow Catalan, a sculptor Pixtor, nor from enjoying Odette from time to time. Nor, of course, did it distract him from work and the selling of it. He had met '. . . a Catalan called Cortada, loaded with millions and a miserly bastard . . . thinks of himself as an intellectual but is a pain in the arse'. Cortada was relieved of some of his money in exchange for some pastels. Manach, who was also rather mean, decided that it would be cheaper for his protégé to share his flat at 130 Boulevard de Clichy; though there were only two rooms, he was seldom in residence and Picasso could have the larger of the two as a studio. It was also a way of protecting his investment and of making sure, he hoped, that he really would get all the paintings and drawings for 150 francs a month.

No sooner had work started again than the gallery proprietor Vollard appeared there as if by magic. A shrewd, apparently sleepy man, Vollard was to deal in Picasso's pictures for more than thirty years, sometimes legally, sometimes in defiance of contracts with other *galleristes*. A French journalist met at the Exposition had suggested a one-man show for the young Spaniard—a favourable press would be guaranteed. The show opened on 24 June and in a preview Gustave Coquiot wrote: 'This very young Spanish painter is a lively, inquisitive man, an acute observer of street scenes and the human adventure . . . covering his canvasses in haste, angry at not being able to move his brushes faster. . . . Here are his whores . . . at the café, in the theatre, in bed before and after. For the high-class whores he chooses shades of mother-of-pearl or pink for the flesh . . . the others are seen lying in wait for their prey . . . without mawkishness or brutality . . . Here, too, are the mischievous little girls in pink and grey, with their fluttering skirts . . . and the boys, like seminarists, their faces as cunning as those of monkeys . . . Here is a dance at the Moulin Rouge . . . the work of an artist who paints round the clock.'

For readers in Barcelona, Père Coll wrote in *La Veu de Catalonia* (10 July, 1901): 'Picasso's exhibition at the Galerie Vollard on the Rue Lafitte is attracting collectors who are in search of the latest of the real artists of the future.'

It is interesting to note here that Pablo had virtually stopped using his father's name, even in the full version Pablo Ruiz Picasso, and the art world accepted this decision that he would use only his mother's surname in future. This hatred and contempt for his father, which seems to have welled up during the abortive trip to Málaga, was perhaps the reason why he went on searching for girls who looked like José Ruiz. As one of his fellow painters put it: 'Anything long and stringy, the more it looks like the Eiffel Tower the better.'

The Père Coll review was invaluable, after the Sala Peres exhibition, in keeping Picasso's name in front of the local public; on 19 July *Juventut* published a series of drawings, and the Catalan press was to follow him closely all his life. He also had a letter from Vidal Ventosa, a picture restorer of some repute, congratulating him on his work, and this is evidence, perhaps the first, of the good relations Picasso always enjoyed with the trade. Many artists have complained about being exploited by gallery proprietors (they had to get up very early to exploit Picasso) or being snubbed or patronized by them, have threatened never to show in this or that gallery again, and so on, have quarrelled with picture framers and art materials suppliers. Picasso always paid for his paints and frames, kept the stuff coming along, sent it to whoever would show it and sell it, and pocketed whatever was offered with only the mildest protest.

The poet Max Jacob went to the Vollard exhibition and liked what he saw. He invited himself to 130 Boulevard de Clichy and liked what he saw there, too: 'I spent a whole day looking at piles and piles of paintings. He was doing one or two each day or night and selling them for 150 francs each in the Rue Lafitte . . . When he wasn't working, he used to go to the Jardin des Plantes at night to see the animals, then on to the Moulin Rouge, the Casino de Paris and other fashionable music halls. He found a way to get himself introduced to some ladies in high society, like Liane de Pougy and Jeanne Bloch, and did workmanlike portraits of them.

One day, I remember, he just upped and left for Spain'. (*Cahiers d'Art*, **6**, Paris, 1927).

With his pockets full of money, Picasso went back to Barcelona and took his mother to dinner, to the theatre, to a soirée given by the Rector of the School of Fine Arts. Arm in arm they strolled down Las Ramblas, more like brother and sister than mother and son; Maria had worn well, and Pablo had aged considerably. She said she was proud to be with him, and not just because he used some of the money to get his hair cut, buy a man-about-town outfit and a top hat (which he later gave to Max Jacob). He also shut up the studio in Calle de la Plata, a final gesture of separation from his father, whom he avoided throughout his stay.

He found a studio in the Calle del Conde del Asalto, with

a terrace from which he could watch the world go by, and started to paint. By now the daily routine he was to follow all his life had been more or less set. Sir Roland Penrose, an admirer, called it 'a monotonous regularity in his working hours'. Far from keeping to the promise of bed by midnight, he seldom went to sleep until about three in the morning, chucking out time at *Els Quatre Gats*; sometimes he did not go to bed at all but went home with the *bodega* girl, and then walked the streets until eleven o'clock. Then he would set out the work for the day and draw in what he would paint later on. By half past twelve he was ready for *Els Quatre Gats* again and a long lunch and a short siesta, then work until eight or nine in the evening. A walk up Las Ramblas and across to the Cathedral Square and *Els Quatre Gats* would complete the cycle. Once a week he would take his mother out to dine (never at *Els Quatre Gats*), and sometimes went to the theatre with her.

Most of his paintings were portraits, of Sabartés, de Soto, rich and poor whores including the *bodega* girl. He enjoyed the life, as an artistic lion who had 'made it' in Paris, but he knew he could not stay. There was only one substantial gallery, the Sala Peres, and it could not sell enough of his output to guarantee him the sort of income he had had in Paris; like Dryden in his day and in another genre, Picasso loved money.

In the late summer of 1902 he went back to Paris, and from then on France was his *patrie*. He decided to move out of Manach's flat and find a home of his own. Having no real preference for any part of the city he asked the barman at *Le Zut* in the Place Ravignan if he knew of a studio large enough to live in. Freddie, the owner of *Le Zut*, a well-known meeting place for whores and their pimps, was to some extent in Picasso's debt because the previous year he and his friends had painted every square metre of the inner room (the cobwebs and peeling paper on the dripping walls had earned it the name The Hall of Stalactites), and he did know of just the place. It was not, however, very luxurious. Picasso replied that anything would be better than the Hôtel des Ecoles or the Hôtel du

Maroc between which he had been moving. The place turned out to be a block of studios round the corner in the Rue Ravignan. It would be ready 'soon': one of the painters who lived there was dying.

Undeterred by the macabre prospect, Picasso gave the good news to Max Jacob who said that until the happy event, they could share Max's flat in the Boulevard Voltaire. It was really just a big room with a little kitchenette, on the fifth floor, but Max would be out all day at a department store where he had taken a job.

Picasso later said that this period, from the death of Casagemas in 1901 until his first ménage in 1904, was really one of slow detachment from both Spain and his mother. She was always beckoning to him, as he put it, offering him an illusion of security—he was back in Barcelona in the New Year, 1903—but it was an illusion. The rash expenditure on new clothes, the haircut and the evenings spent dining and at the theatre with his mother were a part of it; his father's deliberate absence from home on each visit, translated into an obsession with girls who looked like his father—a sort of prolonged sexual assault on José Ruiz—were another. The fuss he made over Lola, and the exaggerated *bonhomie* at *Els Quatre Gats* were frantic efforts to be what he was not, in a place to which he did not belong. He knew this, of course. A letter to Max Jacob written from Barcelona in January 1903 says sadly: 'I think about the room on the Boulevard Voltaire, and the omelettes, the beans and the Brie and the fried potatoes.'

There were, of course, temptations apart from his mother's devotion. The local critics were sycophantic: 'Picasso, the well known Spanish artist, who has had so many triumphs in Paris, has recently sold, for a respectable sum, one of his latest works to the Parisian collector M. Jean St Gaudens' (*El Liberal*); and there was much more in the same tone. Picasso liked flattery and critical respectability but he was also a realist. He knew that he was not the best known artist in Spain and, given the strength of the Establishment, and his own temperament, he was unlikely to become *the* painter of his day. Even the painting to which *El Liberal* had drawn attention (it was a morbid scene, *La Vie*, painted over *Derniers Moments*) was not at all 'one of the few truly solid works that has been created for some time'. Even among the habitués of *Els Quatre Gats* there were better known intellectuals, doing better work—men like the Utrillos, Santiago Rusinol, Ramon Reventos and Pixtot (Pichot, who commuted from Paris) and Iturrino. It was not Picasso who had won the Grand Prix at the Paris Exposition but Sorollo-Bastida, and the French critic who collected comments for the commemorative volume noted Eliseo Meifren and Luis Pidal Menender as just as promising as young Picasso. A lot of Pablo's work was plain hack work done in the same spirit as Victor Hugo's verse ('Give Victor 5 francs and he will write you a sonnet on how to boil an egg'). It was a time of great stress and indecision.

Fortunately for the future, the stress and indecision purged Picasso of much that was meretricious, and prepared him to cut the umbilical cord.

The change manifested itself in the slow predominance of paintings virtually all in blue. The Blue Period (the word has appropriate echoes of the Blues of the American negro) dates from the death of Casagemas, the one emotional rival to his mother, and its first notable work is the view of the Boulevard de Clichy and Rue de Douai through a window in what is a blue room—the walls are blue, the bath and all the furniture, and the light and shade are tones of blue. The *Burial of Casagemas* (also 1901) has the mourners dressed all in blue, and *Woman with a Chignon, Child Holding a Dove* (which is a pigeon) and the important *Harlequin* are all suffused with the same colour.

The contrast between these works and the brightly coloured street, brothel and music hall scenes intrigued his friends and upset Vollard, who could not sell any of them. In the end Vollard refused to have any more in his gallery and Picasso had to store virtually the whole of the Blue Period canvasses with Pixtot at his *atelier* in Montmartre. Picasso went back to Barcelona in January 1903 with only a few hundred francs in his pocket. Undeterred, he went on painting '. . . beggars turned out of town, conversation pieces of dumb, shapeless figures at dark crossroads . . . Old men and women in their second childhood, goitrous children with lack-lustre eyes, coming and going or seated hopelessly in doorways . . . blue-eyed, blue-skinned prostitutes with gentle, sad invitations in their smiles . . .' (Coquiot). In a rare analysis of an artist's work Carl Jung noted: '. . . [among painters] two groups may be distinguished: the neurotics and the schizophrenics. The first group produces pictures of a synthetic character, with a pervasive tone. When they are abstract, and therefore lacking the element of feeling, they are at least definitely symmetrical or convey an unmistakable meaning. . . . The second group produces pictures which immediately reveal their alienation from feeling . . . From a formal point of view the main characteristic is one of fragmentation . . . a series of faults (in the geological sense) which run right through the picture. The picture leaves one cold, or disturbs one by its paradoxical unfeeling and grotesque unconcern for whoever is looking at it. This is the group to which Picasso belongs . . . A series of images begins as a rule with a symbol of the Nekyia, the journey to Hades, the descent into the underworld of the unconscious, saying goodbye to the world above. . . . Thus Picasso starts with the still, objective pictures of the Blue Period—the blue of night, of moonlight and water, the Tuat blue of the Egyptian underworld . . . He conjures up crude shapes, grotesque and primitive . . . Harlequin wanders like Faust through all these forms . . .'.

Picasso always maintained that he painted easily, just as ideas came to him, and it is difficult to imagine that an anti-intellectual (as he was) ever troubled himself with analysis. The paintings kept coming, even though nobody seemed very interested.

There was an odd incident early in 1904, after a move into a rather splendid studio in the Calle de Comercio (Vollard still had enough of the 'old stuff' to sell and Manach occasionally sent his *mensile*). His father suddenly turned up, with a ready prepared canvas, in the hope that a reconciliation could be achieved in paint; Picasso reacted by leaving the canvas almost bare but colouring every square metre of the walls.

The incident with his father, and the news from *Le Zut* that the unfortunate tenant of the studio in Rue Ravignan had passed away, took away the savour of Barcelona for the last time and he left for Paris. His farewell dinner with his mother was not particularly cheerful; she said his father was dying, and when he had gone she would go back to Málaga, leaving the flat to Lola and her fiancé when they got married. He would always be welcome, of course. He knew that he would never go there again. When he had a bullfighting scene to sell, he would describe himself as a *malagueno*, which gave the work, Manach said, more authenticity; but Málaga was even worse than Barcelona. Only Rome and Paris were natural homes for artists. As Barzini noted: '. . . some good, others the struggling young, the old failures and the young hopefuls, the successful and those who will never amount to anything—they know it and do not care . . . There are all kinds: writers, painters, dancers, musicians, actors, sculptors, poets or followers of new and as yet unnamed arts . . . dabblers, dilettanti, people whose love for art is much greater than their modest capacities and talents, who somehow eke out a living in artistic surroundings on the margin of the art world.'

Sabartés always said that it was an article in *El Liberal* (24 March 1904) by Carlos Juner-Vidal which made up Picasso's mind. The article began: 'Pablo Ruiz Picasso! Here is an artist hardly known to anyone, since even those who "know" him do not know him well enough to understand what he is about.' After observing that Picasso had seen in the State galleries 'the great men on whom posterity has set the seal of immortality', he went on to say . . .' if he wished, he could produce and sell as much as he liked but he refuses to please the Philistines or consider that Art is just a trade or pastime for anyone. . . . Picasso's work cannot be compared to anything else in this country . . . He will return soon to Paris and there he will be properly judged.'

Within forty-eight hours of his arrival, Picasso was installed in his first real home in Paris, at 13 Rue Ravignan. Max Jacob, who helped him collect his paintings from the various hotels, from Pixtot (who soon moved in upstairs with his wife, Germaine, the girl who had driven Casagemas to suicide), the Rue Gabrielle and Boulevard de Clichy, named the squat block of a building the *Bâteau-Lavoir*, after the laundry barges which plied the Seine. The *Bâteau-Lavoir*, said Graham Sutherland, was to become the 'most famous artists' slum in Paris'.

For the first few weeks, when he was not painting and drawing feverishly, Picasso spent the day renewing old acquaintances, getting an advance from Vollard and trying to find Manach. The Blue Period was a flop, though the drawings still sold well and Vollard told him to 'put the stuff away somewhere'.

Giovanni Ruggeri wrote in *Gente* (Milan, 1986): 'His blue harlequins were lost, defeated like him. One day, overcome by frustration, he rolled up all the Blue Period canvases he had in the studio and threw them into a cupboard. If they had got lost, there would have been no Blue Period because everything he had painted in that way would have disappeared and the few survivors, if any, would have been rated aberrations.' This is, of course, nonsense. Picasso knew very well that one day, the paintings would come into their own, made famous and saleable by something else he had painted which had found a market. A policeman in the quartier had said to him one day: 'We do not always catch the thieves for stealing. Sometimes, we get them because they do not pay the gas bills or beat up a friend. But we get them in the end.'

Picasso may have been 'blue' and despondent but he was not despairing. He always believed in himself. One day Germaine Pixtot rushed down to his studio and told him that her husband was threatening to commit suicide.

'Bring him down here.'

'He won't come. He thinks he is responsible for your mad paintings because he has taken Casagemas's place.'

Picasso took a huge canvas, half completed, a portrait of a

syphilitic, tubercular prostitute grotesquely celebrating her end. He shouted up to Pixtot:

'Oye! Before you throw yourself off that balcony onto the street, remember I've got this and a couple of others to finish. Give me a few hours and I'll get them done, so when the Press comes to ask questions, I'll have something to show them.'

Pixtot recovered rapidly and wrote to Picasso's mother that her son was settling in nicely.

Fernande

'The man whom I have heard discourse most abundantly about women and love was one of my servants, and neither I nor anyone else was able to learn that he had ever had more than one love affair, and that with a German woman who made eyes for mechanical dolls.'

(Ezra Pound)

André Salmon has left a description of the studio at 13 Rue Ravignan: 'There was a wall cupboard for paints, made of planks nailed together, a round table you could have found in any middle class *salle* (he bought it from the junk shop down the road) and an easel. In the middle of the room was an enormous zinc bathtub, which usually had books in it. In one corner, he had made a sort of inner room with a divan and a mattress on it. We used to call this the maid's room, and we used the divan at parties if we wanted a quick fuck; this went on, of course, until Fernande Olivier arrived' (*Souvenirs Sans Fin*, 1955).

Fernande gave her own account of how she arrived. She wrote (*Picasso et Ses Amis*, Paris 1933): 'As I lived in the same house, I often met him going in or out or on the stairs. He seemed to me to be always on his way to some bar or café and I remember asking myself when he ever did any work. Then somebody told me he preferred to work at night, that during the day there was a steady stream of visitors, mostly Spaniards. One day I ran in from a sudden downpour of rain and he stopped me in the corridor outside his studio and would not let me pass. But I did not get angry with him because he was laughing and had a little kitten in his arms which he offered me. I laughed, too, and he took me into his studio. . . . This was my introduction to the world in which I was to live and love for so long.'

This was, as is perhaps to be expected, a rather romanticised account of what was a carefully planned meeting. Fernande Olivier was a Parisienne whose parents had a hat shop in the suburbs and who had been sent to live with an aunt in the country when her mother died. At the age of sixteen, this seemed to be something like immolation and she looked about for some distraction—a man. She found the local schoolteacher, an amateur sculptor, and before he knew where he was, he had married her. He went mad soon afterwards, and she was on her own again, so she decided to go back to Paris and see what her native intelligence, youth and beauty could get for her. She was not immediately successful and had ended up in the *Bateau-Lavoir* (she would have preferred the present name of the site, Place Emile-Goudeau), doing a bit of washing for any of the tenants who wanted it and lifting her skirts for the local coal merchant when she ran out of money. She had watched with interest when this new tenant, with his friends Junyer y Vidal (dressed like an off-duty bullfighter) and Max Jacob (in top hat and frock coat), had moved in. He was younger than she was and shorter, but to compensate for this he was said to be very virile (the girls who had been to the maid's room compared notes loudly in her presence) and, more importantly, was said to be already launched on a profitable career. She planned very carefully an assault on this far from impregnable fortress and within two months was installed.

Like any woman who moves in with a man, she saw it as her duty to tidy up her new home: 'Huge unfinished canvasses stood all over the studio, and there was an air of hard work everywhere, but Oh God what a mess everything was in!' Picasso watched bemused as she put everything in order (later he was to break a huge unfinished canvas over her head) and for a time rather enjoyed the new regime. He was by nature a domestic animal and as far as he was concerned his mother had been replaced by a young, attractive woman who not only swept his floor and cooked on a paraffin stove, but also warmed his bed whenever it wanted warming. She knew virtually nothing about Art, but she had lived long enough in Montmartre to hear a lot of talk about it, and, of course, the *quartier* lived off the painters, sculptors, their students and clients who bought their food in the local shops, ate and drank in the bars and restaurants and gave regular employment to policemen, postmen, plumbers, electricians and whores. She was, however, better educated than her lover. She had taken a course which qualified her to teach in elementary schools (though she had never done so), and she certainly taught him how to read and write in French. Picasso was very impressed by this, and by her enthusiasm in bed. He became very jealous, hid away her shoes so she could not go out, insisted that she lie down on a couch (from the same junk shop as the table) and read aloud to him while he painted; in fact, she acquired a reputation for being very lazy, which was unfair.

Of his work at the beginning of the new regime she wrote: 'He was working at the time on what has become a famous etching of a couple at a table in a bistro . . . poverty and the effects of alcohol show in this wretched, starving couple . . . Picasso has since painted over another of a cripple leaning on his crutch and carrying a basket of flowers . . . The man was haggard, gaunt and miserable . . .'

Fernande was not a fool. She did not presume to tell Picasso what or how to paint, though she encouraged him to draw because she knew they could sell as much as they wanted to of his drawings. Nor did she try to change his habit of buying and wearing the cheapest possible workman's overalls, though she was amused to note that he always wore good, even expensive, matching underpants and socks. She found tactful ways of getting rid of visitors, though she entertained 'useful' friends warmly and produced miraculous meals on the little stove; she had some difficulty discouraging the coal merchant, though she did find a way to keep his hands off her and still have the coal that winter, at a reduced price. Picasso found himself drawn out of the bars and restaurants before the night was too far on, tempted by what he knew was waiting for him on the bed; when he allowed her to come out with him, she would remind him of this before he got to the second bottle of wine. She knew he had to have eight hours' sleep a night, and that he produced more if he could stick to his routine. Above all, she brought to an end the waste of time which had always irritated him.

The first fruits of her influence were soon visible. The Blue Period came to an end. In that first autumn he did several beautiful watercolours of Fernande naked on the bed, as he himself stands by and enjoys the sight; portraits of local people, one of Fernande's washerwomen colleagues, an actor, and innumerable circus performers from the Cirque Médrano nearby. What came to be known as the Rose Period had begun.

The first exhibition of the 'new style' was held at the Galeries Serrurier, 25 February–6 March, 1905. This had been arranged by Charles Morice, a journalist and general fixer who had taken the place of Gustave Coquiot as Picasso's principal contact with the Press; Morice's *Mercure de France* was more influental than Coquiot's *Journal*. As Picasso wrote to Jacinto Reventos on 22 February: 'I am forced to deal . . . because of interest and need—have to eat but ought not to have to waste so much time . . . It teaches you a stupid but important lesson, one, anyone learns in business in Barcelona—grab what you can. [Charles Morice] is in charge. . . . He always does well by whatever he has his sticky fingers in . . . we'll see what comes of it . . . God willing, I'll sell everything.'

He did not sell everything, but he sold enough to enable him to accept an invitation to Holland, where a Dutch writer called Schilperoort invited him to stay at his home at Schooredam, and a holiday in Spain. When he got back from the short trip to Holland, he confided in André Salmon: 'Fernande is a big girl, but those Dutch women are enormous. Once you got inside them you'd never find your way out again.'

The holiday with Fernande, in late August and September, in Tiana in the wine-producing Maresme, north-east of Barcelona, was more to his liking. A friend wrote: 'Ramon Reventos used to say whenever Picasso was discussed [that] the ochres of his harlequins were stolen from the golden colour of the vineyards of Tiana, and he knew it.'

In the 'Thirties, when Picasso was already a millionaire, Fernande always tried to cast herself in the role of the mistress who had made his life bearable when they were 'oppressed by poverty'. Though her reaction is understandable, and common to all abandoned mistresses in her situation, it established a myth which is far from reality. The steady stream of Spaniards of which she complained came to Picasso's studio because it was the one place they could be sure of finding something to eat and drink. There were also rich collectors and gallery proprietors at the door of 13 Rue Ravignan. Olivier Sanserre, a Councillor of State, was one of them and he bought Picasso's works for cash. Manach and Vollard had rivals in Serrurier and Clovis Sargot as dealers in Picasso's work; Leo Stein bought a canvas in 1905 from Sargot for 150 francs and followed that up with purchases worth 800 francs at the studio. Fernande complained that she had to 'smile' at the coal merchant ('He liked my eyes') to get coal for the stove during the winter of 1904–05, but she was only keeping alive a useful connection. The dog, Frika, was supposed to have brought home a stolen string of sausages 'which kept us alive', but local grocers were quite happy to deliver on credit, and they are not known internationally for their philanthropy. Paco Durio was supposed to leave 'a tin of sardines, a loaf of bread and a litre of wine' outside the door because they had nothing to eat, but he said that it was only an ashamed way of repaying all his friends' hospitality. Picasso's drawings and his new paintings sold everywhere, even to a former wrestler who kept a junk shop and bought art (he sold Picasso a Douanier Rousseau as a canvas to paint over). When Fernande complains that they had to eat out at *Le Lapin Agile*, successor to *Le Zut*, for 2 francs a head, she fails to add that it had the best food in Montmartre.

The truth was out, of course, even then when Picasso and Junyer celebrated their return to Paris in 1904 with a set of drawings showing them getting 'a bag of gold' from Duran-Rouel, one of the richest collectors in Paris. What Fernande did not say in her memoirs was that Picasso put his money away in the bank like a squirrel and only let her have handouts when she had pleased him more than usual, or on the rare occasions on which he felt expansive.

Picasso's circle of acquaintances suggests that he habitually dined out on more than a tin of sardines. In addition to the Spaniards, Pixtot (Pichot), Zuloaga, Canals and Manolo Hugue, not to mention Paco Durio (a friend of Cézanne), there were the French and foreign collectors, Max Jacob, Alfred Jarry and Apollinaire (*not* a connoisseur of sardines).

The exhibition Morice had organized gave Picasso the entrée into all Parisian intellectual society. Morice had written a long review in *Mercure de France* and produced an excellent catalogue with an introduction by Guillaume Apollinaire (Kostrovitsky). Apollinaire wrote two reviews, one in *La Revue Immoraliste*, and the other in *La Plume*. The reviews were eulogistic: 'More than any other poet, sculptor or painter, this Spaniard chills our bones. His thoughts are there, laid bare . . . He has come from a long way away, from the opulence, brutality and colour of seventeenth century Spain . . . The colour is flat as in a fresco, the lines are clear . . . placed on the frontiers of life, animals take human form and vice versa . . .'

Max Jacob remembers his first meeting with Apollinaire, the Polish critic and poet: 'One morning, I met Picasso for breakfast and he said he had spent the previous evening in a bar on the Rue d'Amsterdam with a marvellous man who had reviewed his exhibition. I was to meet him later in the day . . . When I did, I was immediately impressed. He was sitting on a leather-covered bench with his back to the wall in a restaurant, with books everywhere on the surrounding tables. He gave me his hand and that began the friendship *à trois* which lasted until his death. . . . We used to wait for him outside the bank where he worked in Rue Lepelletier and had lunch and dinner together. Picasso and Apollinaire were like brothers—Picasso painted harlequins and acrobats and Apollinaire put them into his poems. . . .'

Most of Picasso's paintings in 1905 were circus scenes. This irritated Fernande who rashly suggested that he paint some of the local churches, maybe the Sacré Coeur which was proving to be such a tourist attraction; he retaliated by making a mock altar above her bed, with two vases as candleholders and her blue slip as an altarcloth. To prove the point that he was making a serious inquiry into the way circus people lived, their mixture of clannishness and friendliness, the tragedy of the old acrobat and the arrogance of the young, he embarked on the largest painting he had done so far. *The Acrobats' Family*, over seven feet square, followed a large watercolour, *The Circus Family*, and there are elements common to them both. The acrobats are joined by people from the painter's early life, a malagueña off to church in a mantilla, the girl from La Coruña, and an old clown who is his uncle Salvador, but somehow they all form part of a whole, a 'mystery' which fascinated Rainer Maria Rilke and inspired one of the Duino Elegies.

The fat clown also appears in some pieces of sculpture Picasso attempted during the winter of 1905–6 (he had done very little until then) and was joined by portraits of Fernande and Alice Princet (later Derain's wife). Tristan Tzara was the first to notice that people were being joined more and more by animals in the paintings and even as part of the sculpture—the usual animals, horses and dogs, and exotic creatures like peacocks and hippopotami. Picasso was so pleased with his sculpture (Vollard made a lot of money having them cast in bronze) that he rashly offered to buy Fernande some perfume (she had complained that she smelt only of paraffin from the stove) and told her to take the money for it from his wallet (always bulging). She did as she was told and came back with a bottle of her favourite scent worth eighteen dollars at that time—an enormous sum; it was the first and last bottle she ever had during the years she lived with him.

Pleased with his portrait sculpture, and three portraits in

oil, *Woman with a Fan, Woman in a Chemise* and *Boy Leading a Horse*, he decided to try a painting with Gertrude Stein as his model. She was a bit taken aback, knowing that he very seldom used live models as he was too mean to pay them, but she agreed. She lived to regret it, she used to say, as he made her sit for him eighty times and never offered any refreshment. She had plenty of time to study his painting techniques, however, and left some interesting notes on it: 'Picasso sat very tight on his chair and very close to his canvas, and on a very small palette which was of uniform brown grey colour, mixed some more brown grey and the painting began'. Sometimes he sat on the floor and took the painting off the easel, propping it up against a chair. Sometimes he had the canvas on the couch and knelt in front of it. Fernande was always hovering about, 'the *femme decorative*', smelling sweetly now.

Picasso's choice of a lesbian as a subject for a picture is odd seen in the context of his macho Spanish character, but she was after all his most important collector and the one who had made his work known to the international community. It would be unkind to suggest that he thought of her only as an investment. There was a genuine mutual liking and respect for many years and Gertrude Stein could boast truthfully that her flat in the Rue de Fleurus was the only place where Picasso dined regularly for over thirty years. The portrait, however, did not go well. One day in early July he painted out the whole of the head and said he could do no more. He was off to Spain for a rest.

Fernande was glad to be out of Paris during the hot summer, and packed everything, including the perfume and the paraffin stove, for the trip. They took the train to Barcelona, where she met his family for the first time, then worked their way back towards the French frontier to a village called Gosol high in the Pyrenees; the last part of the journey was done on the backs of mules. It was a tiny village, a score of stone houses round the little square. The air was cool and fresh, the sky blue and Mount Cadi like a Spanish Fuji with its white snowcap. The place smelt of the fruit ripening in the orchards, of coffee, olive oil and wild thyme. While she lay about reading he painted more than thirty scenes of village life—with no trace of the all-pervading blue of his work only two years before. She could certainly congratulate herself on having brought back warm colours to his palette, and he seemed to want no more than to enjoy the place and her company.

The holiday came to an end one evening when the visiting doctor told him that he had two cases of typhoid in the village. Always a potential hypochondriac and fearful even of the common cold, Picasso ordered Fernande to pack. They left the following morning and did not stop until they reached the *Bâteau-Lavoir*. A household tragedy restored his good humour—the cat had eaten the white mice he kept in a drawer in his paint cupboard.

Picasso always refused to exhibit at the *Salon des Indépendants* in the spring and he was unlikely ever to be invited to show at the autumn *Salon*, but he had been to the *Indépendants* that year to see some paintings by Matisse and his followers (known as the *fauves*, or wild beasts). Leo and Gertrude Stein, who had introduced Picasso to Matisse at their home, bought the centrepiece of the show, Matisse's *La Joie de Vivre*, a splendid picture alive with bright patches of colour. Picasso loved the picture and from then on he used to take Fernande at least once a week to Matisse's studio to see what 'the old man' (he was twelve years older than Picasso) was doing. Fernande described him as 'a very attractive person, just what you would expect of a painter, with a wonderful red beard. Though he seemed to be hiding behind his spectacles he always spoke very clearly and his ideas were easy to understand. Picasso always seemed a bit subdued, while Matisse really shone'.

Matisse had started a collection of wood sculpture from the French African and Caribbean colonies. Max Jacob believed that there lay the birthplace of Cubism, or at least the genesis of Picasso's part in it: 'At Matisse's he saw negro sculpture for the first time . . . Cubism was born from negro sculpture. Picasso started some figure drawings of men with their noses growing out from between their eyes . . . he used to think about them a lot, simplifying the outlines of animals and things in general until he got it all into a single line, like the drawings you see in historic caves.'

André Salmon agrees: 'He had taken to negro sculpture and said it was better than the Egyptian [but] it was not just an appetite for the picturesque. He said that the Polynesian and Dahomeyan approach was reasonable enough even if it revealed a world which looked different from the one we had learned to see. . . . Faces whose noses were seen full on, even further flattened, like isosceles triangles . . . the enchantment of Oceania and Africa . . . the noses became white and yellow and touches of yellow and blue lit up the bodies.'

Daniel-Henry Kahnweiler, who had abandoned merchant banking in London for a career as a collector and dealer in Northern Europe, saw these experiments develop into the famous portrait of *Les Demoiselles d'Avignon*. Shrewder than Salmon, Kahnweiler knew of other influences, the cave paintings at Elche, the odd portraits of Steinlen (the painter of cats on the famous posters advertising milk, and the donor of the cat which ate the white mice), *objets d'art* from Martinique, not to speak of literary ideas. While Fernande was working on Picasso's basic grammar and syntax, Max Jacob was guiding him through what he considered significant books, among them Rabelais' *Gargantua*; this late literary education was probably just as important as the enthusiasm he shared with Matisse for exotic sculpture. Salmon reports without explanation an example of 'literary interference': 'One evening, Picasso suddenly left a group of friends who had been talking about poetry, went back to his studio and took down a painting of a young workman he had not touched for a month—he gave it a crown of roses and turned it into a masterpiece.'

Les Demoiselles d'Avignon seems to have had a literary origin, too, because its author always referred to it as 'the philosophical brothel'. Salmon believed that the picture had grown out of a series of nudes of Fernande, *Women Dressing, Woman Combing Her Hair* and others of 1905–6, but Kahnweiler noted that paradoxically 'the nudes had been stripped . . . to a strange, large painting of women, fruit and drapery. . . . There is in it a beginning in the spirit of 1906 and there is one section which is all 1907. The nudes, with big eyes, stand as stiff as tailors' dummies . . . bodies with flesh tints and black and white—that was the 1906 bit. Then in the fore-ground there is a bent figure with a bowl of fruit, bright blue, loud yellow, white and black . . . This was the beginning of Cubism, an attempt to solve all painting's problems at once . . . those of representing three dimensions and colour on a flat surface . . . the simulation of shape by using chiaroscuro . . . the problem of reconciliation of the whole. Foolishly, Picasso decided to try to solve all these problems at once. He put sharp-edged images on the canvas . . . in the brightest colours, yellow, red, blue and black. He put the colours on in threads to give direction and to build up, with the effect of the drawing, a three-dimensional effect. . . . But after months of hard work, Picasso realized that a solution to these problems did not lie along that road'. (*Der Weg Zum Kubismus.*)

Max Jacob once observed to Fernande (whose friend he remained even when Picasso threw her out) that the problems were mostly invented by painters themselves, and interested only painters. Most people who bought or merely looked at pictures were moved by a 'general effect' and not by technique. Look at Jacopo Bellini, he used to say, with his perspective boxes and wax figurines, brought to Venice from Florence in 1429, not to speak of Tintoretto with his dolls' houses, rain and wind machines and all the other little laboratories to test the effect of light and shade. Was anybody impressed in Venice? No, Bellini had to move to Padova to find an audience.

Kahnweiler thought the failure worthwhile and the effort inseparable from the personality of a serious painter, whatever the general public thought. Anyway, 'an artist with genius always produces works of aesthetic value . . . his innermost being makes beautiful'. And, he might have added, saleable. He had so far infiltrated the Picasso establishment that he had been added to the list of dealers. In the autumn of 1907, there was a major retrospective exhibition of works by Cézanne, which showed his experiments with cylinders and cones and with hatchings on plain colour surfaces (mistaken for negro art); some of what he learned was used by Picasso to take *Les Demoiselles* still further.

Fernande was mystified by this new enthusiasm, and not pleased to have the large unfinished canvas always on show; always conscious of her status as a married woman living with another man, she thought a scene from a whorehouse inappropriate as a centrepiece for her establishment. Luckily, she acquired a new friend, Gertrude Stein's lover Alice B Toklas who had just moved in at the Rue Fleurus; Fernande's morality did not buckle at lesbianism. Alice has left a record of their first meeting: 'Pablo and Fernande, as everybody called them at that time, walked in. He was small, quick-moving but not restless, his eyes having a strange faculty of opening wide and drinking in what he wished to see. He had the isolation and movement of the head of a bullfighter at the head of their procession. Fernande was a tall beautiful woman with a wonderful big hat and a very evidently new dress, they were both very fussed. "I am very upset," said Pablo, "but you know very well, Gertrude, I am never late but Fernande had ordered a dress for the *vernissage* tomorrow and it didn't come." '

Like Fernande, Alice was an intelligent but not intellectual woman and they both rather resented being in the shadow of the great, the more so since they were living with and being supported by them. They enjoyed talking about feminine frivolities, especially perfume and hats; the story of the eighteen dollar bottle stayed in Alice's mind for years. Picasso had apparently made Fernande a small dress allowance after years of keeping her in rags, and what was most on her mind was not the birth of Cubism but how she should apportion the money between dresses and hats. She shared a passion for hats with Alice (whose 'autobiography' was, of course, written by Gertrude Stein and emphasizes all these failings), who observed: 'She liked hats, she had the true French feeling about a hat. If a hat did not provoke some witticism from a man on the street the hat was not a success. Later on once in Montmartre she and

I were out walking together. She had on a large yellow hat and I had on a much smaller blue one. As we were walking along a workman stopped and called out, there go the sun and the moon . . . Ah, said Fernande to me with a radiant smile, you see our hats are a success.'

Picasso, who knew that Gertrude and Alice were a lesbian couple, felt that Fernande was safe with them. Anyway, he was becoming rather irritated by her. She was hinting, not very subtly, that they should leave the *Bâteau-Lavoir* and set up a superior establishment where she could entertain properly. He was now a famous man, and he had the money. What was the point of putting it all in the bank, at the age of twenty-five? She thought she had found the right psychological moment after the *Salon des Indépendants* in 1907 when Vollard made a substantial offer to buy all Picasso's work, cutting out all the other dealers. She stamped her foot, made her characteristic Napoleonic gesture of poking her index finger at the ceiling, and demanded a move.

'You move,' said Picasso.

Tearful, Fernande hurried to see Alice to tell her the news. She had hoist herself with her own petard, she was told. She had to leave and hope that Picasso would ask her to come back. They interceded with Pablo and got her a small allowance, which she spent quickly installing herself in a 'proper apartment'. She began to give tea parties to all her friends, using Germaine Pichot as a source of news about Pablo and his state of mind, as he used Germaine to find out how she was getting on without him. Neither really enjoyed the separation. Fernande pretended that it was the little things she missed, like the American comic supplements to the newspapers Gertrude passed on (Pablo hoped to learn English that way). Picasso missed the domesticity and told Gertrude that Fernande would come back when her money ran out and she had sold her last piece of jewellery. Alice tried to help out by taking French lessons from Fernande, and was impressed by how many of the *cercle* had remained loyal to her; Max Jacob took her out to dinner when he could, Van Dongen painted her portrait and paid her a sitter's fee, Germaine Pichot offered discarded lovers, Alice Princet (who brought along Derain, with whom she was living) gave her a dog.

Gertrude Stein said it was not enough. She would go back, even to the Rue Ravignan. Alice's 'autobiography' says: 'Gertrude Stein said to me suddenly, is Fernande wearing her earrings? I do not know, I said. Well, notice, she said. The next time I saw Gertrude Stein I said, yes, Fernande is wearing her earrings. Oh, well, she said, there is nothing to be done yet, it's a nuisance because Pablo naturally having nobody in the studio cannot stay at home. In another week I was able to announce that Fernande was not wearing her earrings. Oh well, it's alright then, she has no money left and it's all over, said Gertrude Stein. And it was. A week later I was dining with Fernande and Pablo at the Rue de Fleurus. I gave Fernande a Chinese gown from San Francisco and Pablo gave me a lovely drawing.'

Back in the *Bâteau-Lavoir*, Fernande found to her horror that in her absence, Max Jacob and Apollinaire had persuaded Picasso to smoke opium. She had to try it, too, and she comments on the bad temper which followed the morning after nights of 'confident, tender, indulgent friendship'. Fortunately for them a young German painter died of sniffing ether nearby, and that was an end to drugs in the household. Picasso was painting again and celebrated her return with some warm nudes, as well as carrying on with his Cubist experiments, but she noticed that he seemed to be growing out of Montmartre. He had never taken any interest in any sport other than bull-fighting, and seldom took any unnecessary exercise, but now she found herself walking across Paris every Tuesday to see what was going on across the Seine—in particular at the *Closerie des Lilas* where Max Jacob held court, with André Salmon and Apollinaire. On Fridays they were always at Gertrude Stein's, on Thursdays it was a walk to the Matisses'. Vollard gave dinner parties in the basement of his gallery and there were weekends at Apollinaire's mother's house at Le Vesinet, where she was astonished to see Picasso start to box with the poet.

Encouraged by this restlessness, and by the necessity to give the occasional dinner party to repay hospitality, Fernande began to entertain on a new scale. Gertrude Stein said later it was to show Picasso how inadequate their establishment was. In 1908, a dinner party in honour of 'Douanier' Rousseau seems to have been the high point of the season. The guest list reads like a *Who's Who* of Parisian intellectual life—Apollinaire, Gremnitz, Leo and Gertrude Stein (and Alice), André Salmon, the Pixtots, Max Jacob, Jacques Vaillant, Marie Laurencin—30 people at table for dinner and more afterwards. It seems to have been a lively affair. The guest of honour was so moved by it all that he sat still under a dripping wax candelabra until a dunce's cap of candlewax formed on his head; as they scraped it off, he played his violin. Marie Laurencin had been drunk before dinner, and Pontins had failed to deliver the elaborate meal ordered so what there was to eat was a scratch affair but nobody seemed to mind. Fernande recalled 'the wives and mistresses of the painters wore really original dresses. Madame Agero looked like a schoolgirl in a black smock', that the Americans were not well dressed, and much else of *haute mode* and cattiness. After dinner there were speeches and a sort of spontaneous cabaret.

Gertrude Stein wrote later: 'Guillaume Apollinaire got up and made a solemn eulogy, I do not remember all he said, but it ended up with a poem he had written and half chanted, everybody else joined in the chorus *Le Peinture de ce Rousseau* . . . there were toasts and then all of a sudden André Salmon who was sitting next to my friend . . . leaped upon the by no means solid table (it was made of planks over the bath) and poured out another eulogy or poem . . . seized a big glass, drank what was in it, then promptly went off his head, completely drunk, and began to fight. The men got hold of him, Braque, a great big chap, got hold of a statue in each arm while Gertrude Stein's brother, another big chap, protected little Rousseau and his violin. . . . The others, with Picasso (who though small is very strong) leading, dragged Salmon into the front atelier and locked him in. Everybody came back and sat down'. Fernande has a variant on this last incident: 'André

Salmon and Gremnitz did an imitation of delirium tremens, chewing soap and frothing at the mouth to horrify the Americans.'

After Salmon's performance, whatever it was, 'the evening was peaceful. Marie Laurencin sang some charming old Norman songs in a thin voice. Agero's wife sang some charming old Limousin songs, Pichot did a wonderful religious Spanish dance ending as Christ crucified on the floor, Guillaume Apollinaire solemnly approached me and my friend and asked us to sing some Red Indian songs . . . Rousseau, gentle and blissful, played the violin and told us about plays he had written and memories of Mexico . . . About three o'clock in the morning we went into the atelier where Salmon had been deposited . . . and there he lay sleeping, surrounding him half chewed were a box of matches, a *petit bleu* and my yellow fantasie. . . . All of a sudden, and with a wild yell, Salmon rushed down the hill. Gertrude Stein and her brother, my friend and I, all in one cab, took Rousseau home.'

Shortly after this memorable dinner (it took Germaine and Fernande two days to clear up the mess), Picasso decided he would like to spend the summer in the country. A friend offered him a cottage on a farm near the Forêt de Hallatte, in the green countryside watered by the Oise, and with Fernande, the cat and the dog, he set off for La Rue Des Bois (the postal address of the hamlet nearby). It was not a very comfortable cottage, but they had their own well (there was only one tap for the whole of the studio complex at *Bâteau-Lavoir*) and plenty of good, fresh food. Though he did some experimental work with perspective and masses of colour, many of his pictures were recognizable still lifes and portraits of the local people.

Paradoxically, Braque spent the same period painting under the influence of *Les Demoiselles d'Avignon* and had a picture rejected by the jury of the *Salon d'Automne* because it was 'Cubist', probably the first time the adjective was used to describe the 'new style'. Matisse, who was on the jury, apologized for 'a lack of comprehension' but Braque was converted and Kahnweiler organized a Cubist exhibition for him in

November which was a great commercial success. Braque said later that he and Picasso were working together 'in search of an art form which would render the signature of the artist unnecessary because they would achieve the ultimate anonymous artistic personality' but Picasso never confirmed this.

Gertrude Stein suggested that it was during a holiday at Horta del Ebro in 1909 (he wanted to show Fernande where he had convalesced as a boy; they also met Sabartés there) that: 'Picasso painted three landscapes which were extraordinarily realistic and all the same, the beginning of Cubism [*Houses on the Hill*, and *The Reservoir* bought by the Steins, and *Factory at Horta del Ebro* bought by the Russian collector Shchukin]. Picasso was experimenting with photography and he had taken some photographs of the village he had painted and it always amused me when everyone protested at the "fantasy" of the pictures making them look like the photographs when of course the photographs looked like the pictures . . . Cubism began with landscapes but inevitably then he at once tried to use the idea he had in expressing people. . . . Landscapes and still lifes were inevitably more seductive to Frenchmen than to Spaniards . . . The head, the face, the human body, these are all that exist for Picasso. I remember once we were walking and we saw a learned man sitting on a bench, before the war a learned man could be sitting on a bench, and Picasso said, look at that face, it is as old as the world, all faces are as old as the world' (*Picasso*, Paris 1938).

Braque's comment was that 'Miss Stein understood nothing of what went on around her . . . she has entirely misunderstood Cubism which she sees simply in terms of personalities'.

The truth, if there is any such thing as truth in art history, is probably that 'Cubism' was just one approach to painting and drawing which interested Picasso for a time during his long and variegated career. He had no time for theories and Fernande has said that he was anything but an intellectual. Every painting was for him an experiment, no one more important than another. When an American journalist tried to 'classify' Picasso and his work in the May 1910 issue of *The Architectural World* (which contains the first reproduction of *Les Demoiselles d'Avignon*), Picasso wrote to Leo Stein at Fiesole that he should read it, that Burgess's article would give him a good laugh.

On 17 June 1910 Fernande wrote to Gertrude Stein to report that Picasso was painting harlequins again: 'We have made friends with some clowns, acrobats, bareback riders and tight-rope walkers and spend all our evenings with them.' She also reported that 'we are definitely going to Spain . . . There are too many painters going to Collioure . . . so Pablo decided not to. We shall go to Cadaques, on the other side of the frontier, just about the same distance . . . We shall be there until September.'

Pixtot (he used the Catalan version of his name when at home) and Germaine had invited them to share their house, on the Catalonian coast where the beach was inviting. Fernande and Germaine bathed in the sun while the two men worked, inside the house. Most of the paintings were 'domestic'—the various things to be found in almost any house, bottles, plates, cups, glasses, a guitar—and suggest that Fernande's influence ('Even when you are thinking about the new style you must do some things we can all enjoy') was still strong. There were even some drawings of fishing boats which would not have surprised a collector of seaside postcards. There was one nude, however, a development of one he had done before he left, which shows the way his mind was working; the nude is rather like an elaborate Japanese kanji, giving a vague impression of the real object (a woman) in which it originated, but not directly recognizable as such. It posed one of the problems for Cubists, that of identifying the subject to the person looking at the picture; Braque tried on one occasion to get over the idea that his was a picture by painting a realistic nail at the top as if to say that the work was really hanging; Kahnweiler said they should all label their paintings carefully, *Seated Nude, Bottle and Glass*, and so on, just so there would be no mistake.

One of their visitors was Dérain, about to marry Alice Princet with whom he had been living almost since her honey-moon with her husband, an insurance salesman. There was a great mixing of men and women in Picasso's entourage, though Sir Roland Penrose is exaggerating when he writes that Picasso 'with unexpected concern . . . interested himself in the happiness of his friends'. For Pablo, relationships between men and women were not to be taken seriously. He was as indifferent to the comings and goings of Alice as he was to the pairing of Apollinaire with Marie Laurencin or Braque's marriage (he had once tried to marry Braque off, for a joke, to a barmaid).

The next move in his own domestic life was a consequence of years of nagging by Fernande. They took a rather grand apartment on the Boulevard de Clichy, at no. 11, immensely superior to the attic at 130 he had shared with Manach. There was a large studio and a suite of rooms facing south over the tree-lined street. It had to be furnished, of course, and it soon resembled the junk shops from which he had bought his first pieces. Fernande seems to have had no say in the decor, which she should have taken as an omen (another was his plea that he had to keep on a studio in the *Bâteau-Lavoir* to store all his work in progress). Some of the furniture was of the rustic style in oak to be found in Spanish country homes. There was a grand piano, though neither of them could play, and a piece of vulgar Italian marquetry from his mother. The two Chippendale chairs 'from England' were placed in the dining room, for his use only, and on the dining room walls, to point the contrast with his father's pheasants, he had straw-framed lithographs 'fit only for the concierge' (Fernande). Here and there were *objets trouvés* which might just come in useful, bottles, bits of tapestry, old frames, negro masks, some ivory (all Fernande got out of this enthusiasm was an ivory bracelet). The studio was not to be swept, for fear the dust should stick to the great slabs of paint he was putting on his canvasses at that time, so it soon resembled an old rubbish dump.

There were some splendid paintings, a Braque, a Corot, several Matisses.

As a form of revenge, Fernande said she would refuse to entertain at the weekends. They would go to Gertrude Stein on Saturdays, Matisse on Fridays, and on Sunday 'into the country'. Only when people were really at a loose end would she have them round. What was the use of having a maid if all she could show them into was a flea market? Some of Fernande's disappointment showed to their friends. One Saturday evening 'Picasso, very lively, undertook to dance a Southern Spanish dance not too respectable, Gertrude Stein's brother did the dying dance of Isadora, it was very lively, Fernande and Pablo got into a discussion about Frederic of the *Lapin Agile* and apaches. Fernande contended that the apaches were better than the artists and her forefinger went up in the air. Picasso said, "yes apaches of course have their universities, artists do not." Fernande got angry and shook him and said, "you think you are very witty but you are only stupid." He ruefully showed that she had shaken off a button and she very angrily said, "and you, your only claim to distinction is that you are a precocious child." Things were not in those days going any too well between them'.

Another bone of contention was his sudden absences from 'home' for a day or two at a time while he was 'working on an important picture with a model'. It was well known that he never used models, and this one, Fanny Tellier, had a reputation for romping with her artists. Fernande never descended to physically spying on them, though she arranged that Germaine should 'pop down from time to time to see if they wanted anything', but the picture confirmed her worst fears. *The Girl With a Mandolin* is recognizably a portrait, though it has been given the Cubist treatment in the face. The hair and the folds of the dress are very seductive and the centrepiece is really her right breast which almost hangs out of the canvas as if it were a ripe pear. After some not too subtle nagging, the girl did not turn up one day for a sitting and he was discouraged from finding out why.

The frost between them was healed temporarily when Picasso discovered 'the sensibility of the English'. A friend brought him a copy of *The Nation* of 3 December, 1910, and translated it for him: 'Picasso is quite different from Matisse in the vehemence and singularity of his temperament. In his etching of *Salome* he proves his technical mastery beyond cavil, but it shows more, a strange and disquieting. . . . Of late years, Picasso's style has undergone a remarkable change. He has become possessed of the strangest passion for geometric abstraction, and is carrying out hints that are already seen in Cézanne.' Picasso, who knew how important the 1907 retrospective of Cézanne had been for the whole world of art, praised Fry's perspicacity and said no French critic had seen the connection.

Who was this English writer, Fry? He must be invited to Paris. Gertrude Stein noticed that about this time the number of writers in Picasso's entourage increased at the expense of painters and sculptors (she once found herself in a room full of 'little men who were poets'). She put this down to the fact that 'knowing how to paint as he did, what could he get from friends who were painters? He did not need the company of painters every day. What he needed were ideas if he was to paint. He wanted to know people with ideas, new ideas. . . . He was born knowing all he needed about painting'. On his escapes from his new establishment to the *Bâteau-Lavoir* or Max Jacob's new flat on the Boulevard Barbes, Picasso confessed to Leo Stein and others that he found painters very greedy and French painters more so than others, always trying to borrow money. Foreigners, now, they bought pictures, and foreign writers obviously thought more about art.

Fernande was not loth to entertain American and British critics and gallery proprietors and be entertained in return. She also found *les Anglais* very refined. She persuaded him to let her tidy up the living quarters in the Boulevard de Clichy and take his *objets trouvés* to the Rue Ravignan. The Chippendale chairs were moved to the hall to make a good impression, a mirror and a hat and umbrella stand set near the door. The lithographs were removed from the dining room walls and the Corot and a Cézanne hung there with several of his paintings, mostly recognizable portraits including Vollard and Kahnweiler (*les Anglais* liked businessmen). The marquetry horror went into the bedroom, which was soberly curtained, and the maid was redressed to look like something off the London stage. He bought three Siamese kittens and a little monkey (*les Anglais* liked animals), and a tweed sports coat for himself. Not to be accused of taking things lightly, he began to forgo his aperitifs and wine for English beer, and a whole series of paintings, drawings and collages feature Bass at this time; it is astonishing that Bass Charrington has no records of where these paintings are and has never used them in advertisements—perhaps they do not think of 'frogs' as serious beer drinkers.

The pictures *Roast Goose* and *The Letter* date from this English period, as does a curious incident in a restaurant. From his new British, mostly English, friends he had heard of the political tension between Great Britain and the Kaiser's Germany; one evening he was sitting at the next table to some German painters, and when they came over to congratulate him on his work he pulled out a pistol and fired several shots into the air.

He started to read Shelley and Keats, and convinced himself that he was tubercular. His doctor, seeing the massive healthy frame, dark curly hair and face glowing with bucolic vigour, told him that if he had a cough it was because he smoked too many cheap cigarettes. He changed doctors immediately until he found one who would prescribe a placebo which he swore did wonders for him.

His anglophilia was reinforced when the Americans upset him early in 1911, and it took some smoothing of ruffled feathers by the Steins to restore their old relationship. An article by Arthur Hoeber in the *Globe and Commercial Advertiser* (New York, 21 April, 1911) was responsible for the upset. Hoeber wrote: 'Over at the little gallery of the Photo-Secession on Fifth Avenue and 30th, Mr Stieglitz still holds out with his show of the work of Pablo Picasso, which, save to the high-browed in art, remains still an unfathomable mystery. Men and women come and go, and still the wonder grows. Here and there Mr Stieglitz manages to make a convert, and there are those who, refusing to accept these weird things, yet maintain they are stimulating! An enormous crowd of visitors have trailed down to these galleries, however, though very few have remained to pray. There are astonishing travesties of humanity here, that, unless you happen to be of the cult, appear sublimely ridiculous, with faces and forms twisted out of all recognition, while two or three efforts appear to be the design of some ill-balanced brain for a fire escape, and not a good fire escape at that. Yet we are informed seriously that these emanations are representations of the human figure. There is a watercolour of a tin cup over which the informed grow enthusiastic, and there is a charcoal drawing of a dish of bananas that seems a possible effort for a first year kindergarten pupil, though bad even for that youthful age.'

When the time came to leave Paris for the summer, it was decided to go somewhere new. Frank Havill had bought an old monastery at Ceret on the French side of the Pyrenees, and had given several rooms to the sculptor Manolo who had spoken enthusiastically of the place to Picasso. Taking with him Fernande, the menagerie, a French oil cooking stove, Max Jacob, Braque and his wife, Picasso descended on this small town and took over the whole of the first floor of the monastery—'the Vatican of Cubism'. Ceret had never seen artists before, certainly not so many and (people said) so many famous men and their women. The local priest was worried about the fact that there seemed to be a certain *informalité* in these couplings, and an inappropriateness about their living in a former monastery, but after a while he was seen, too, on the terrace of the Grand Café taking his aperitif or digestif with them. His host was often Picasso, the wealthiest of the group, who liked the place because the food was French and the spirit of the people Catalan. He had two large studios overlooking the lush countryside where the apricots were ripening, the vineyards promising a good harvest and fat cattle grazing in the fields. He only painted one landscape, however, and a few scenes in the narrow cobbled streets. Braque and he spent most of their working hours on portraits in the 'advanced Cubist style', *The Poet, The Accordionist* and *The Fan* among them. They were recognizable as portraits (apart from the indication given by their names) because what is obviously a human figure occupies the centre of the canvas, but there any resemblance to the traditional portrait ceases. The idea of a chair is given, the idea of a body, a face from all angles on a single plain and black lettering offers clues to the different parts of the scheme. When he was accused of destroying his subjects, he said: 'A painting is usually an ensemble of things added to the original idea. In mine it is an ensemble of destruction.' When Fernande protested that he made everybody look so ugly, he replied: 'Anybody who wants to create anything must make ugly things—to generate the intensity of feeling necessary for creative activity, a bit of brutality is necessary. Afterwards, the artist makes the ugly beautiful because he has purged himself of ugliness and brutality.'

When they returned to Paris, he was comforted by some more appreciative writing by the refined *Anglais*. Huntly Carter (23 November, 1911) commented: '*The New Age* is the first journal in this country to show an intelligent appreciation of the latest stage in M. Picasso's remarkable development, that is at present generally misunderstood and derided, just as the comparatively commonplace early work of the pre-Raphaelites was jeered at and spat upon. . . . This is how the famous Mr Lewis Hind lets himself go in *The Daily Chronicle*: "The Cubists . . . who are geometricians first and painters second, arouse interest with their figures and architecture, and still lifes emerging from canvasses that look like coloured, symbolical frontispieces to editions of Euclid . . . [can] any lover of the old masters avoid feeling displeasure before a geometrical, cubical landscape by Picasso?" He is apparently quite ignorant of the fact that the old masters at least saw light reflected at angles just as cubists do, but they were not intelligent enough to give their vision the Picasso wideness of expression. Picassoism is thus summarily brushed aside to the satisfaction of Mr Lewis Hind, whose efforts to make board and lodging in recent years in the daily press out of the advanced movement in painting has probably done the movement more harm than he will ever be able to repair.'

Carter quoted a letter from Middleton Murry suggesting

that Picasso was a practitioner in the school of thought of Plato who turned artists out because he thought their form of art was photographic as we should call it now. Middleton Murry followed this up on 30 November, also in *The New Age*, with the modest disclaimer that 'a speculation such as mine on the relationship of the art of Picasso and the aesthetic of Plato [is] of no great value in itself. I frankly disclaim any pretensions to an understanding or even an appreciation of Picasso. I am awed by him. . . . That his later work is unsaleable confirms my conviction that Picasso is one of those spirits who have progressed beyond their age . . . Picasso has done everything. He has painted delicate watercolours of an infinite subtlety and charm. He has made drawings with a magical line that leaves one amazed by its sheer and simple beauty—and yet he has reached a point where none have explained and none, as far as I know, have understood. . . . A great friend of mine, a leader of the Modernists in Paris, a woman gifted with an aesthetic sensibility far profounder than my own, said once as she was looking at a Picasso, "I don't know what it is—I feel as though my brain had been sandpapered" . . . Those who condemn Picasso condemn him because they cannot understand what he has done in the past, and are content to assume that all that is beyond their feeble comprehension is utterly bad.'

Picasso said he was amazed. He had never read 'such intelligent stuff' by French critics. These English critics must have 'heads as big as balloons' to contain all that knowledge. Who was this Plato? Fernande and Max Jacob tried to give him a résumé of *The Republic* over lunch one day, but as he never understood even the Futurist Manifestos of Marinetti, he fell back on a general apreciation of *les Anglais* and said he must go to London soon. He would send this Murry and this Carter a copy of *The Siege of Jerusalem*, a book of poems by Max Jacob which he was illustrating. In London he would see 'the real police'.

The reference was to an unfortunate incident in September, during the hysteria which followed the theft of the Mona Lisa from the Louvre. The thief, a Belgian, had given Picasso a couple of statues years before, and they had found their way into an old cupboard in the *Bâteau-Lavoir*. Apollinaire had remembered this and when Picasso got back from Ceret had gone with him to search for them, and hand them over to a newspaper, *Paris Journal*. They had both been arrested and gaoled, freed only because the thief had confessed before going home to Belgium.

From Max Jacob, Gertrude Stein and Apollinaire, there are letters to suggest that the winter of 1911–12 was an unhappy time for Fernande. She had lost her way with his paintings. She no longer complained about the unsaleability of the Cubist works (there were hundreds of saleable canvasses, drawings and etchings at home and in the Rue Ravignan) but about the way she appeared in them. She enlisted the help of Vollard, who had just had his portrait done again: 'In front of these portraits of women with three eyes, a knee where the breast should be and hands which wave at you from every side of the canvas, I thought at first it was all a joke (like the time Picasso painted a work with a donkey's tail and had it accepted at the *Salon des Indépendants* as *Twilight on the Adriatic*) but it is not a joke: Cubism consists of taking apart forms and volumes.' Fernande did not want to be taken apart. Other artists liked her to sit for them—Marie Laurencin, Pichot and his sculptor friend Marcoussis. They did not take her apart. Gertrude Stein tried to console her: 'In this phase, the subjects are unrecognizable. Picasso paints portraits of women which he seems to have put through the mincing machine, though it is possible to recognize the different anatomic parts and put them together again mentally.' But it was a phase, she said, and Fernande should be patient and wait until it had passed.

Unfortunately, Fernande had lost her patience. She had forgotten that not so many years ago she was a married woman without a husband, reduced to living in a slum and doing other people's washing, not to mention obliging the *charbonnier*. The grand apartment, the English friends, the fame, had all gone to her head. She began to think of herself as an authority on art, and to 'recommend' to Gertrude Stein artists whose work she should collect. She had so lost her head that she forgot even the survival skills of the woman at large. As anyone could have told her, if you have a rich and famous man and an attractive girl friend, you make sure that they never meet; if you do not, you will certainly lose them both. In the cause of promoting the work of Marcoussis, Fernande asked if she could bring him and his mistress, Marcelle, to dinner one Saturday.

Gertrude Stein remembered: 'Fernande had at this time a new friend of whom she often spoke to me. This was Eva (Marcelle), who was living with Marcoussis. And one evening all four of them came to the Rue de Fleurus, Pablo, Fernande, Marcoussis and Eva. It was the only time we ever saw Marcoussis until many years later. I could understand perfectly Fernande's liking for Eva, small and negative like Evelyn Thaw (an American woman Fernande admired).' In the setting of the Rue de Fleurus, Picasso saw Marcelle (it was he who rebaptized her) for the first time well dressed and made up (Marcoussis kept her in rags at his studio).

Not long afterwards, Gertrude Stein and Alice B Toklas went to see Picasso in the *Bâteau-Lavoir*. 'He was not in, and Gertrude Stein as a joke left her visiting card. In a few days we went again and Picasso was at work on a picture on which was written *ma jolie* and at the lower end painted in was Gertrude Stein's visiting card. As we went away Gertrude Stein said, "Fernande is certainly not *ma jolie*, I wonder who it is?" '

Picassos's affair with Eva went on throughout the spring. Fernande was unaware of it. The portraits he painted of his new 'jolie' were unrecognizable and anyway she had decided to put her faith in Gertrude Stein's belief that this painting phase would pass. Maybe there were other women: they would pass, too. Fernande believed that most couples were held together by inertia, mostly by the inertia of men who cannot be bothered to move and set up house again, changing their bars and friends. She had a rude awakening when she left for Ceret with the Pichots, expecting Picasso to follow in his own good time. Follow he did, with Eva in tow. There was, of course, a terrible row and the two women came to blows in the best (Anglo-Saxon) traditions of jealousy. Eventually, their mutual friends' persuaded Picasso to go away, taking Eva and a big Pyrennean dog they had acquired, to Avignon for the summer (they settled for a house at Sorgues which he rented for 90 francs a month); they were joined there by Braque and his wife, another Marcelle. The two men worked as if nothing had happened.

When the holiday was over, there had to be a reckoning. Gertrude Stein recalled that Pablo had come to see her 'and he said a marvellous thing about Fernande, he said her beauty always held him but he could not stand any of her little ways. Pablo and Eva were now settled on the Boulevard Raspail'.

Fernande realized that there was nothing to be done. She had had her share of the life of this strange man, and must hand him over with as good a grace as possible to her successor. Once she had put her emotions in the proper place, she could talk about money. She insisted on keeping the apartment in Boulevard de Clichy 'until something more suitable comes up' and he ought to leave her some money, and the paintings he had done of her. They settled for some paintings and drawings and a bundle of notes Picasso had taken to carrying in his pocket. All he wanted from the Boulevard de Clichy was the rest of his work, the marquetry object and the Chippendale chairs, and of course the animals.

After a brief, brisk argument, he left behind the unused piano.

Eva

'And what is woman? She was obviously placed on earth to amuse and comfort [man], as decorative and unimportant as the dumb girls who aid the magician to do his tricks on the stage.'

(Barzini)

Picasso's friends and acquaintances seem to have taken the dismissal of Fernande without surprise. Kahnweiler managed the move of the pictures and oddments to 242 Boulevard Raspail; he made no charge for this, but took the occasion to go through the work and earmark things he wanted to buy. He had a letter of thanks on 12 June which contained the declaration: 'I love her very much and I shall write her name on my pictures'.

Germaine Pichot and Max Jacob, the two closest to Fernande, showed some disappointment, and it was Germaine who had led the chorus of protest at Ceret which had forced the two lovers to move on to the outskirts of Avignon. Germaine's husband said he was glad in a way that his old friend had found a woman who looked like Maria, small, dark and passionate, as opposed to the tall, red haired girls he had had until now—'at last he has stopped fucking his father'—but warned that Eva had a notoriously bad temper and was as tough as old boots. Germaine herself was less than kind: Eva was as false as her teeth, and such a liar that she had convinced herself that her dentures were real. She was small, but pure poison all through.

Gertrude Stein and Alice B Toklas took the change in their

stride and were soon visiting at the Boulevard Raspail. They took care to tell Picasso that they thought Fernande had behaved very well, in the circumstances, and showed him a letter they had received, 'written with the reticence of a frenchwoman. She said she wished to tell Gertrude Stein that she understood perfectly that the friendship had always been with Pablo and that although Gertrude had always shown her every mark of sympathy and affection, now that she and Pablo were separated, it was naturally impossible that in the future there should be any intercourse between them because, the friendship having been with Pablo, there could of course be no question of a choice . . . that she would always remember their intercourse with pleasure, and that she would permit herself, if ever she were in need, to throw herself upon Gertrude's generosity.'

Max Jacob and Apollinaire undertook to see that Fernande did not find herself in need. For a time she spent every weekend with Apollinaire's mistress, Marie Laurencin, whose portrait of her in a large white hat shows that she had not lost her taste for extravagant millinery or, presumably, the wherewithal to pay for it. Marie Laurencin's mother liked Fernande very much and taught her to do saleable needlework; Marie was very shortsighted and no help in transferring her designs onto canvas. Apollinaire seems to have arranged for the sale of the paintings and drawings Picasso had left her, and to have used his position at the bank to invest the money wisely.

Generations of gossips have tried to explain Picasso's sudden and intense infatuation with Marcelle Humbert. She was not a new acquaintance, though he had only seen her from afar, as it were, in rags at the domestic end of the studio. Her age was not a handicap, nor the fact that, like Fernande, she had a discarded husband somewhere in the background (it was not until later that Picasso began to look with interest at young virgins). She was certainly no beauty, and Marcoussis had knocked her about for years. She was not an intellectual, though she was a former *lycéenne* and so better educated than Fernande. She was certainly very energetic, whereas Fernande had become very idle and flabby, but it was probably her style which appealed most to the young master. The daughter of a senior civil servant, when she was cleaned up and properly dressed she had the air of a person who would never use the wrong knife and fork, and she was certainly popular with *les Anglais* and other distinguished foreigners.

Manolo believed that Picasso saw his aunt Eloisa rather than his mother in 'Eva'. Picasso insisted that everybody call her Eva, that she revert to her maiden name of Gouel, and that a lawyer should search for her missing husband and arrange a divorce; he did not press this too hard—as in the case of Fernande—because if the divorce had been arranged he would have had to marry her.

Whatever the reason for her triumph, Eva wasted no time in establishing herself. She had decided that Picasso should move out of Montmartre across the river to Montparnasse, away from all those Spaniards and circus performers; this was perhaps ungrateful, as it was from a popular song on the Butte— 'O Manon, ma jolie, mon coeur te dit bonjour'—that Picasso's dedication to her came. The *Bâteau-Lavoir* studio had to be closed — she was not going to risk him entertaining other women there as he had done her. She isolated herself from Marcoussis' circle, and put out a stream of splendid slanders— that Picasso had offered Fernande to Marcoussis in part exchange, that Germaine Pichot had given the pox to half Montmartre, starting with Casagemas in 1901, that Marie Laurencin was the bastard daughter of the President of the Republic, and much more. Her friends were not spared either, and she is said to have coined the lapidary remark: 'It is a waste of time for a woman to destroy the reputations of her enemies. She should start with her friends.'

Until she could find somewhere better, she organized the new establishment to keep her lover hard at work and happy. It was not as grand as the Boulevard de Clichy, but the rooms were draught-proof and there was plenty of painting space. She is generally credited with the birth of Picasso's interest in collage. Usually, Picasso was very reluctant to borrow ideas from Braque, the son of a house painter who employed a lot of his father's professional tricks when he had a difficult subject—using a comb to create special surfaces, creating imitation marble patterns, and the like. Eva, who had had a great deal of experience trying to make an indifferent sculptor's work look interesting, saw that there was a way to combine Kahnweiler's insistence that the public should be given some help in understanding Cubist paintings and Braque's *trompe-l'oeil* lettering and hanging nails. Picasso had told her about his early love for paper sculpture and had shown her that he had not lost his knack for it. Why not paste bits of paper sculpture onto the canvas? He had painted in one of Gertrude Stein's visiting cards, on one of his first portraits of '*ma jolie*'. Why not work in real bits of newspaper instead of Braque's lettering? If he needed part of a work to have an uneven or different surface, then instead of Braque's mock marble, why not stick on a paper serviette or a piece of linoleum?

The *Still Life with Chair Caning*, another painting (May 1912) of the early Eva period, has a double *trompe-l'oeil*: a piece of linoleum with the marks of chair caning on it is pasted onto the canvas. Later on he would try triple *trompes-l'oeil*, newspaper cut out to the shape of a guitar, which was surface, message and image all in one. She was not very keen on the Bass, beer or symbol, and urged him to 'splash on the colour, which is what people like'.

Eva liked the atmosphere in Montparnasse and the two cafés, *La Rotonde* and *Le Dome*, where 'a better class of person' gathered in the evening—not whores and acrobats but politicians, both native and those in exile (Trotsky among them), intellectuals of all sorts, and not too many painters and sculptors—'only the ones who sell well', she remarked. She was a genuine lover of the theatre, of which Picasso knew nothing, and the autumn and winter of 1912-13 was his baptism of fire. There was a general revival of interest in Futurism that winter (Marinetti had been a friend of Marcoussis, and Picasso knew Severini very well), and a translation of the *Manifesto of Futurist Painters* drew many artists to the theatres lit up by *Rot Bomb-ance* and *Poupées Electriques*. There were also Futurist 'happenings', throwing down dolls and pamphlets from the Eiffel Tower, and a parody of Napoleon's interment at Les Invalides which led to the Futurist General Staff's second expulsion *en masse* from France.

Under Eva's discreet guidance, most of Picasso's business was done abroad at this time. Apart from the virtually permanent exhibition at Vollard's, his major showings were in London, Düsseldorf, Cologne, Munich and Barcelona; Shchukin in Moscow kept open house to those who wanted to see the Picassos he had been buying since 1907. The refined *Anglais* were still on his side. *The Times* commented very flatteringly on work on show at the Stafford Gallery, Duke Street: 'We believe M. Picasso to be an accomplished and sincere artist possessed by an insatiable love of experience and discovery and haunted by an incessant fear of the commonplace. He will not be literal, he will not be facile, he will not be a virtuoso . . . he begins to see objects as if they were already works of arts before he begins to draw them. Thus his *Vieux Miséreux* seems to be drawn from a statue, and a very fine one . . . We acknowledge his profound artistic seriousness, a seriousness which is shown by his attitude towards everything which he draws, by his desire to discover and express its essential character rather than use it as rough material for his art.'

Notwithstanding a snide remark in *The Observer*—'. . . this kaleidoscopic jumble, in which it is just possible to distinguish a skull which has obviously been under a steamroller . . . childish pen scribbles . . . that should never have been rescued from the wastepaper basket' (P J Konody)—the exhibition moved on with flying colours to the Grafton Galleries (5 October–31 December 1912) as part of the second Post-Impressionist Exhibition. It was praised by Roger Fry as 'the work of highly civilized and modern man trying to find a pictorial language appropriate to the sensibilities of the modern outlook . . . the difficulty springs from a deep-rooted conviction, due to long established custom, that the aim of painting is the descriptive imitation of natural forms. . . . Such a picture as Picasso's *Head of a Man* would undoubtedly be ridiculous if, having set out to make a direct imitation of the actual model, he had been incapable of getting a better likeness. But Picasso did nothing of the sort. He has shown in his *Portrait of Mlle L B* that he could do at least as well as anyone if he wished, but here he is attempting to do something quite different.'

It is interesting to note that Roger Fry's opinions were taken seriously by the Cambridge intellectuals of the day, most of whom (according to Paul Delany in *The Neopagans*, MacMillan 1987) were 'classical, ironic, permissive, homosexual, urban, indoor, young and pacifist'. When Roland Penrose (later Sir) went to call on his brother at King's College, where there were artists and critics including Fry, the Bells and Duncan Grant, he found himself 'in the well-ordered rooms of Maynard Keynes, made impressive by the large quantities of books on economics and philosophy . . . My respect for the great man, whose face always suggested to me wisdom and the cunning of a fox, was greatly intensified by the presence on his walls of pictures by Cézanne, Matisse and the first Cubist paintings of Braque and Picasso I had ever seen'. A friend observed many years later that a man like Keynes, whose economic theories had almost brought the world to ruin, could at least make a shrewd and profitable investment for himself.

Indeed, Picasso's paintings had become a very good investment. In 1912 the successful exhibitions of 1910 in Munich and Düsseldorf were repeated and Eva, always ready with a pencil and paper, calculated that some of the work had appreciated by as much as 300% in two years. There were good reviews, but not such high prices, in Barcelona. *Picarol* welcomed back 'this intrepid artist and fighter, who, coming out of *Els Quatre Gats* with a fury of enthusiasm, has triumphed in Paris after kidnapping Nature herself in cubes'. Josep Junoy in *Arte e Artistas* asserted: 'Wherever Picasso sets his hand, he leaves the imprint of his genius. He has a gift of assimilation unlike that of any other artist. . . . Picasso understands things without loving them; he interprets them ruthlessly. His love is domination.'

This last was a very shrewd observation, echoed by Gertrude

Stein: 'Americans are like Spaniards, they are abstract and cruel. They are not brutal, they are cruel.' Guillaume Apollinaire, in *Les Peintres Cubistes* (Paris 1913), said something similar about Picasso: 'This Malagueno bruised us like a sharp frost . . . those who knew him even in his early days can remember his artistic impertinence . . . he queried even the universe . . . a savage laugh in the purity of light.'

The Germans also detected savagery and ruthlessness in his new work, which did not displease them: 'A logical Cubist like Picasso must have been attracted by the idea of doing without tones . . . forcing out his work . . . in rhythmical lines and planes' (*Was Is Mit dem Picasso*, Pan, Berlin). Schonlank in the same magazine wrote: 'Picasso is the creator of a new order. He has produced it from within himself as a woman gives birth to a child, with frightening strength, the generation of power and suffering in the struggle for life.' Ludwig Collen thought the violence was in the Romantic tradition: 'The Romantic is forced to plumb the depths. . . He has replaced the mechanical space of perspective with the dynamic space of mind.' (*Die Romantik der Neuen Malerei.*) M K Rohe added that: 'This nervous hypersensitivity has been Picasso's strength . . .' (*Pablo Picasso, Die Kunst Für Alle*, Munich 1913).

The Russian Tsarist police thought they detected something revolutionary in Picasso's latest struggles and ordered Shchukin in Moscow to allow the public to see his Cubist paintings only once a week. Chulkov in *Appollon* confirmed: 'In my opinion, two tendencies are at work in contemporary Western art, a nihilistic optimism and a demonic pessimism.' Tugenhold remembered a visit to Picasso's studio, 'the laboratory for his creative experiments, a dungeon in which he tortures objects and tears out their insides.' Nikolai Berdyaev wrote that the world had left the sunshine of Gaugin's Tahiti to wake in Picasso's world, 'where all is cold, gloomy and terrifying. . . . A wintry cosmic storm has stripped off one layer of foliage after another, all the leaves and flowers have gone . . . all flesh has disintegrated. . . . This winter will not only destroy the few remaining leaves but shake the whole material world to its foundations, as the universe disintegrates.'

Nothing could be in greater contrast with Picasso's visible daily life. He would wake up in the morning at about half past ten and sit up in bed in his blue and white striped pyjamas to drink the coffee Eva brought him. They would exchange endearments, and she would tell him what she had in mind to prepare for lunch that day; the room was always neat and tidy, the bed linen spotless, the silk brocade curtains tied back to show the bright, white net which covered the windows discreetly. Even when the bed became the scene of their theatrical sexual activity, she told her friends that Picasso was always very gentle. To look at him, she used to say, you would think he would be violent, but he is really like a lamb. Unlike Marcoussis, he never struck her.

The rest of their home on the Boulevard Raspail had the same sort of atmosphere. The cushions were always plumped up on the English armchairs and the French furniture in the dining room was dusted and polished every day. The cats and dogs knew their place, too, and looked like part of the decor. Picasso's studio was the exception to all the rules, but even there he had a little table on which tea was served in a flowered tea set. During the spring of 1913 Eva found a new home for them in the Rue Schoelcher (no. 5 *bis*). She liked it because it was even more peaceful and she could look out of the windows at the tombs in Montparnasse cemetery. Here the studio was bigger and had better light, and though the flat was farther away from his favourite bars and cafés, Picasso accepted the move without protest.

Picasso's health certainly improved under this tender loving care, and those of his friends who had had doubts about the dismissal of Fernande were reassured. As a tangible sign of their approval, the new couple was invited to Ceret for the summer; Germaine Pichot, who had led the 'opposition' the previous year, was asked to stay away. It was a blissful summer, marred only by news of the death of Picasso's father, but though he dashed across the frontier into Spain ostensibly to comfort his mother, Picasso used the opportunity to go to a series of bull-fights. Eva suggested that they invite his mother to stay with them for a few months in Paris, but he said he did not think she would 'fit in'; perhaps next year they could have her for part of the summer. Anyway, the new flat was not quite finished and his mother 'could be quite critical'.

It was during that summer that Eva began to feel unwell. Max Jacob noticed it and asked if he could recommend a good doctor, but she shrugged it off as fatigue after moving house and 'making a home for Pablo' twice in as many years. In fact she was worried. She had seen her own doctor, thinking, perhaps hoping, that she was pregnant, and in the course of an examination he had discovered a cancer in the early stages of development. The doctor was optimistic about the success of his treatment, but it was a source of anxiety, particularly because of Picasso's horror of illness; she was afraid that if he got to know what was wrong with her he would pack her off to a hospital and she would never see him again except perhaps on visiting days.

However, the holiday did her good and she was back in the Rue Schoelcher to 'pose' for *The Woman in the Armchair*. By 'posing' on this occasion, Picasso meant coming and going and reminding him of what Éluard lists '. . . the features of the little face, the curl of the hair, the delicious armpit, the lean ribs, the froth of petticoat, the soft comfortable armchair, the daily paper'. By contrast the head is outsized and the breasts stuck on as if they were an afterthought. It is a powerful painting. Ironically, Penrose wrote later that it was so powerful 'that a friend to whom I had let my house for a month complained it gave her nightmares and endangered the future of her expected child'. (He had been given the painting to look after, when a Surrealist exhibition in London closed many years later.)

The winter of 1913–14 was full of rumours of war. During the Saturday evening dinner parties at the Rue de Fleurus, the talk was all of Germans: Marie Laurencin's mother had died and she had replaced her with a German, foolish girl; Ronnebeck the sculptor was a fanatic 'with lots of photographs of the German navy which he insisted on showing us. . . . He had a commission to paint a countess who had a magnificent place on the shores of the Baltic'; Uhde was obviously a spy; and so on. On a more positive note, Gertrude Stein announced that she had decided to 'collaborate with Picasso in making portraits'. According to *The Autobiography of Alice B Toklas*: 'This is how portrait writing began . . . I am an extremely good five-minute cook and Gertrude Stein liked from time to time to have me make American dishes. One Sunday evening I was very busy preparing one of these and then I called Gertrude Stein to come in from the atelier for supper. She came in much excited and would not sit down. Here, I want to show you something, she said. . . . In spite of my protests and the food cooling, I had to read. I can still see the tiny pages of the notebook written forward and back. It was the portrait called *Ada* . . . This was the beginning of a long series of portraits. *Ada* was followed by Matisse and Picasso . . . Gertrude Stein printed them in *Camera Work*.'

The acutely observed word portraits had an astonishing effect on Picasso. He began to look again at his friends and painted new pictures of Vollard, Kahnweiler, Sagot, Apollinaire, and Max Jacob, in complete contrast to the Cubist impressions he had done before. He also painted the stream of unusual visitors to Gertrude Stein, remarking that it was not true that tourists came to Paris to look at picturesque artists—they came as ready-made models for artists. One of his favourites was Dr Claribel Cone of Baltimore, 'who liked ease and graciousness and comfort. She and her sister Etta Cone were travelling. The only room in the hotel was not comfortable. Etta bade her sister put up with it as it was only for one night. Etta, answered Doctor Claribel, one night is as important as any other night in my life and I must be comfortable. When the war broke out she happened to be in Munich engaged on scientific work. She could never leave because it was never comfortable to travel.'

There was a flurry of theatrical activity in Paris that winter, to Eva's great delight. Plays, concerts and ballet had record audiences. She took him to see his first ballet (Nijinsky, *Rite of Spring*) given by the Ballets Russes, and kindled his enthusiasm for the art form and the company. Apollinaire was also there . . . 'dressed in evening clothes, industriously kissing various important ladies' hands. . . . The dancing was very fine although our attention was distracted by a man in the next box to us flourishing his cane . . . finally his cane came down and smashed the opera hat another spectator had put on in defiance.'

Kahnweiler was also with them often. Picasso used to tell him that he should take out French citizenship, as his wife was French, and as a German he would be the target for all sorts of retribution. Gallery proprietors and dealers had many enemies in Paris. 'Kahnweiler always replied that he would when he passed military age, but that he naturally did not want to do military service a second time. War came, Kahnweiler was in Switzerland with his family on vacation, and he could not come back. All his possessions were sequestered.'

When war came, Picasso was in Avignon. He had gone there in the spring with Eva because he thought she looked tired, and had been joined by Braque and Derain. The three painters worked with a feeling that time was running out, that war was coming and even if they were not killed, things would never be the same again. There were some arguments about whether or not Picasso should join the Foreign Legion—it was rumoured that a special battalion was being formed for 'superior' foreigners—but Picasso said he felt the war was no concern of either himself or Spain. He did not see why the fact that France had given him a home, fame and fortune should affect his decision in any way. When war was declared, and Braque and Derain left to join their regiments, there was a tense atmosphere at the station, covered by bravado; Picasso used to say that their friendship ended there on the platform.

Picasso and Eva stayed on in Avignon, and he never stopped working. Paradoxically perhaps, most of his collages were more amusing and colourful than before. He enjoyed even imitating the real *papiers collés*, though also glued to pictures 'pieces of marbled paper, triangles of plywood, newspaper cuttings and such and linked them with a few lines of charcoal or chalk. He fixed to a wooden panel all sorts of household rubbish, lids of boxes, inkwells, visiting cards, broken musical instruments, chair seats, sometimes gluing them on, sometimes just tying them on with string . . . what will happen next?'

The first winter of the war was rather uncomfortable, until the black market got itself properly organized. It was a particularly cold winter, which Fernande passed sensibly living with her coal merchant; Gertrude Stein had to bribe a policeman to get fuel for her atelier. There were a few air raids. On the second occasion, Picasso and Eva were dining with Gertrude Stein and Alice: 'By this time we knew that the two-storey building of the atelier was no more protection than the roof of the little pavilion under which we slept and the concierge had suggested that we should go into her room where at least we would have seven storeys above us. Eva was not very well these days, and fearful, so we all went into the concierge's room. Even Jeanne Poule, the Breton servant . . . came too. Jeanne was soon bored with this precaution and so in spite of all remonstrance, she went back to her kitchen, lit her light, in spite of regulations, and proceeded to wash the dishes. We soon too got bored with the concierge's lodge and went back to the atelier. We put a candle under the table so that it would not make too much light, Eva and I tried to sleep and Picasso and Gertrude Stein talked until two in the morning when the all's clear sounded and they went home.'

Eva's health was rapidly deteriorating, and it was 'a grim winter'. Even in the "sumptuous apartment in the Rue Schoelcher life seemed to be menaced by death, cold and decay. There were letters from friends actively participating in the War, some amusing ones from Apollinaire who said he was falling off horses trying to become a good artillery officer, but it was a lonely life, and a great contrast to the days when 'going out' had to be restricted so that time would not be wasted and more work could be done. According to Gertrude Stein: 'The only other intimates at that time were a Russian they called G. Apostrophe and his sister the baroness. They bought all the

Rousseaus that were in Rousseau's atelier when he died. . . . Picasso learnt the Russian alphabet from them and began putting it into his pictures.'

Reports from the Front made for depressing reading and Picasso felt much as any healthy young man feels when he is stared at accusingly by young and old women who have brothers, sons and lovers sitting in the frozen mud of a wartime trench. He hesitated to go out in case he was accused of being a coward, or dodging conscription. He stopped speaking French and always declaimed loudly in Spanish when forced to speak in public, at times even speaking deliberately halting French to suggest that he was a newcomer to the country. From time to time he became very neurotic about his non-participation in the war, and he once even claimed he was making a contribution to the war effort: 'Picasso and Eva, Gertrude Stein and myself were walking down the Boulevard Raspail (they had gone to pick up some mail which had gone to the old flat) on a cold winter evening. There is nowhere in the world colder than the Raspail on a cold winter evening; we used to call it the retreat from Moscow. All of a sudden down the street came some big cannon, the first any of us had seen painted, that is, camouflaged. Pablo stopped, he was spell-bound. "C'est nous qui avons fait ça", he said—it is we who have created that, he said. And he was right. From Cézanne through him they had come to that. His foresight was justified.'

No official authority ever gave him credit for inventing camouflage, and, of course, it was a spurious claim.

He appeared in an equally unlikely role that first winter of the war, as godfather to Max Jacob, Jacob, born a Jew, had been toying with the idea of converting to Christianity since he had had a vision of Christ crucified many years before; friends and acquaintances had been sceptical, putting the trance down to cognac. Not at all discouraged by the scepticism, from time to time he brought up the subject of his guilt, as a Jew, 'responsible for the murder of the Son of God'. He became so fanatical about this that friendly priests in Montmartre who might have given him instruction and arranged for his reception into the Church were frightened off. It was only just before Christmas 1914 that he found a priest, who took him seriously, at Eva's local church in Montparnasse. Though 'the Picassos' were infrequent attenders at the church, he gave their names as Christians who would sponsor him and speak up for him at the official celebration. Perhaps because Eva was so ill, Picasso agreed to be godfather and offered one of his own baptismal names, Cyprien, as the saint under whose protection Max should be received. The event is recorded on the flyleaf of *L'Imitation de Jésus-Christ* which Picasso gave to his godson: 'To my brother in Christ, Cyprien Max Jacob, as a souvenir of his baptism, Thursday 18th February, 1915.' Max Jacob, whose health was also uncertain, was only able to work from time to time and it seems that Picasso sent him money to get him through the winter, as he did to the Futurist poet Severini who was starving and suspected of having tuberculosis.

In the spring, Picasso decided to move to Avignon, to get a change of scene and perhaps some more cheerful company. Eva had rallied and seemed quite her old self, as she set up an establishment for them in the old town itself. While they were away, Gertrude Stein and Alice B Toklas enrolled in the American Volunteer Ambulance Service (American Fund for French Wounded); a taxi driver taught Gertrude to drive and soon she turned up in Avignon, too, as it was a rest area for the wounded. Braque remembered: 'I was convalescing when she and Miss Toklas arrived in their Red Cross Ford. They looked extremely strange in their boy-scout uniforms with their green veils and Colonial helmets. When we went out with them onto the Place Clemenceau, as it now is, their funny gear so excited the curiosity of the people in the square that a large crowd gathered round us, making humorous remarks. The police arrived eventually and looked at all our papers.'

Gertrude's hilarious adventures, chronicled in the *Autobiography of Alice B Toklas*, were recounted first hand to Eva and Picasso, and there was a moment when Picasso himself thought of volunteering as an ambulance driver. Unfortunately, he could not drive and never did learn; on the few occasions when he went out on the road between Avignon and Sorgues to learn, he was so inept that Eva had hysterics and the attempt had to be abandoned.

The holiday ended earlier than usual when Picasso had a talk with a local doctor and learned how seriously ill his mistress was. As she had feared, he insisted that she be moved immediately to a hospital and they returned to Paris. He found a private nursing home half an hour away from their home and assured her that he would pay for the very best treatment available. He wrote to Gertrude Stein in November to say that Eva was 'comfortable' and was as well as could be expected. He went to see her every day and 'spent half the day on the Métro or at the hospital'. He seemed to regret the waste of time travelling and sick visiting more than the absence of his *amie*, but added in the letter that he had found time to go out and meet some circus people, who had cheered him up, and had painted some acrobats and harlequins which had turned out rather well.

A photographer came to do a photo-reportage on him and the stills show him in the working dress of the day—an English ratting cap on his head, his English tweed sports coat and a pair of very old patched trousers covered with paint (he wiped his hands on his trousers when he was painting or eating). His face is as grim as the winter he had just passed but he does not look ill-nourished; since the tuberculosis scare he had taken to smoking an English pipe and he has it firmly clasped in one hand or between his teeth. He has the air of a chucker-out at a working men's club in the North of England.

There was nothing to be done for Eva, as everybody knew, and it came as no surprise when she died just before Christmas. The funeral was a low-key affair, with Spanish and French friends, only eight in all, to see her buried. Pablo seemed to be genuinely moved by the occasion and to have resented Max Jacob's attempts to cheer him up by telling jokes at the graveside; Max's misguided efforts cost him a drawing of Christ Crucified which was to have been a present on the first anniversary of his reception into the Church. Picasso wrote to Gertrude

Stein in the New Year that he was very sad that his poor Eva had gone '. . . she was always so good to me', and hoped that they would be able to meet soon and restore his morale with some good talk. (8 January, 1916.)

As it was very depressing to have to look out of his windows at a cemetery having just seen his mistress die, he began to look for somewhere else to live. He felt rather lost, a tribute perhaps to the amount of space Eva had managed to occupy in his life during four short years. Friends said he toyed with the idea of taking up again with Fernande, but soon dismissed the idea as foolish; anyway, she was living with the coal merchant, a lasting source of warmth. He told Max Jacob he thought of going to Spain and staying with his mother or Lola and her new husband, but that idea soon lost its appeal; so recently, in Spanish terms, after his father's death, they would still be mourning or pretending to mourn. He did not, in fact, go anywhere because he had nobody to go with and he hated to travel alone. He drew the curtains and sought solace in painting. In a way, he was benefiting from Eva's last legacy. She had convinced him that for the sort of painting he was doing it was a waste of money to buy expensive artist's oil paints. Braque always had a cupboard full of decorator's Ripolin, which was very good and had to be long-lasting to please the customers. To foreign visitors who came to worship at the shrine of Cubism he said: 'They are all that is healthy in colours, paints, *la santé des couleurs.*' As Gertrude Stein noted on a brief leave in Paris: 'At this time he was making constructions in paper, in tin and in all sorts of things, the sort of thing that made it possible for him to do the famous stage setting for *Parade*,' for Jean Cocteau.

It was Cocteau who rescued Picasso and found him a house in Montrouge. 'We went out to see him. He had a marvellous rose pink silk counterpane on his bed. Where did that come from, Pablo?, asked Gertrude Stein. Ah ça, said Picasso with much satisfaction, that is a lady. It was a well-known Chilean society woman who had given it to him. It was a marvel. He was very cheerful. He was constantly coming to the house, bringing Paquerette, a girl who was very nice, or Irene, a very lovely woman who came from the mountains and wanted to be free. He brought Erik Satie and the Princesse de Polignac and Blaise Cendrars.'

It was again to Eva that he owed his acquaintance with Erik Satie, a composer who liked writing music for the theatre. He was a Norman like Marie Laurencin (who had given up Fernande because she disapproved of the coal merchant) and Braque (who had just about foregiven Picasso for not joining the Foreign Legion), and they spent many happy evenings at the Rue de Fleurus drinking calvados and telling lies. One day as the winter drew in, 'Picasso came and with him, leaning on his shoulder, was a slim, elegant youth. It is Jean, announced Pablo, Jean Cocteau, and we are leaving for Italy'.

Cocteau had convinced him to help him with his ballet, *Parade*, to the disbelief of everybody in Montparnasse and Montmartre. Cocteau said in his diary: 'I dragged him into it. His clique didn't believe I could do it, because this was the tightest period of Cubism. The things you could find on a café table and only those were what you were supposed to paint. To paint a stage setting and above all for the Ballets Russes (those eternal adolescents who worshipped Picasso had never heard of Stravinsky) was terrible. . . . The worst crime of all was to join Diaghilev in Rome . . . All journeys anywhere in the world except between the Place des Abbesses and the Boulevard Raspail were forbidden. Despite the absence of Satie, who was to do the music (he said he could not leave Arcueuil), we laughed to see the painters waving on the platform incredulously as they disappeared into the distance behind the train . . . We created *Parade* in a cellar in Rome where the company was rehearsing. We called it Taglioni's Cave. . . . What I think it is important to record is the ease with which Picasso adapted himself to the theatre and its special demands, just as he had adapted himself to everything else in his past, of course . . . I shall never forget the studio in Rome. The rough drawings for *Parade* were kept in a sort of small box which showed where the fixed objects would be, the trees and the barracks, for example. . . . At a café table, Picasso painted the Chinaman, the American, the horse (the Vicomtesse de Noailles said it looked like a tree laughing) and the blue acrobats Marcel Proust said looked like the Dioscuri.' He added that most actors get bored, anyway not inspired to give of their best, if they have to walk in front of lacklustre drops every night, but 'Picasso charged the scenery with emotion'.

The Parade project was Cocteau's second attempt at an 'integral ballet'. He said that most ballets in the past seemed 'bitty' because they were composed at different times by different people: for example, *Giselle* was choreographed by Adam after an idea by Gautier, and had changed producers and scenery many times—it would be better if everybody concerned had got together at the outset and made something 'integral'. The Satie-Picasso-Nijinsky-Diaghilev-Cocteau 'team' would devise something which would change the history of the theatre—or so Cocteau said.

Picasso certainly made the best use of his time in Italy. He wrote to Gertrude Stein, on 17 April, 1917, that he was working all day and staying up all night 'with some Roman ladies'. When he was not painting backdrops, he was caricaturing Diaghilev, Bakst, Massine, doing a few portraits and drawing the scene painters. He met Marinetti again when the Futurist leader came home on leave (he was one of the first tank commanders, twice decorated for bravery) and was given the *Manifesto Della Danza Futurista* and an unintentionally funny book which was just about to appear, *War, the Only Hygiene in the World*. He also met Enrico Prampolini, one of the other young lions of the Futurist Movement. Prampolini later recalled (*Incontro Con Picasso*, Novara, 1943) the day when Cocteau, Bakst and Picasso came to see him at 8 Via Tanaro, 'home, studio, editorial offices of avant-garde newspapers and magazines and a secret meeting place for painters harassed by the police; it was here the *Casa d'Arte Italiana* and Ricciardi's *Teatro Del Colore* were founded. There was not much room and the walls were covered with futuristic paintings and drawings. All over the place were easels, furniture, bits of sculpture, constructivist objects; wire sculpture hung down from the ceiling and abstract shapes in bright colours added to the confusion. "This isn't a studio, it's a conjuror's box," said Cocteau, bouncing in. Bakst followed him, fat, dressed in black like a tax collector, with old-fashioned gold-rimmed spectacles. Picasso stood by the door for a minute, thick set, with bright eyes, a black forelock brushed sideways in a way that was fashionable in Italy six or seven years ago . . . He looked about him delightedly, like a child in a playroom . . . Mon Dieu", he said, "my poor Eva would have had a heart attack if she saw all this" . . . but he was at home in that magic box. . . . Marinetti, Boccioni and Cocteau had told him about me in Paris . . . We all went out to the *Caffe Greco* where Armando Spadini and Massine were waiting and sent a card to Erik Satie, a heart with our signatures through it like lovers' arrows.'

Picasso seems to have enchanted his Italian hosts, with 'his laconic, musical voice, just like his paintings'. They took him to the Vatican Museum and he saw for the first time the Sistine Chapel frescoes and the Raphaels in the Stanze. Prampolini went to see him at the Albergo di Russia in the Via del Babuino and found the room decorated with 'the first classicist drawings he had made in that serene Roman climate. The world of Renaissance humanism left its mark on him, on a portrait of Cocteau and the painting *Three Women*. His artistry had been enriched. . . He wanted to know everything. . . He went for a few days to Naples and Pompeii to look at Roman painting at its point of origin in time, and came back with new syntheses of colour, form and space which showed in what became known as his Classical or Antique period from 1917 to 1923, following Synthetic Cubism . . . the famous large pastel heads of women (inspired by what he saw in Pompeii) and the monumental *Les Grosses Femmes* and *Les Baigneuses* are among the most representative and important evidence of the influence exerted by Classical Roman art on his work.'

During the late spring and early summer Picasso went, with a Spanish-speaking Italian girl Prompolini had found for him, on a visit to Florence and Venice. The Tuscan capital was full of British and Americans 'all criticising the way the Italians are fighting the War, the incompetence of the General Staff and the way they are shooting one in ten of regiments which run away'. When he got to Venice, much nearer the Front, he found more of the 'Allies', 'like visitors to an abbatoir'. Hemingway swore he first met Picasso in Venice on that trip, but as the painter, according to the girl Alicia Gomez, spent most of his time trying to escape from the heat and mosquitoes, this is unlikely. Picasso did not like either Florence or Venice, notwithstanding the works of art at every street corner; he complained of the food and fleas in Florence and of the heat and stench in Venice (his hotel room overlooked a *rio* into which the good Venetian housewives dumped their rubbish every morning).

When the work in Rome was finished, he was glad to get back to Paris. Alex Salto did a pen portrait of him about this time, at Montrouge: 'He had on a green sweater and baggy corduroy trousers. French artists still wear them. He is short but built like a bullfighter. He is olive-skinned, his black eyes are set close and his mouth is strong, the lips full and clearly outlined. He reminded me a bit of a racehorse . . . There was something huge and supernatural about him and I could well believe what they said about him, that he could cast spells and see into the future. But he was very friendly and showed me all his strange objects, including a sort of magic lantern into which you looked and you could see angels flying in the sky. I saw Henri Rousseau's picture of European statesmen at the outbreak of war, paintings by Derain, Matisse and Cézanne (a watercolour). Over his bed hung the first picture he ever painted, at the age of twelve, a golden-haired girl in a red skirt. . . . *Les Demoiselles d'Avignon* was there, the size of a wall, a bit wider than it is long. . . On an easel in the middle of the room, among pots of Ripolin paint, was a box without a lid and inside it there were bits of wood fixed at various angles so he could study the effect of light casting shadows . . . here and there he had moveable flaps of paper. . . .'

The performances of *Parade* in Paris were not a success, in spite of great advance publicity and an introduction in the programme by Apollinaire, who said it heralded a new era in the history of cooperation by great artists. Picasso's scenery was striking enough and looked like the scene for a party behind scenes at the circus. Acrobats, animals and everything else on the drop curtain looked like what they were—there were no 'Cubist problems' for the audience. Even the backcloth showed houses in normal perspective, and the costumes were bright and cheerful. Unfortunately the music was incomprehensible. Satie had put together a collage of sound which he believed mirrored Picasso's collages of paper, linoleum and other materials. Of course, he had refused to go to Rome with the rest of the collaborators in the 'integral ballet' and so had had no idea what Picasso had really painted—he had just assumed that he would go on making collages, in the theatre and outside. Satie's collage of sound was remarkable, and many years later was copied by an American 'fun band', Spike Jones and His City Slickers; the score sounded like that for a village band, and not too big a village either. In addition to more or less recognizable musical sounds, the startled audience heard sirens, the humming of car dynamos and the rattle of typewriters, trains passing and planes flying overhead.

The cast did not help to simplify the ballet. In addition to the dancers proper, there were three 'managers', an American, a Frenchman and a horse; the American carried a megaphone and a poster, the Frenchman (his back painted to look like the trees on a boulevard) a long, white pipe and a stick, and the horse wore an African mask. Massine danced the role of a Chinese conjuror and when he came on, after an introductory *pas* or two, he produced an egg from his pigtail and ate it, then brought it out, whole, from the toe of his shoe, tried to eat fire and burnt himself, put out a fire he nearly started and then partnered a little girl who 'runs about, pretends to ride a bicycle, imitates stars from the silent films, runs after a thief with a revolver, boxes, sleeps, mimes a shipwreck, then goes to sleep on the grass'. The other two dancers were acrobats who did a *pas de deux* and at least looked striking in Picasso's blue and white costumes. The 'managers' moved in and out among the dancers, grumbling that it was only a rehearsal and they were still waiting for the real actors to show up.

The catcalls and the jeers did not discourage Cocteau, who put the show on several times before giving up and going off with Diaghilev to Barcelona; *Parade* was not in the repertoire. Picasso gladly accepted an invitation to go with them to Barcelona, as he had nowhere to go and nobody to go anywhere with. Anyway, he was anxious to see how his mother had got over the death of his father, and to meet his new brother-in-law, Juan Vilato, a doctor like Uncle Salvador.

His mother was fine, still telling everybody she was on her way back to Málaga, and did not like Barcelona since her son had 'gone away to a foreign country with a foreign woman'; her daughter Lola would have been only too happy to see Doña Maria go, because her mother had moved in with her after her marriage 'just to help you to get the house running' and showed no signs at all of moving out. Picasso did not like Vilato, and to the relief of all moved into a hotel by the docks, not far away from his old studio.

It was good to be back in Barcelona and be lionized by the 'old gang'—Utrillo, Iturrino, de Soto and Canals were still there and gave him some good parties. *Els Quatre Gats* was closed (though it was to reopen in one of the many refurbishments it has had until the present day), so after the ballet they revelled along the Parallelo; Juan Miró first saw Picasso (and his first ballet) during that visit and said it was like an old hero coming home from the Moorish wars. As always, Picasso painted. The landlord of his hotel, when he found out that he had an internationally famous guest who was filling the bar and restaurant every night, cleared out the linen from the drying room on the top floor and converted it into a studio. From the windows he could see the whole of the docks from the Estación de Francia, and he did a series of paintings which show the windows and the scene beyond, with the shutters framing the boats, sellers of this and that, beggars and the sea. He used to entertain there, too, and the landlord gave him some tables and chairs (the amount of food and drink they consumed staggered him, but as he had never made so much money in his life as a hotelier before, they could have anything they wanted to eat and drink it on). A whole series of 'window paintings' followed, with one of the tables drawn up to the window itself and covered with the sort of objects which had covered his café tables in Montparnasse. There is also a painting, which dates from this stay near the docks, which shows one of the most bloodthirsty bullfight scenes he ever did. It is a fight between the bull and the picador's horse (the picador has disappeared, presumably unseated). The bull, which seems to be untouched by the matador, is goring the horse, has in fact disembowelled it and holds it in its death throes in the sand.

Some biographers have explained the presence of this scene of violence at the *corrida*, in a collection of peaceful scenes of everyday activity, as an explosion of sexual energy (Penrose). There is no evidence to suggest that his sexual energy, which was always explosive, was any greater than usual. Women and men came and went at the former laundry floor of the hotel. In the early hours, the men usually left and one of the women remained, a scene familiar (and not just to painters) all over the world.

It is true to say that there was a certain amount of pressure on Picasso to marry. He was the only male child and Doña Maria hoped to see grandchildren from her Pablo before she died; she also hinted that there would be legal complications if he did not marry, that the vineyard, now producing grapes again, and 'everything else', would go to his sister and brother-in-law. However, his brother-in-law does not seem to have discouraged the idea of marriage, and his sister was in favour of it, perhaps so that she would have somewhere else to dump their mother when she became too cantankerous. Doña Maria even kept the paintings *Science and Charity* and *The First Communion* unframed, the better to be able to go, even abroad, to check up on a daughter-in-law.

As he always did, Picasso took his mother out to dinner and to the theatre. He explained that his 'own' ballet, *Parade*, was not on this time because more work had to be done on it,

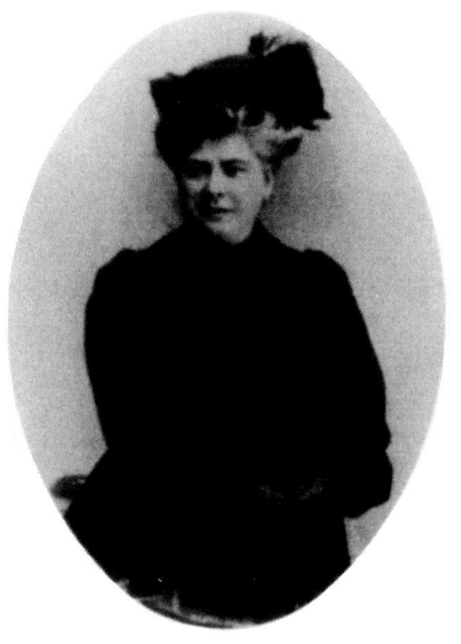

Picasso's Mother.

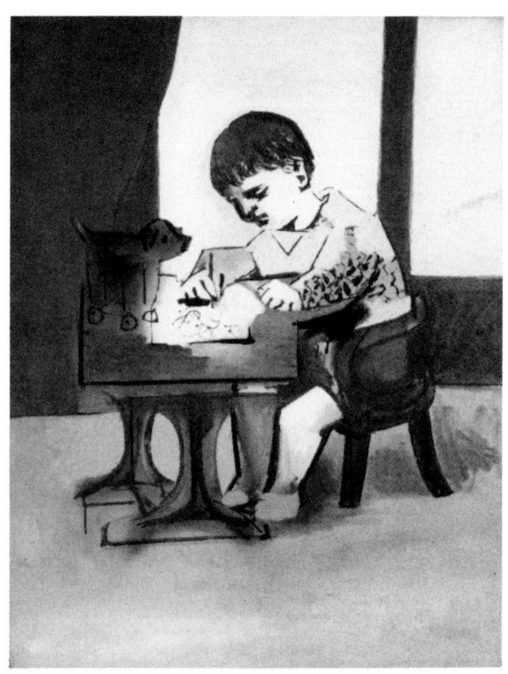

Painting by Picasso—*Paul Drawing*—1923.

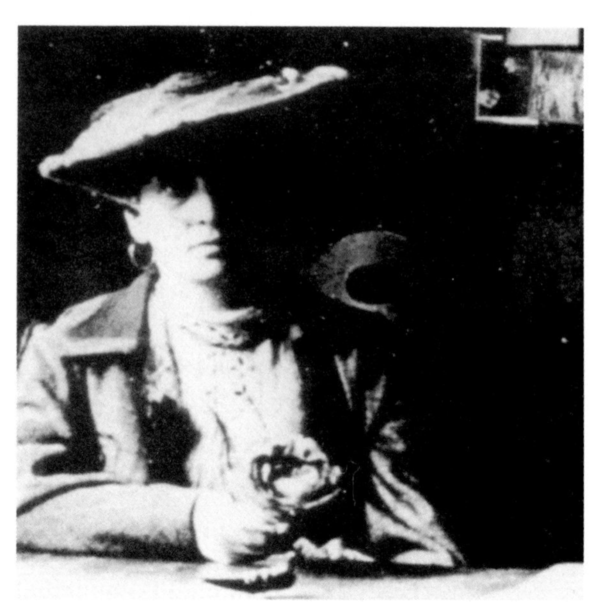

Fernande Olivier

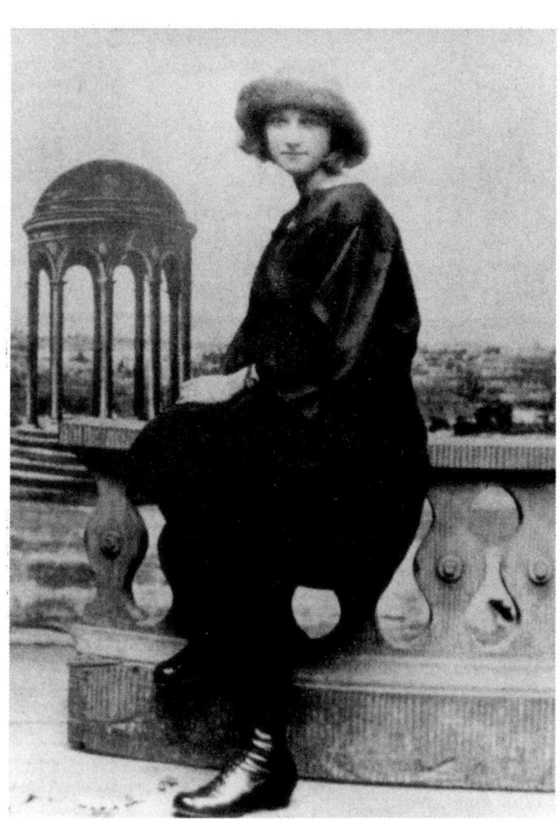

Marie Thérèse Walter.

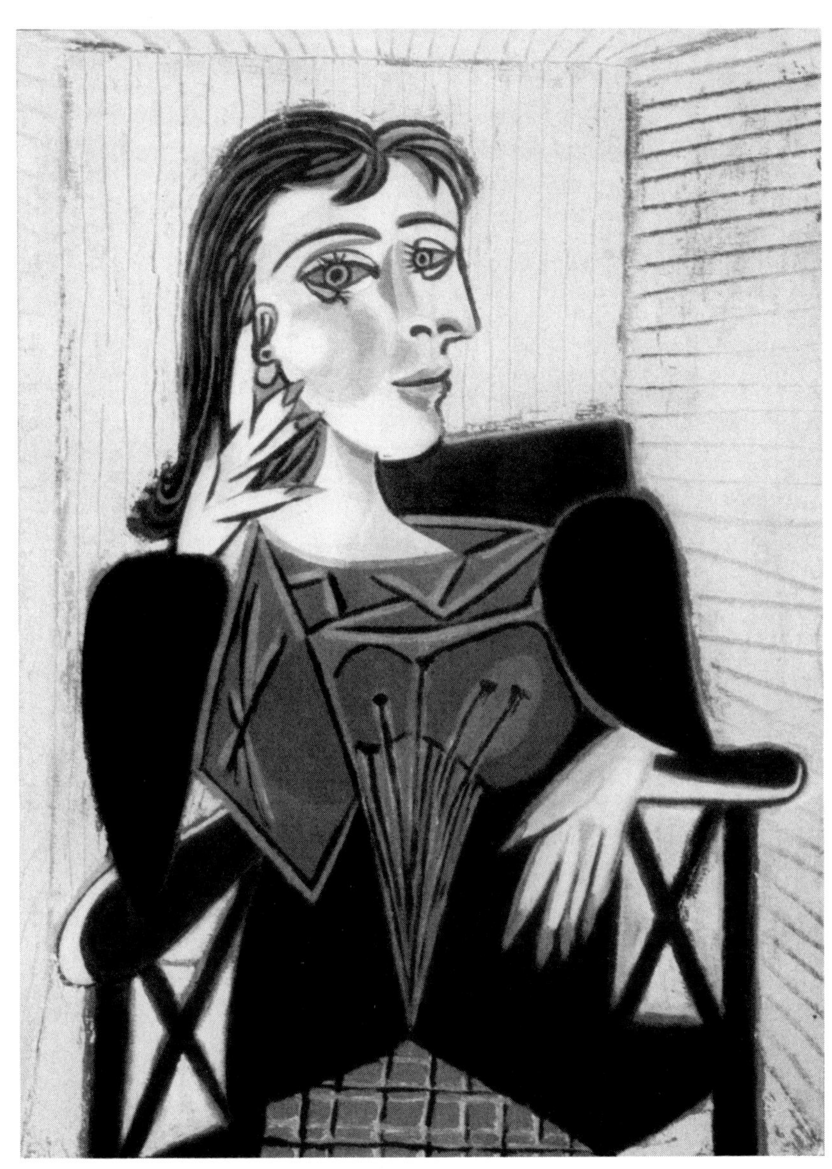

Picasso's portrait of Dora Maar

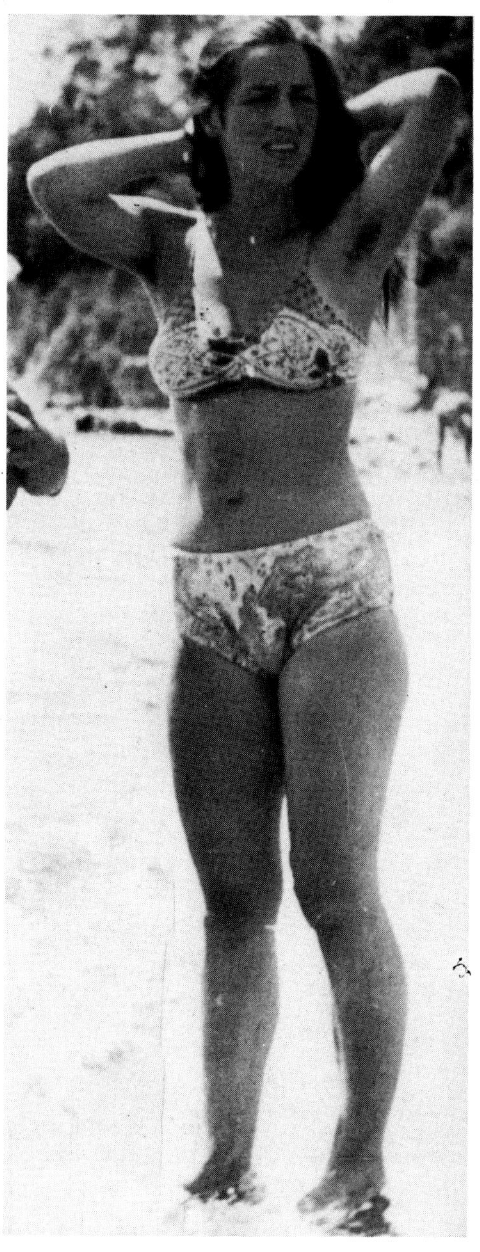

Françoise Gilot who was Picasso's companion for 8 years. Photographed after her announcement that she was to leave him. (The Keystone Collection).

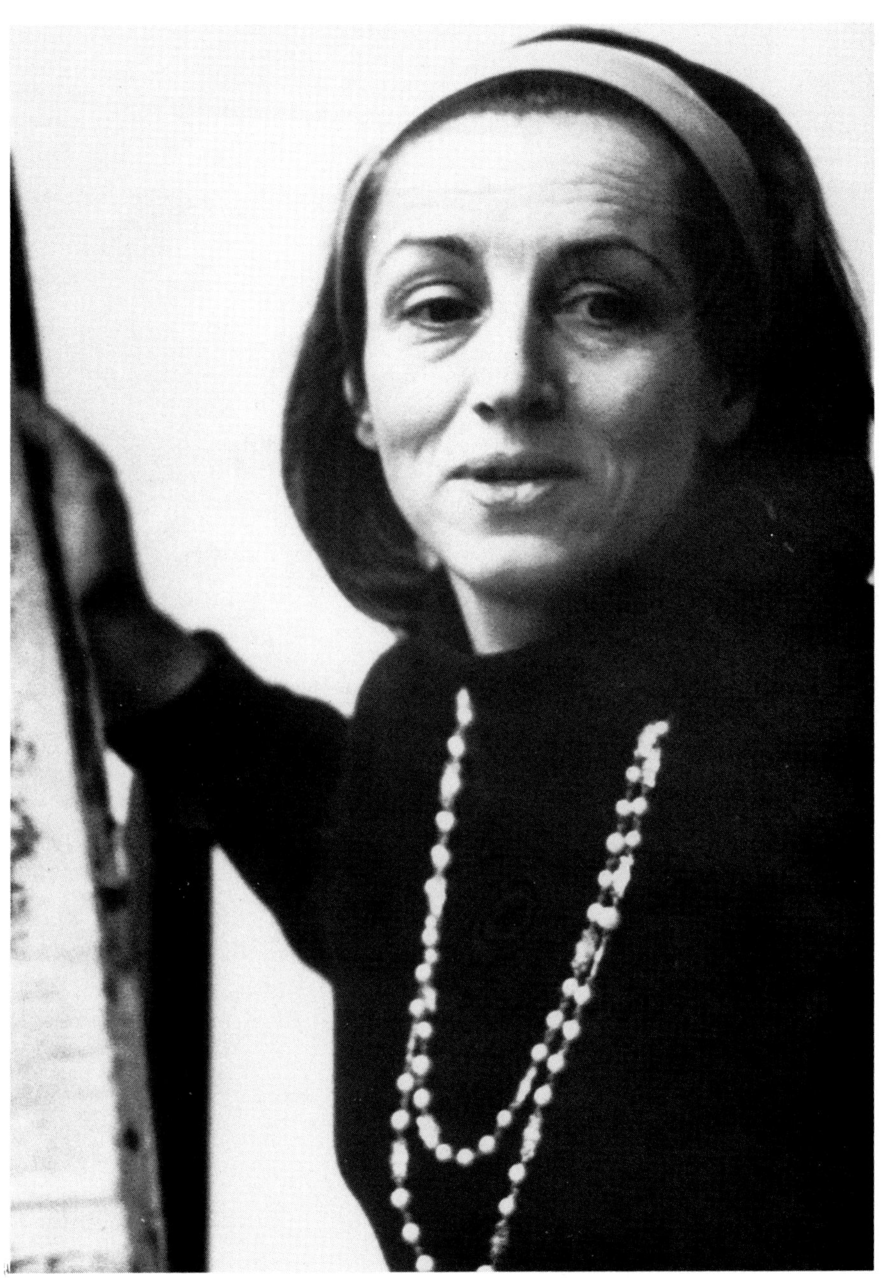

Francoise Gilot photographed in London after the death of Picasso in 1973. (The Keystone Collection).

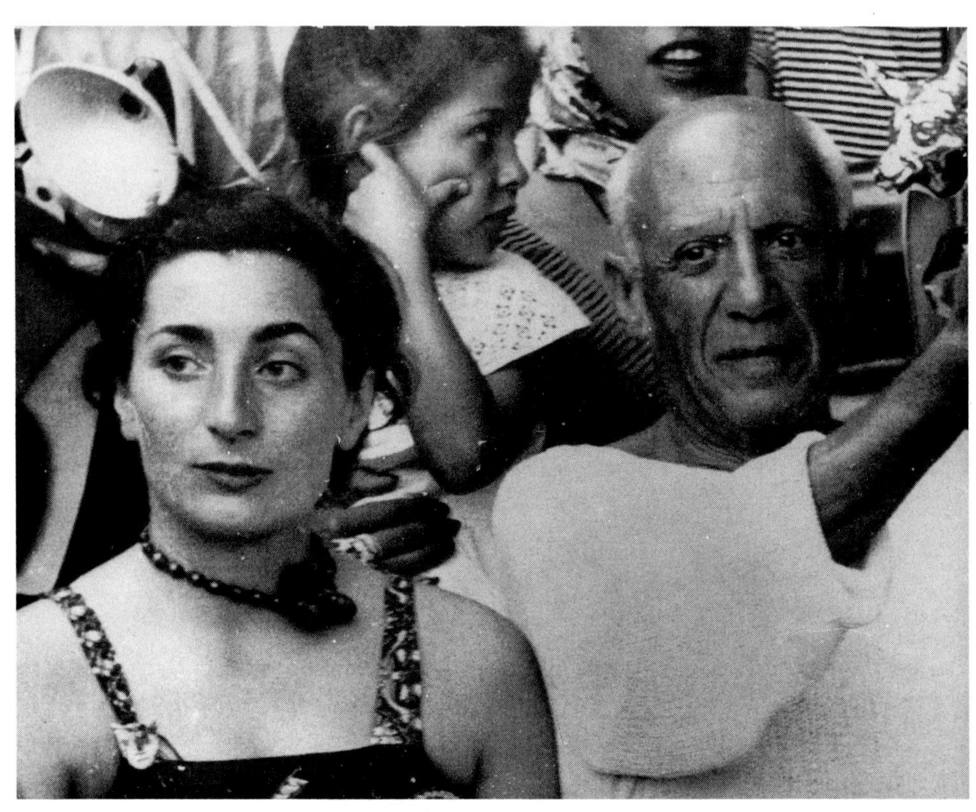

Picasso with Jacqueline Roque, his second wife, whom he married in 1961. (The Keystone Collection).

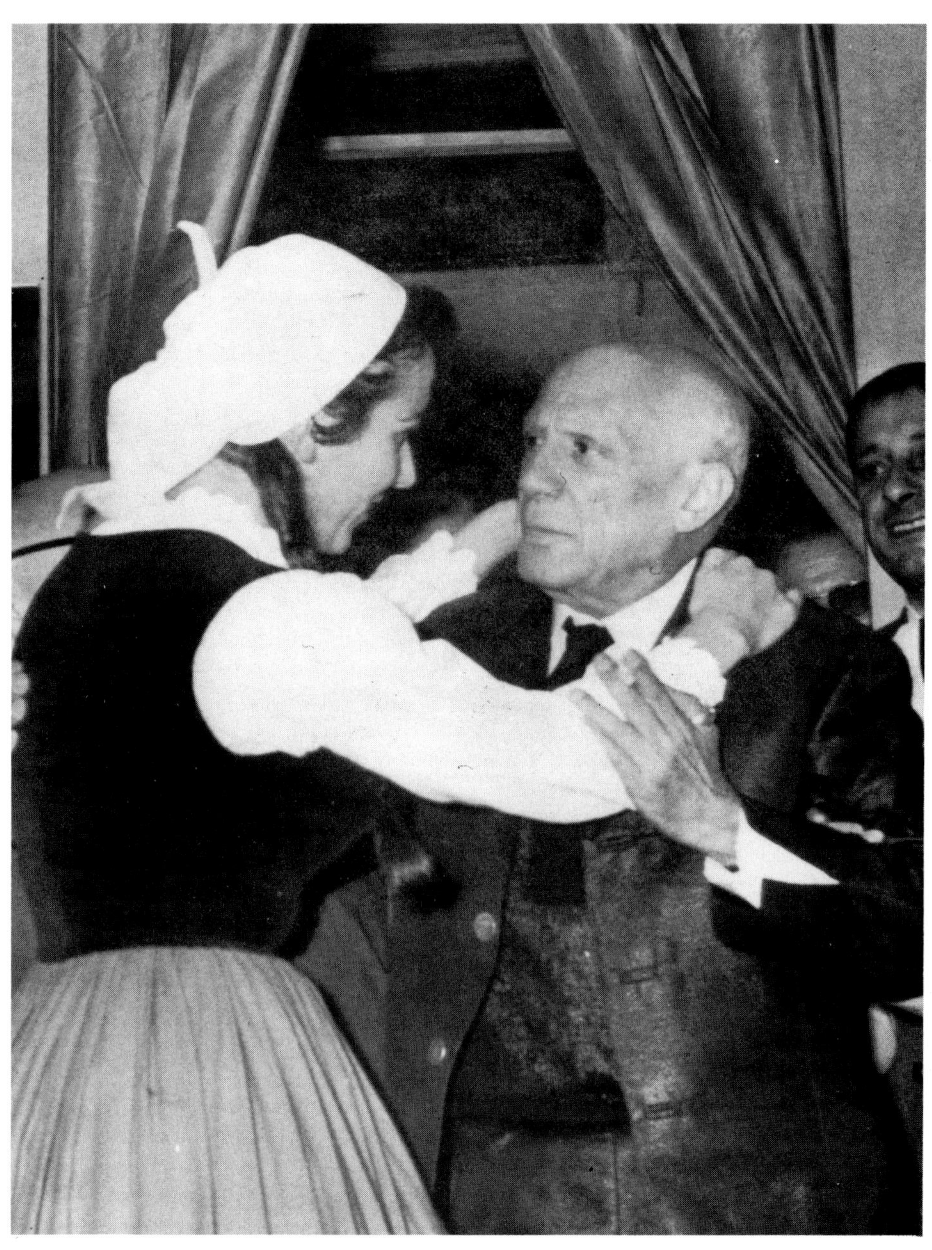

On his 80th birthday Picasso received a hug from a 20-year-old provincial girl. (The Keystone Collection).

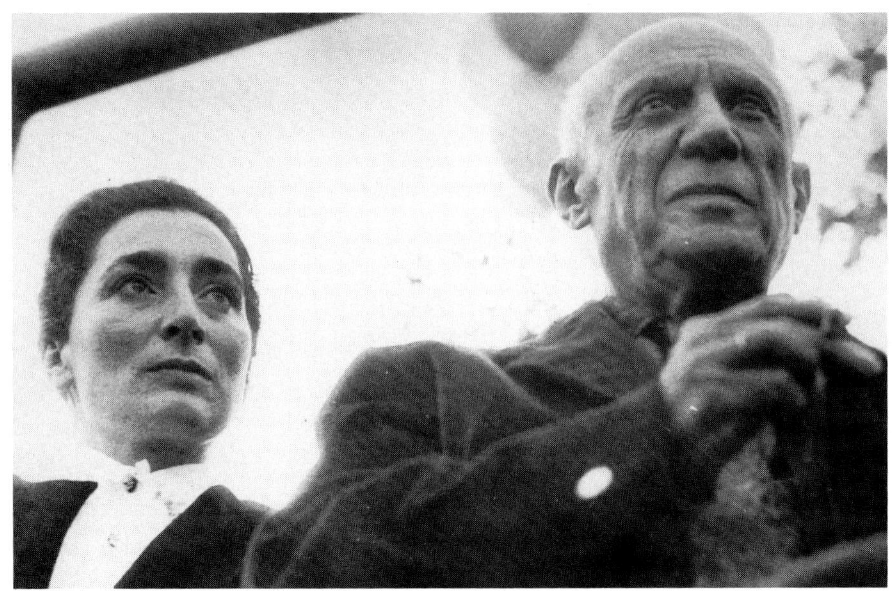

Picasso with Jacqueline, whom he married in 1961, the heir to his massive fortune. (The Keystone Collection).

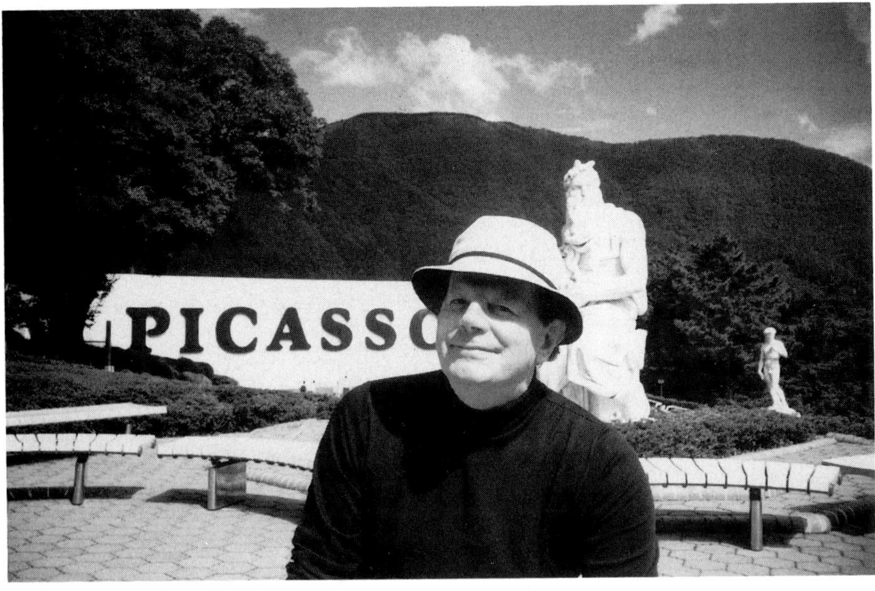

The author, Roy MacGregor-Hastie, outside the Picasso Museum in Japan.

but there were other ballets, white ballets from the Ballets Russes she would like to see. One of the things she saw twice was a ballet called *Good Humoured Ladies*, because one of the four soloists, she said later, had captured her son's heart.

Picasso had met Olga Koklova in Rome. It had been explained to him that Diaghilev recruited half his dancers from among those with a genuine talent, and half from among the daughters of good families with ready cash. When she had been taken on, Olga had been the daughter of a rich and powerful Tsarist General, a fact which had guaranteed her a place in the *corps de ballet*. Unfortunately, the war and the Russian Revolution (Lenin and the Bolsheviks seized power while the company was in Barcelona) had left her father an impoverished ex-General, and Diaghilev was anxious to get rid of her. When he heard of Picasso's interest, he was very pressing. Did she not know that this famous artist was also rich and the leader of an important movement? Yes, she did. She may have had little talent, but she was intelligent and well-read. Her father had been a friend of Shchukin and she had seen Picasso's paintings at the house; later, friends noted that she knew quite a lot about contemporary art, and about the Russian painters influenced by the Cubists, Grigoriev (*Man In a Cellar*), Exter, Tatlin, Larianov (whose portrait of Tatlin resembles the first portraits of Vollard and Kahnweiler), Malevich, Kandinsky, Archipenko and Shukkaev (whose *Women Bathing* is Picassoesque). Well, then, said Diaghilev, this man loves you! Go to him!

In Rome and in Paris Olga had ample proof of Picasso's devotion, but she also noticed that she was not the only one. In Paris, he had taken her to see the house at Montrouge, the neat housekeeper, not to mention the animals and birds, but she had found it very 'suburban' and in great contrast with the life-style of tenant and the women, traces of whom she found everywhere. She refused to move in with him, or even let his hand stay for long up her skirt. Cocteau and Diaghilev pleaded, but she would not relent.

In Barcelona, the pursuit went on. Picasso was mystified.

This was not a rich girl. She had no future as a dancer. Her father was in exile, competing with thousands of other Tsarist exiles who would provide Paris with its taxi-drivers and restaurateurs for decades. She was not even particularly beautiful, though she was very soignée in the ballerina style which promises so much more than there is to give; on stage she even perspired freely, he had noticed during a visit back stage, 'and dripped wet white onto the boards'. Who did she think she was? He did not need her in his bed. When he got to Barcelona all his old friends competed to 'fix him up' with something they had finished with or something newly arrived in one of the thousands of brothels—a 'nice girl' who was only doing it to save up enough money for her dowry. Nevertheless, the image of the girl Olga was never far from Picasso's mind and traces of her appear in some of the hotel paintings. He seems to have been really intrigued by the thought that marriage would get him the vineyard. Maybe the Russian Revolution would not last: *les Anglais* would put it down as they had got rid of Napoleon. Maybe if he married this girl—that was obviously what she wanted, she had said as much in no uncertain terms—he would inherit a large estate like Tolstoi and have serfs (his knowledge of history, especially Russian history, was very sketchy).

Whatever it was that decided the issue, Diaghilev left Spain without Olga or Picasso in tow, and at a dinner in Barcelona the engagement was announced. If there was no other way to have her, he would have to marry her and hope there would be other, even material, compensations. He had in mind a civil marriage at the *Mairie* when they got to Paris, but Olga was outraged and had the vociferous support of Doña Maria and Lola. Of course, there must be a big church wedding and all the famous people must be there. Olga decided that there would be a very big wedding, at the Russian Orthodox Church in the Rue Daru. He could choose his own witnesses (they were to be Max Jacob, Apollinaire and Cocteau) and she would have the whole company. She needed time to prepare for the wedding, of course, at least six months. She also needed money. As a special exception to the rule, she would allow him to pay for anything.

Picasso got his own back while he was waiting for 'the Day': he painted her in the same mantilla he had used for a similar portrait of Fernande.

Olga

'A life of first nights followed by nice little dinners followed by hysterical scenes.'

(John Richardson)

Picasso's first marriage was ill starred from the outset. Olga moved out of the house at Montrouge because 'it would not be proper to be married from there', and ran up bills for herself and her friends at a hotel. Then she was 'too busy' to go to the wedding of the man closest to her future husband, Guillaume Apollinaire, in May 1918, at the Church of St Thomas Aquinas near his home in the Rue St Guillaume. She made a third mistake when she underrated the importance, in French law, of the civil ceremony at the *mairie*; it was only at the last minute that one of her friends told her that the later wedding at the Russian Orthodox Church would have no validity—and there was a mad scramble to collect the right number of French citizens as witnesses. To add to the last minute turbulence, she refused to invite Gertrude Stein and Alice B Toklas, saying that homosexuals were understandable—they had harsh mothers— but lesbianism was an insult to femininity and those who practised it had no place at a wedding.

With all these omens in the sky, it was perhaps surprising that the wedding took place at all, on 12 July, 1918. The civil ceremony was extremely dignified, with Apollinaire, Max Jacob and Jean Cocteau as witnesses. The religious ceremony, which lasted for three hours, tried the patience of all except the Russians present, for whom it was an occasion to exchange notes on the experience of exile; most of them knew that Picasso's hope of a Romanoff restoration (and a noble land-holding) was doomed to extinction. After the feasting, there was some bickering. Olga refused to go to Montrouge, saying she would never enter that house again, it smelt of too many other women. Pablo offered her a taste of the *Bâteau-Lavoir*— the Pichots would move out for them and they could enjoy artistic surroundings; luckily Olga was warned about the living conditions there. In the end, they settled for a small hotel at Nevers, registering under false names, then slowly approached Paris via a few nights at Versailles and Fontainebleau.

The problem of where to live was solved by the rich Chilean lady who had supplied the pink silk counterpane for Picasso's bed. Madame Errazurix had a sense of humour and was also extremely shrewd. She was not at all put out by the thought that this young ballerina had dragged Picasso to the altar, and, with the utmost discretion, kept the news from the bride that she had been his mistress at Montrouge. She also knew that in his present euphoric state, Picasso would be painting like mad and would leave behind at least some of her walls frescoed and worth more than the cost of board and lodging; she was certainly right about the white walls of their bedroom, on which he painted nudes with some lines of Apollinaire, to the effect that love wounds wise men as well as fools. There were also some paintings done on the beach and some recollections of his life with Olga's company in Rome. There are also some very realistic portraits, the most important of which is *Madame Rosenberg, With her Child*.

The Rosenbergs, Paul and Leonce, were Jewish art dealers. Leonce had been an early believer in the commercial potential of Cubism, and dealt almost exclusively in the works of Picasso, Matisse and their followers; earlier that year he had organized a very successful sale, the first post-war sale on any scale, with Paul Guillaume in the Faubourg St Honoré. Paul Rosenberg was less committed to Cubism but saw the potential of Picasso in any of his moods. He understood that Picasso was not the founder of any school, but, as Gertrude Stein had seen immediately, painted as he felt. As Apollinaire put it: 'He changes direction, goes back to where he started, begins again even more sure of himself, always becoming greater.' Paul, as shrewd as Errazurix, whose lover he was, hit on the idea of taking for Picasso two floors of Rue de la Boétie in the fashionable centre, and opening a gallery himself next door. He had no difficulty in persuading Olga that this would be a most suitable address for her, and Pablo was still euphoric.

In the autumn, the move from Montrouge was made with as much fuss as possible. There was incessant squabbling over the fate of the cats, dogs, birds, monkey and other fauna. Eventually they compromised—the menagerie would be on the upper floor, the 'artist's studio floor', while she had the right to arrange the public rooms and their bedroom on the lower. She took the more polite paintings to hang on her walls, and he took the best of the Rousseaus, Matisses, Cézannes and Renoirs and stacked them on the floor.

It was a time of mixed emotions for Picasso. He missed the Saturday evenings with Gertrude Stein (she did not speak to him for three years) and the company of his old friends—'Ah, le Pablo, on le trouve maintenant dans les beaux quartiers'—in Montmartre and Montparnasse. Braque and Matisse thought he was a traitor and wished him ill of the *beaumonde*. Apollinaire had been his only supporter but shortly after the move to Rue de la Boétie, he fell ill; this came as a shock and surprise to his friends because the 'poet-hero' had apparently recovered from his war wounds and was really enjoying his marriage. On the day the Armistice was declared, Apollinaire died.

Picasso's gloom was only relieved by painting and by the prospect of a trip to London. In September, Diaghilev had taken the Ballets Russes to the British capital, determined to stay for a year and cash in on the celebratory mood. A new production of *Parade* was scheduled for 'later', but Diaghilev, finding that Picasso had admirers among the London intellectuals (Fry and Clive Bell had been pushing his name for a decade), wrote to ask him if he would design a new ballet, to the music of De Falla, based on a folk tale *El Sombrero de Tres Picos* (*The Three-Cornered Hat*).

Olga was as excited as her husband. She had realized that she had made some grave mistakes at the beginning of her marriage and was anxious to give her husband some new glory associated with her, or at least with her past, as a dancer—she even tried to persuade Diaghilev to let her take part in the new ballet. Early in the New Year they left for London and were put up at the Savoy Hotel; when he heard that he would not have to pay for their suite there, Picasso agreed to let himself be fitted out with a wardrobe appropriate to the London season. Innumerable shirts and ties were bought in the Savoy Arcade and suits ordered from the Savoy Tailors' Guild; he even bought a dinner jacket which Derain (who always wore the same blue suit when he was not painting) said was ridiculous, but secretly envied. Olga spent a lot of money on her wardrobe, but cash seemed to flow in from Diaghilev, galleries and newspapers, and on most evenings they dined out at other people's expense. Olga, helped by Polunin's English wife Elizabeth, did a bit of matchmaking, trying to pair off dancers with rich Englishmen while the going was good; they had some success and later Lydia Lopokova managed to get Maynard Keynes as a husband just as his star was really in the ascendant.

They seem to have met everybody, Keynes, Lytton Strachey, Fry, the Bells (Vanessa and Clive) and all of Bloomsbury, extracting from their hosts a promise to dine with them in Paris. They made a lot of customers, and gave Picasso a new taste for portrait-painting; when they got back to France in the summer he embarked on a whole series of portraits, mostly of poets (Olga thought them much superior to painters, in mind and manners), among them Aragon, Valéry, Breton and Reverdy as well as old friends like Max Jacob (out of favour with Olga because of his 'vulgar' jokes at the wedding).

That summer of 1919 they recuperated at St Raphael. They seem to have been fully reconciled—she was promised a Renoir for the dining room—and they both liked the place. Their hotel was cheap and their rooms so large they reminded him of the former laundry floor he had taken over at the hotel in Barcelona; many of his paintings at the windows are virtually indistinguishable from the Barcelona series, with their shutter frames, table at the window as an altar for still life objects, and so on. This summer holiday began a long affair with the South of France, which did not end even when tourism *en masse* destroyed the ambience; by that time Picasso had his own establishment and did not have to eat the disgusting food served to Nordic holidaymakers—and he also enjoyed the loud vulgarity and the naked female flesh to be looked at free of charge on the beaches.

It was a good year for business, too. Paul Rosenberg was proving to be an even better businessman than Kahnweiler. In October there was an exhibition at the gallery next door in Rue de la Boétie, which was handy for Picasso who liked to chat with prospective customers and was always good for an autograph; the catalogue had a drawing of Olga on the cover, which did no harm upstairs. At the same time the Leicester galleries in London put on a show of watercolours, etchings and drawings (from 1902) and this made quite a lot of money, too; Olga was discouraged from going shopping, but redoubled her zeal in learning English.

Kahnweiler was having a great deal of trouble convincing the French authorities that he was entitled to have back the contents of his gallery, confiscated at the beginning of the war. He had never been disloyal. His wife was a loyal Frenchwoman. The artists he was showing were all patriots, with the exception of Picasso, and most of them had served with honour in the French Armed Forces. For the whole of 1920, there was a great coming and going to ministries by the artists concerned, Picasso, Braque, Gris, Léger and others. During the summer, when Paris shuts its doors, there was also some discreet lobbying at summer residences, but that seemed to have little effect. Olga was very worried, because 132 paintings by her husband were involved and though he was a prolific painter, this still represented a lot of work. When Paul Rosenberg asked her why she was so upset—Picasso had been paid for many of the works and it was Kahnweiler who stood to lose the most—she called him a fool. All those works put up for auction at one go would depress the price of Cubist paintings on the market and make it impossible to sell new work for the sort of money her style of life made necessary. She was only quietened down when she discovered that she was pregnant.

Picasso was overjoyed at the news that he was about to become the father of a legitimate child. He swept Olga off to Juan les Pins and installed her in the very best hotel. She did not need any encouragement to rest and play the role of the fragile mother-to-be, though she was always well enough to go shopping 'for the baby' or to interview prospective nannies. She was, of course, concerned to get an efficient and ugly nanny—not so ugly that she would frighten the child, but ugly enough to discourage her husband from taking an interest in her. She favoured middle-aged Dutch women, but at about this time he began to paint large Dutch women from sketches he had made in 1905 and never developed. He said they were scenes celebrating maternity and that of course he had done them for her, but she was not convinced. In the end she settled for a Breton peasant woman who had had ten children of her own, would stay with her throughout the pregnancy and see how she liked the establishment in Paris thereafter.

There were visits from Diaghilev, who commissioned some drawings for a ballet derived from the Italian *commedia dell'arte*, with a Pulcinella and Pimpinella as well as Harlequin and Pierrot, and Picasso started work at Juan les Pins immediately—the harbour at Naples becomes, in fact, any fishing harbour in the South of France—and Olga found the sketches entrancing, promising herself that when she was a normal shape again she would have some of the costumes made up into day clothes and others into clothes for the many parties to which they were invited.

The birth of their son, in February 1921, at an expensive clinic in Paris, gave Olga the excuse for climbing another rung up the social ladder as she saw it. In London she had learnt that English gentlemen have large houses in the country, from which their wives and daughters go up to the capital for the 'season'. These gentlemen often have a flat in Town, or stay at their clubs, or both, but the country house is the base from which they operate. This was good enough for her. She told Picasso that they needed a large and comfortable establishment not too far from Paris, in the French Home Counties, as it were. One was found easily enough—like the English, the French were abandoning them as being too cold, draughty and expensive to run—at Fontainebleau, a substantial villa at a low rent. There were gardens, flowerbeds, lawns and gardeners. The nanny was joined by a maid, a cook and a manservant and genteel entertainments were planned for the spring and summer. A series of sickly portraits of mother and child, of mother playing the piano, of mother walking in the salon or writing a letter at her desk, show how far Picasso had been dragged down; perhaps the high peak of Olga's influence can now be seen over the christening—Max Jacob's offer to be a godfather was refused.

By the beginning of the summer, however, Fontainebleau had begun to pall and Picasso found excuses for frequent extended trips to Paris, staying at the Rue de la Boétie. There was the first of the auctions of Kahnweiler's property—no fewer than 381 Cubist paintings among others were sold between 1921 and 1923—and the need to be there to stimulate public interest. It came as a shock to him to discover that the French Government had given the technical supervision of the sale to Paul Rosenberg's brother, Leonce. He met Braque at the saleroom and a communion of interests helped towards a renewal of civility, if not friendship; after working himself up into a state about Picasso's bourgeois clothes and the human condition of painters in general, Braque was so enraged by the smug satisfaction on Leonce's face that he walked up to him and thumped him (his war record saved him from retribution), earning a round of applause from the public.

In the end, helped by Kahn, Lefèvre and Dutilleul, and the Belgian René Gaffe, Kahnweiler was able to buy back most of the paintings and keep prices more or less in line with what they would have been.

Though she pretended to be pleased by the way things had gone, and admired Braque's 'manliness', Olga refused to have any of the 'old crowd' at Fontainebleau. There was no way of getting her out or them in, and Picasso grumbled to the gardeners that he would like to see at least a Paris street lamp, or, even better, a *pissoir* in the middle of the lawn to bring the place to life. He liked poets in moderation and Russian Counts not at all, and the place was always full of them. He retired to a complex of studios at one side of the house and locked himself in for hours every day; his wife explained this behaviour as the 'sensitive artist's need for solitude'.

A bright spot in his life that year was the arrival in Paris of Tristan Tzara, who was to come and go for forty years as Picasso's women decreed him *persona grata* or *persona non grata*. Apollinaire had spoken about Tzara, the Romanian leader of a new movement called Dada (the words for 'Yes Yes' in Romanian) founded by Hugo Ball in Zurich in 1916. Marinetti, Modigliani, Arp and Kandinsky all showed their work at the Voltaire and contributed to the magazine *Dada*. This lively journal often attacked Picasso as having caused Cubism to drift towards a 'hateful aestheticism' but Picasso was never offended, and he was amused when Tzara, on his appearance in the Paris cafés, also attacked Marinetti (who had become with Mussolini the founder of the new Fascist Movement in Italy) and everybody else. This witty, coarse Romanian was such a contrast to the rather effeminate French poets with which the country (and the household at Fontaine-bleau) was oversupplied, that his impact was enormous. He and his followers virtually took over the magazine *Litterature* which had been founded by Breton, Aragon and Eluard, and during the winter of 1921–22 attracted a numerous, noisy claque to all his 'shows' (exhibitions outside police stations, 'happenings' in the lavatories of grand hotels and so on). Olga mistakenly allowed Picasso to invite him to lunch one day ('A Romanian poet—how amusing!'), and he delighted his host by remarking, after a tour of the house and grounds: 'Russian ballerinas get very greedy when they leave the stage and start to breed. Be careful of this one. She will have you goldplate her cunt.'

Picasso had been hoping to get to the South of France for the summer of 1922. The bawling brat, Paulo (Olga had Italianised his name, misspelling it, to remind her of the country where they met), was getting on his nerves and he had told his wife they would have to give up Fontainebleau (he bribed the owners to tear up the rental agreement). In the South there would be plenty of rough, hairy, sweating peasant girls and fishermen's daughters, and he was in the mood for a little extra-marital activity. There was the added attraction of Gertrude Stein. Gertrude, though her language was more refined than Tzara's, had seen what a golden cow Olga had become (though Alice B Toklas remained devoted until the end) and was prepared to accept the explanation that it was she who had banned the inhabitants of the Rue de Fleurus from the wedding. There was a reconciliation at a gallery: 'We were somewhere at a picture gallery and Picasso came up and put his hand on Gertrude Stein's shoulder and said, "Oh hell, let's be friends". "Sure", said Gertrude Stein, and they embraced. "When can I come to see you?" said Picasso. "Let's see", said Gertrude Stein, "I am afraid we are busy but come to dinner the end of the week." "Nonsense," said Picasso, "we are coming to dinner tomorrow", and they came.'

Dinner with Gertrude Stein reinforced Olga's determination not to go to the South of France and she said her doctors had spoken very highly of Dinard, on the coast of Brittany. There would be *les Anglais* and a chance to shine in society and the coast. He could paint and draw seascapes which were all the vogue in London, and so the holiday would more than pay for itself. Reluctantly Picasso took a house, but with a reduced staff, and settled down to draw some banal but intelligible scenes of life at Dinard and St Malo; they did, in fact, sell well. He also painted a number of interesting still lifes which give an overall impression of light shining through fishing nets or shutters. Some of the juxtapositions of unusual objects are

Cubist in manner, and there are the usual collections of café table props, but the interest lies in the handling of light; perhaps he was under the influence of some *Anglais* like Turner or Constable. He also found a bar and some Breton cronies, and met his son's nanny's family, a mob of drunken fishermen and their women, with whom he could relax. The shame of this, he said later, caused his wife to fall ill and there was an alarming drive back to Paris, with Olga groaning, and little Paolo being carsick all over the nanny. In Paris, the doctors said that Olga was 'not quite in place after the delivery of the child', but was successfully operated on. 'There you are,' said Tzara, 'she was goldplating her cunt.'

Back in Paris, Picasso found the Dadaists in good form, planning a whole season of 'negative events'. He agreed to be a guest at their *Soirée du Coeur à Barbe* at the Théâtre St Michel, the more willingly because some of his wife's poets, including Breton and Eluard (who had just constituted themselves the Surrealist Movement) were threatening a 'counter-event' which was really only in the spirit of Dadaism. Unpardonably, the Surrealists did not let Tzara's show get under way and jumped onto the stage to prevent it. There was an exciting riot, and one of the Dadaists suggested that they should get the police to join in (*flics* always followed Tzara in large numbers). Picasso shouted to Tzara: 'No police', at which the Surrealists panicked and later blamed Tzara for their undignified flight from the St Michel. It was months before peace was restored at the rival cafés.

The Picassos spent a quiet winter in the Rue de la Boétie, while Olga recovered her good health. They came to an understanding about sharing the house and cutting down the entertainment, though there was still too much of this for his liking. He was at an unsettled stage with his work. He was tired of Cubist experiments which did not seem to be leading him anywhere, but not satisfied by the Neo-Classical drawings and paintings which, though they sold well, were not leading anybody else anywhere, either. It is certainly true, as he always said, that he was not a 'leader' in the sense of actively directing a school of painters (Braque always had pupils who were drilled in his ideas), but it is also true that he liked to start artistic hares and see who would run after them. Not being an intellectual, he felt lost during the debates, often acrimonious, between the Dadaists and Surrealists, though he could see that the debates were more serious than the public events which mirrored them. He agreed to allow Man Ray to photograph some of his work for a new magazine, *La Révolution Surréaliste*, but refused to write a manifesto because he said he had nothing to declare.

During the annual summer holiday, in 1923 at Cap d'Antibes, he met Diaghilev again and agreed to collaborate in what turned out to be his last ballet (though his paintings were used for years in other people's creations). The attraction lay largely in a chance to repair the damage done in *Parade* by the physical separation of Picasso from the composer Satie. This time, Satie and he would work together and there would be no 'misunderstandings'. The ballet, *Mercure*, is not important and it irritated Picasso to learn that its first performance was to be at a private party to be held by one of his wife's socialite friends, the Comte Étienne de Beaumont, but it helped to pass the time and restore a certain equilibrium. There were plenty of opportunities, in the costume and scene design, to show off his virtuosity to admiring girls (drawing their portraits with one line, never taking the pen or pencil off the paper, for example), and the visual impact of it all was very pleasing; there were no harsh shapes or colours (the decor was mostly brown and grey) and the music was, for Satie, subdued. The plot, a sort of satire on Greek tales from Mount Olympus, was insignificant and the whole affair, as Cyril Beaumont wrote later, was 'stupid, vulgar and pointless'.

The first performance of *Mercure* was interesting only to society columnists and those Picasso-watchers who reported his doings to Montmartre and Montparnasse; he looked particu-larly out of place in a matador's costume he had designed for himself.

The summer at Juan les Pins marks the beginning of the end of Pablo's life as a social butterfly. On their return from Cap d'Antibes the previous year he had found his expensive English wardrobe largely eaten by moths (it had been uncared for at Fontainebleau). The best of the cloth had been eaten away and only linings and stiffenings were visible, with the occasional bus ticket and, in one instance, a pipe hanging out of a nonexistent pocket. This he took to be an omen and the matador's costume was his last excursion into the world of well-dressed men. Photographs taken between 1924 and 1927 show him getting shabbier and shabbier. His dinner jacket was the last to go, though his Harris tweed sports coats looked no worse then (or even after the war) than they had done the day they were bought in London. Some of the suits, or the parts of them which survived, were drafts to service in the studio, and he could be seen sometimes in black and white pinstriped trousers, straw slippers and a cricket sweater with the moth-holes cobbled up by himself. Braque thought it was a great improvement.

It was not only Picasso's façade which seemed to crumble. During her illness after the holiday at Dinard, Olga was for a time too weak to care for her toilette, and her husband discovered that her hair was not jet black after all, but a sandy-red colour like his father's. During convalescence, the dye was put back again and her hair stayed black until after the Second World War, but the damage had been done. The illness also reinforced the strong features of her face, giving it an almost masculine quality. The soignée ballerina disappeared forever from the canvasses and drawings.

Back at work seriously, Picasso re-examined what he had been doing since the first Cubist ideas had been mooted, to see what, if anything, he should do to revive them. After the success of the Juan les Pins drawings in no. 2 of *La Révolution Surréaliste*, Breton became a frequent visitor to the studio, trying to wean Picasso away from Tzara and attach him to the 'orthodox wing' of the Movement. It was during one visit that he was rummaging about, with Picasso's permission, looking for a striking painting to reproduce in issue no. 4. Suddenly he came across a very large canvas, rolled up like a carpet, and carefully unrolled it on the floor. It was *Les Demoiselles d'Avignon*. 'That's it', said Breton, and he was the first person to reproduce the (still unfinished) first manifestation of Cubism in paint. At the first Surrealist exhibition in the Galerie Pierre, in 1925, Breton tried to root Surrealism in Cubism, denying any debt to Dada: 'The position held by us now could have been delayed or lost if it had not been for the iron will of this man.' This tactic failed, as did Breton's attempts to stop Max Ernst and Juan Miró designing a new production of *Romeo and Juliet*—for some reason Breton was convinced that nobody who belonged to the new intellectual aristocracy (of Surrealism) could have anything to do with ballet. Olga was furious to learn of this last heresy, and from one of her poets, too, and urged her husband to make a demonstration of solidarity with her art. She wrote to Diaghilev and had an answer by return of post inviting them to spend the late spring and summer in Monte Carlo before going to the house they had taken at Juan les Pins. She was as unsuccessful in her way as Breton in his. Picasso discovered that he had lost interest in ballet as such, but placated his wife by doing a series of paintings of dancers.

Just as he was finishing his first drawings, the news came from Paris that Pixtot (Pichot) had died. Olga was shocked at the impact the news had on her husband. He was drunk for three days, for the first and last time in his life, then shut himself away and started work on a canvas which has become known as *Three Dancers* (Tate Gallery). Penrose's description of it as 'a nodal point in the work of Picasso' cannot be bettered: 'It is the first to show violent distortions which have no link with the classical serenity of the preceding years. . . During the following years, the human form was to be torn apart, not with the careful dissection practised during the years of analytical Cubism, but with a violence that has rarely been paralleled in the work of any artist.' As Picasso explained many years later, it is not a portrait of three dancers at all, but of women as monsters who destroy men. He had in mind Pichot's widow, Germaine, who had destroyed his friend Casagemas, and perhaps Olga, too; Pichot's shadow glowers at the right of the picture, a menacing shade against the window space. Olga was so worried that she sent for reinforcements, his mother from Barcelona and Gertrude Stein from Antibes. When his mother arrived they tried to distract him with happy memories from his childhood. Gertrude Stein wrote: 'They [talked] about Picasso when [she] first knew him. He was remarkably beautiful then, he was illuminated as if he wore a halo, "Oh," said Madame Picasso, "if you thought him beautiful then, I assure you it was nothing compared to his looks when he was a boy. He was an angel and a devil in beauty, no one could cease looking at him." '

During this bout of nostalgia, Cocteau, who had embarked on a biography of Picasso, sent a little light relief in the form of a telegram asking him for the date of his birth. 'And yours', telegraphed back Picasso. Hemingway was sent for, too, and organized a series of fancy dress beach parties, but Picasso sat on the the periphery of it all, dressed rather like an off duty waiter in a white shirt buttoned up to the neck, without a tie, with a rather odd white felt hat like a golfer's.

In the end, they left him alone with his grief and some young painters and sculptors who had come to pay homage. He had been toying since Apollinaire's death with plans for a commemorative sculpture—'something that corresponds to the monument described in *Le Poète Assassiné*, that is a space with a void, of a certain height, covered with a stone'. He might have done it had Alberto Giacometti not appeared on the scene, with his brother Diego. He had brought with him a portfolio of sketches for pieces of sculpture based on a Western rein-terpretation of African art (one of the sketches was to become *Spoon Woman*), and seeing them took Picasso back again to those days of heady excitement before the war and *Les Demo-iselles d'Avignon*. Though he was very kind to the Giacomettis, he was seized with a sort of fury, and ran about the seaside markets shouting in a mixture of Spanish, Catalan and French that he had lost his way, that he had been seduced by evil women, that he was the new Samson ruined by not one Delilah but many, and much more. The fruit and vegetable sellers and shopkeepers, who knew that this apparent madman was not only an artist, but, more important, had money and paid his bills, took it all in good part and waited for the mistral to either drive him completely off his head or calm him down. Level wrote that he sometimes made a palette out of the paper linings of fruit and vegetable boxes, crushing their contents to make colours in which he 'painted' violent flowers like those of Van Gogh; the more shrewd traders kept them, and sold them at a very handsome profit a quarter of a century later.

By the end of the summer he seemed to have calmed down, and took his mother back to Barcelona. It was a wise decision on his part because he found himself in an ambience in which he no longer had any enemies or rivals. It was also a relief to be able to speak Spanish all day without having to force himself to speak either the 'correct' French on which his wife insisted or the other varieties of French spoken by everybody else but Olga. He was fêted not only by his old friends but by the younger generation of Miró, already among the 'converts' to whatever he cared to do. His sister was pregnant and did not feel like having him in the house—he detracted attention from her—so he took a suite of rooms for his mother and himself in the cathedral square. His mother was happy to be able to go to Mass without discomfort or fatigue at any time of the day, and he was only a hundred metres away from what was to be the latest incarnation of *Els Quatre Gats* (Romeu was dead). In a book published under the auspices of *Els Quatre Gats*, Josep Palau i Fabre notes: 'A Barcelona, a questa vegada, Picasso ana a veure l'exposicio d'un jove pintor que prometia, que feia molt d'enrenou, a les Galeries Dalman, ara al Passeig de Gracia, Era Salvador Dali.'

The meeting with Dali was important for both artists. Dali had been a bit suspicious of all the adoration doled out to Picasso in his absence and poured over him on his rare appearances in the city. He found a modest genius, still disturbed by the death of Pixtot, and anxious only to get on with his work as best he could. For Picasso, it was refreshing to meet a 'jove pintor' who had no doubts. Dali approved wholeheartedly, as many painters in Spain did not, of his senior's excursions into other art forms, of his photography as well as the painting and sculpture, of the scenery and costume designs for ballet. This 'generosity of spirit' was in keeping with his own beliefs that an artist had to exert his influence twenty-four hours a day in whatever ambience he happened to find himself. He listened approvingly to the tales of the painting with fruit and vegetable juices on wrappings to hand, and during their several meetings talked of the artist as 'designer'; he was later to turn this to commercial advantage long before the couturiers realized that a name made famous in one métier could be used to sell the products of others.

Somewhat cheered by this and other casual encounters, Picasso gave a number of interviews to local journalists, some of them amusing and malicious. He gave one interview to a Catalan language paper in which he talked about his friends in Paris, especially those known to the readers of the paper. How was Cocteau doing, he was asked (Jean had made a hit with the homosexual community during the visit of the Ballets Russes). Picasso said he was doing very well as far as he could judge. His poetry seemed to be reaching the audience it deserved and you could find a book of Cocteau's verse on the bedside table of any fashionable hairdresser. One of the local homosexuals sent a translation of the interview to a Parisian paper, which printed it with heavy sarcasm. For days afterwards, Picasso, who had returned to Paris, had to shut himself up in his studio to avoid Cocteau, who was demanding an apology or denial of the authenticity of the story. Gertrude Stein notes that 'the first evening the Picassos went out they went to the theatre and there in front of them was seated Cocteau's mother. At the first intermission they went up to her, and surrounded by all their mutual friends she said, my dear, you cannot imagine the relief to me and to Jean to know it was not you that gave out that vile interview, do tell me that it was not. And as Picasso's wife said, I as a mother could not let a mother suffer and I said of course it was not Picasso and Picasso said, yes, yes of course it was not, and so the public retraction was given.'

Peace may have been restored to the local scene but Picasso soon became depressed again and fell into frequent troughs of misery out of which he climbed in a rage. He began making some collages which were really vicious cartoons. He had another go at Cocteau, who annoyed him more and more with his airs and graces, his pretence of being eternally thirty years old becoming more absurd with age; Cocteau was satirized in one of these 'cartoons' in a 'portrait' which consisted mostly of the tails of one of his shirts stuck onto a board. A more vicious effort was the work known as *Guitar* which consists of an ordinary kitchen dishcloth held to the base with nails poking out at the world; he said he had intended to sew razor blades everywhere so that anybody who was thoughtless enough to touch the work would cut his hands, and a good thing too. This was finished before they went again to Juan les Pins in the summer of 1926.

That summer he began a new collection of objects he said showed more artistry than any man could give them. He would wander up and down the beach for hours, picking up things which took his fancy, old sardine cans battered and rusted in an interesting way, bits of driftwood, empty seashells and pebbles. Olga would watch him go and nervously entertain her poets and Americans under coloured parasols, hoping he would not return in time for the elegant lunch served with exaggerated style at one o'clock. Of course, he always did appear, carrying a bag of the morning's *objets trouvés* which he would empty in front of her guests, deliberately invading tablecloths. Ignoring her frozen looks, he would hold forth on what he had disco-vered ('Think of what has happened to the beans which were once in this can—here is a new way of thinking about time'). At the best of times, when he was not being deliberately provocative, he would take two or three apparently unrelated things and turn them into a plaything for Paolo or a piece of barbaric jewellery for the wife of a guest. Sometimes the artifacts were very beautiful. Paolo was always pleased to receive his father's attention—though he was now five years old, he was not allowed to go on the beachcombing expeditions—and the women who received the unique and wearable pieces were intelligent enough to know that they had been given something of value. The tension grew again after lunch, when Picasso insisted on taking all his stuff back to the house and, unless Olga were careful, taking some of the detritus of lunch back with him, too.

There was trouble in store on their return to Paris. After Lenin's death, the Russian Revolution and Communism had become less of an immediate threat, or so politicians wrongly believed. Soviet diplomats began to circulate, embassies and consulates opened and Soviet writers and artists began to travel. As the writers and artists who were allowed to travel were all Communists, many Western self-styled intellectuals came to the conclusion that this really was a new, creative society, that the stories of atrocities before and after the civil war had been exaggerated, and that maybe they had something to learn from what had been,—who knew?—the second great Revolution after the French. Soviet journalists, especially art critics, came to call on Picasso. The Party line was favourable. *Ogonyok* (2/ 1926) summed it up by saying that Picasso's works had been known now for twenty years, and 'are a reflection of the whole culture of our time, in both its good and bad aspects'. Georghi Yakulov, a Party hack, noted that the painter lacked a sense of unity, '. . . is good at analysis but poor at synthesis', but felt that this was not really his fault but the fault of the (decadent) Western European culture of which he was a creature. However, he made some intelligent observations about Picasso's attitude to perspective: 'Perspective in itself is nothing but the unfolding of objects. The Middle Ages used a conventional flat perspective, the Renaissance a three-dimensional one, while nineteenth-century perspective was purely photographic . . . Picasso's main achievement from a purely historical point of view is to have created a new perspective for our time.'

This and many other articles which arrived and were translated by Olga for the benefit of her husband and her friends prompted some lively debates, and also the thought that not nearly as much debate went on in France about the new directions art was taking. This concensus of opinion confused Olga. On the one hand she was intensely patriotic and pleased to discover that her country was thought of as being in the avant-garde in some sphere of activity relevant to her husband's profession. On the other hand, they were Communists, and with the coming of the Soviets her father had lost his job in the Army and all he owned in Russia. Some of the oilier pre-Soviet diplomats who had been given posts again in the new Foreign Ministry assured her that there would be 'compensation' and 'apologies for mistakes made in heat of revoluntionary enthusiasm', which she took to mean that her family's property might again become theirs, or better still, hers. These hints that 'all will be put right', and the first invitations to the Picassos to visit the Soviet Union turned her head in favour of Stalin (after all, he *had* been to a seminary) and induced her to receive Soviet journalists in large numbers and in style.

Picasso avoided most of the journalists but spent a lot of time with friends and colleagues discussing 'art criticism'. It was unfortunately true, they agreed, that most writing about art was in the newspapers, mixed up with crime and politics, and served only to promote the work of artists in whom the journalists had a personal or financial interest. There was nothing else except the 'little magazines' promoting new sects and cults, read only by devotees. It was Christian Zervos (Xervos) who convinced Picasso that the time had come to launch a magazine for the professional and the intelligent layman. Just as Johann Joachim Winckelmann, with the publication of *Geschichte der Kunst des Altertums*, gave birth to a new discipline, art history (Barzini), so it can be said that Xervos' *Cahiers d'Art*, founded in 1926, gave birth to the 'art press', to a series of publications which were neither for the connoisseur, nor the intellectual nor the dealer exclusively, but for the 'professional' no matter what his interest in art, and for the lay fringe which might even contribute more new ideas than those directly involved in 'art work'.

Picasso and Braque were both flattered to learn that the first issue of *Cahiers*, planned for the following year, would feature a discussion on their 'quest for Cubism'; Picasso was so pleased with the first layouts of the magazines that he offered some illustrations of his own (and was to contribute to the magazine, throughout its long life, until 1960).

It was working with the journalists and artists of *Cahiers* that autumn that concentrated Picasso's mind. One of *les Anglais* who came to see him had left him a copy of *Gray's Anatomy*, over which he pored with Tzara at the *Dome* (the Romanian poet was under an interdict in Rue de la Boétie). Tzara was most interested in the drawings of female genitalia, and said he had had no idea they were constructed so ingeniously—'But I am glad I did not know when I was young. Mystery, that is romance; *les Anglais* are not interested in women because they all know how they work'. Picasso was fascinated above all by the way parts of the body join together, and by the way the editors of this classic text for medical students dealt with each part separately. He found the illustrations superb, and during the winter of 1926-27 produced a score of drawings and a dozen paintings which would have enlivened any lecture.

Picasso's 'anatomical paintings' began with a series of studies of the human head. Some of his friends said that his wife was his model and that what she called the 'gross distortions' were part of a plan of reprisals. Certainly, many of the drawings seem to have been taken from a mad hairdresser's catalogue and he had never ceased to tease her about the colour of her coiffure. Hairs appear here, there and everywhere in these drawings and some of the paintings. Where hair is conventionally accepted as necessary and desirable, it vanishes. Where women spend a fortune eliminating natural hair it is shown as a forest. All the appurtenances of the head change places as if a surgeon was being given advice on how to graft imaginatively. Eyes and ears change places. Attributes which are paired are still paired, but unusually—two eyes on one side of the face, two ears below the chin, and so on. The mouth sometimes takes the place of an ear, and vice versa. The nose emerges from the forehead. All of them sprout hairs.

When the ménage moved to Cannes during the summer of 1927 (*les Anglais* said that Nice and Cannes were superior to Juan les Pins), he turned his attention to the women who were finding some excuse to take off their clothes on the beach. He was struck by the irony of the existence of little huts for undressing, airless and always locked, when the whole point of *la plage* was to get undressed. Around the huts he spawned a whole circus full of women with their fingers gripping keys and fondling locks. The women are out of *Gray's Anatomy*, but later found their way into Henry Miller's books, especially the *Tropics* trilogy. Those parts of the female body which are generally larger than men's, breasts and buttocks in particular, appear swollen beyond even the worst nightmares of professional beauties, and, not surprisingly, they do not always appear in pairs. Sometimes the big blobs of paint suggest women without any logical explanation. There are many shapes which look like the cross-sections familiar in *Gray's* and sometimes things which only suggest certain individuals if the viewer is in on the secret—like the beads which represent his mother and a piebald pube which is Olga. Picasso explained to those who protested: 'Nature and art are two different things. Art is about what nature is not.'

Olga complained bitterly that his involvement with 'those monstrosities' was taking up all his time; last year it was collecting junk from the beach, this year her guests saw virtually nothing of him. Hardened by now to her incessant complaints, he said nothing but went away and made an even more 'monstrous' picture of her. She tried to persuade Gertrude Stein and Alice B Toklas to come over from their summer home at Belley on the Rhône, hoping that they would get him out to do his duty, but received only a polite refusal. It was not a happy holiday and it was a great relief when it was all over and she could get back to Paris and her social circle.

Nothing changed during the autumn and winter, as far as she knew. He was either shut up in his studio, or out and about with Tzara and his other 'disreputable friends'. Had she taken the trouble to go upstairs to the studio she might have found something new, and not to her advantage. Tzara had only one remedy for a nagging woman, and that was to change her for another. Though he was as short as Picasso and slightly built, he had a penchant for large buxom blondes, whom he said had a calmer temperament. (His tastes never changed. Many years later Jack Lindsay was walking down the Boulevard St Germain, to his Hotel, in la Place de l'Odéon, when he thought he saw a man being smothered at a café table. 'A very large woman was engaged in these smothering operations. . . I glanced across and saw the man disengage himself sufficiently to show his face round one side of the woman, and to my surprise recognized Tzara. At the same moment, he recognized me. I had halted irresolutely, uncertain whether or not to walk on, but Tzara with considerable agility shook the woman off like a dog shaking off the rain, stood up, and with dignity unimpaired came smiling across to us.")

What Picasso needed, Tzara had decided, was a big blonde. He had several in his retinue at the tile but none of them would do. A new adventure was called for and it took place on 8th January, 1928 (though for some reason everybody claimed it was a year earlier). Olga had become, to quote Richardson 'silly and unredeemably square . . . infatuated and jealous to the point of insanity . . . an obscene yenta crowned by a grotesquely dainty hat.' Picasso had been sleeping at Tzara's flat in the Rue de Lille and had crossed the river for a brisk walk around the Opera. As he passed in front of the Galeries Lafayette, he saw the big blonde of Tzara's dreams standing in front of the store. She used to say that she was waiting for a friend, but the truth was she had run away from home and had found neither fame nor fortune. She had run out of money and was hoping for a job as a shop assistant.

The blonde, Marie-Thérèse Walter, was so opulent and inviting that Picasso said it was obvious that anybody could open her body like a wardrobe; it was just a question of finding the right key. She looked silent and rather stupid, which after Olga's rantings was just what he was after. After walking round her once or twice just to make sure she was real, he approached her without too much finesse. She was hungry and accepted his invitation to breakfast, and he watched amazed as, instead of picking away genteely at a croissant, she demolished a plate of bacon and eggs, a whole basket of rolls and four cups of coffee. He asked her if she was English, as he had never seen anybody who was not English or American eat like that so early in the morning. She said she was Swiss and spoke German and French but no English (she had, in fact, learnt German in Wiesbaden). At other times (especially when Greta Garbo was a film star) she claimed to be Swedish (her grandfather was Swedish) though she had been born on 13th July, 1909 at Perreux, outside Paris. She said she could not stay too long because she was waiting for a friend, but thank you for the breakfast, this is the name of my hotel not far away and if you would we can meet again some time maybe this evening. . Then she strode off, wiping the crumbs from her chin as she went back to the store.

Picasso did not have Tzara's experience in intrigue, and asked him for advice. His first concern was not to make his life at home any more difficult than it was. Olga must not find out about this affair, as he was sure it was going to be. This girl did not look like the sort who could be taken to a hotel indefinitely, so it would be necessary sooner or later to keep her in some sort of establishment of her own. But where? In Paris he was very well known and there would always be somebody anxious to stir up trouble by reporting the girl's name and address to his wife. And what would happen then? There would be terrible scenes at home and she would certainly go to the girl and maybe even attack her physically—she had been known to throw shoes and plates. The girl must be set up at a discreet distance. But then, how would he get to see her? He could not spend his life on the Métro, being shaken to a distant destination and finding the fires of his passion, as he put it, spent when he arrived—the Métro always gave him a headache.

Tzara was very understanding. At first he offered Picasso the use of his flat, even offered to put the girl up there. Occasional use was welcome, but it would be too much of a temptation to Tzara to leave her there unattended. Tzara agreed.

'A lover must be mobile and independent', he said. Picasso must buy for himself an automobile and that would solve all his problems. He could put the girl where he liked and join her in his own good time.

During February and March, Picasso slowly raised the temperature of the relationship and had his first sexual encounter at an hotel at Neuilly. At the same time he was taking driving lessons with one of the three schools Paris boasted in those days. As a lover he made good progress. As a driving pupil he was a failure. By the time he was getting ready to take himself and his family to the South of France for the summer he had almost lost interest. He would have to let the girl go. Tzara would take her over—they got on well together.

It was Olga who rekindled his interest. Her first mistake was to refuse to go to the South of France. They were to go to Dinard again. Picasso reminded her of the disastrous end to the holiday they spent there in 1922, but she was undeterred. Paolo was now seven years old and attention had to be paid to his education. The peasant nanny was a good woman but barely literate, and the tutors who had followed each other in quick succession were 'too French'. What she had in mind for Paolo was an English education, maybe Eton. The nanny and the tutors could be replaced by an English governess. It would be cheaper and better. She had the names of several who would be at Dinard with their families. They could go there, return the nanny and interview the governesses. Anyway, it was all arranged. She had had the good fortune to meet some English people who had given her the address of a large villa with a garden near the harbour.

Gloomily, Picasso accepted this *diktat*. His wife had hired a car to drive them to Dinard, which was another mistake. Picasso struck up a conversation with the driver and told him of his unsuccessful efforts to learn how to drive—in his wife's presence he spoke loudly about the benefits to the child of regular excursions into the countryside. Both Olga and the driver were intrigued, for different reasons. Olga thought it was high time they had a car of their own, anyway—maybe an

English car, a Rolls Royce. The driver, Marcel, said there was nothing to beat the Hispano-Suiza and it was hard to get repairs done to a Rolls Royce in France. And as it so happened, he was looking for a situation with a family as he was thinking of marrying and settling down. By the time they got to Dinard it had been virtually agreed that Marcel should join their household, and should look around to see which model of the Hispano-Suiza would suit them best.

Elated by the prospect of being able to take on Marie-Thérèse, Picasso was nevertheless depressed by the size of the Art Nouveau nightmare his wife had rented. However, even that had its compensations. It was large enough for him to be able to set up a studio and see his wife and the English governess (immediately engaged after three lightning interviews with the candidates) only at mealtimes. He could paint in the garden, too, and escape through a gate to the quayside to draw the fishing boats and the ferries. On the third day, he was further consoled by the arrival of Georges Hugnet, a poet and publisher who had been introduced to him by Gertrude Stein. Hugnet, who lived at the other ferry terminal at St Malo, was putting together an edition of Gertrude Stein's pen portraits with illustrations by the artist's subjects—Picasso had contributed a self-portrait, one of Apollinaire and one of Satie, Berard had done himself and Virgil Thompson, Tonney one of himself and Bernard Fay, and Chelichev one of himself. Hugnet was a young, dynamic, cheerful man who had impressed Olga with his seriousness and his command of English, and he was able to take the heat off Picasso at mealtimes during his frequent visits.

Meanwhile, during visits from Paris by Marcel, with reports of what was on offer in the car market, Picasso had tested Marcel's discretion and had been assured that 'a good chauffeur looks only through his master's windscreen' and much more of that nature. If he needed any extra incentive to make up his mind about Marie-Thérèse it was his wife's report that the new English governess had been scandalized to see that they slept in a double bed after ten years of marriage. An English lady

needed more privacy for her toilette after such a long time . . .
And anyway, double beds were unhealthy. In many English
bedrooms there were twin beds, but she did not think Picasso
would like them—he was too wide and they were too narrow.
They would have separate rooms, but to avoid scandal in Paris,
her bedroom would have twin beds. She had thought it all out
very carefully.

Picasso was even more scandalized than the English
governess. His whole Spanish macho personality was outraged.
How could a normal wife not want to sleep with her husband,
even if they were not as sexually active as he would like? There
were no twin beds in Spain, he said. Single beds were for
children and nuns. He went on about this for several days until
he was sure he had scored some psychological points, then
found an excuse to go up to Paris with Hugnet. There he
explained to Marie-Thérèse what had happened, that all would
be well and arranged when he got back at the end of the holiday.
Meanwhile, why did she not go with her friend to Switzerland
and tell them the good news that she was to become secretary
to a famous artist. There were even public galleries there which
had his pictures hanging on their walls.

Back in Dinard, Picasso painted with gusto as he thought
of all the blonde benefits which were to accrue to him shortly.
Penrose describes these pictures as full of 'dynamic exuberance',
which certainly does justice to the great splashes of joyful
colour. From time to time when Olga annoyed him more than
usual, he would break off and do a portrait of her as an octupus,
or as a jumble of driftwood, broken glass and seaweed on the
shore. But then he would take a new canvas and splash away
like an infant given his first set of colours.

There was no doubt about it. Marie-Thérèse had arrived.

Marie-Thérèse

'While she is at school, a girl's brains should stay inside her
head. When she leaves school, they will slip down to between
her legs, but by the time she is twenty-one they should have
found their proper home in her handbag.'

(French saying)

Picasso was in a fever of excitement when he got back to Paris
from Dinard. Having engaged Marcel and hired a car until the
new one could be delivered, he was anxious to get Marie-
Thérèse set up properly as soon as possible. She was responding
to regular sexual activity and glowing with satisfaction. Picasso
was not by nature a jealous man—perhaps Olga had cured him
of this native Spanish trait—but he did not want this glow to
be shared. He had a slight suspicion that Tzara might, as it
were, take a slice or two of the cut cake hoping it would not
be noticed, especially as the Romanian did not conceal his
admiration for her physical attractions; he was sceptical about
her intelligence and it was not reassuring to hear Tzara say that
if she got hold of a good novelette and a box of chocolates,
'she could be fucked without being distracted'.

It was Marcel who made the excellent suggestion that the
girl be moved to Montrouge. This was one of the many French
equivalents to the St John's Wood stucco love nests in London,
and he was known in the neighbourhood; if Olga's spies saw
him there, he could always say he was collecting some canvasses
he had forgotten, and none of the local people would betray
him as they did not like Olga. He explained to Marie-Thérèse

that this was a temporary arrangement, that what he had in mind was a little flat in the centre and a place in the country, when he could find them. She accepted this arrangement, as indeed she accepted every arrangement proposed over the years; whatever her faults, she was neither ungrateful nor a natural troublemaker. She was happy to make love when asked to do so, and to laze away the rest of the time wherever it was warm and comfortable and food could be got without effort.

During the autumn he divided his time between her (she must have given satisfaction, because Tzara complained that he no longer toured their favourite brothels to see if there was anything fresh or especially highly recommended to try out) and his painting. *The Studio* and *The Painter and his Model* are important works completed at this time and there are some happy paintings and drawings of his son in various costumes, not to speak of 'portraits' now recognizable as of Marie-Thérèse. He rediscovered a passion for sculpture and evolved both the linear patterns of his "work in space" and the practice of working on paintings and several pieces of sculpture at the same time; if an idea came to him in one medium he would transfer it to the other, sometimes literally sticking on pieces of cardboard, paper, string, where a piece of sculpture seemed to demand it. Occasionally, the years of frustration he had survived with his wife came to the surface in an explosion of hideous colour, but not only in horrific caricatures of Olga but also of himself, as if he had suddenly realized that it was his own fault that he had allowed himself to be dragged down into the social morass of the 'successful painter'; in one painting of himself and his wife at one of the Etienne de Beaumont soirées, he sees himself as a willing victim of a Russian Borgia, drinking a trickle of liquid arsenic offered by the monster next to him.

But all in all, he was at peace with himself, and in 1929 he moved his legal ménage again to Dinard. There his wife had her own circle of émigrés and *les Anglais* and enjoyed entertaining them, and the boy Paolo seemed to like the place and the sea air. It did not seem to worry his wife when Picasso took off with Marcel with one excuse or another—a sale, a meeting to plan a new exhibition, some new articles for the Surrealist press. Some of the Surrealists, Olga's favourite poets, appeared in Dinard during the season and she was able to show them off to English intellectuals who were anxious to be in on the latest mode. A special number of *Documents*, which Georges Bataille hoped would really launch his new magazine, was to be devoted to Picasso with contributions by Bataille himself, and by Desnos, Jouhandeau and Prévert. During these improving soirées Olga received many compliments on how she had kept him looking so young—he would soon be fifty, who could believe it looking at him, and at the quantity of work he still managed to do?—and she may have consoled herself with the thought that he would soon be too old to cause her any jealousy.

She would have been alarmed had she heard him describing his days and nights with Marie-Thérèse as 'wading through the seas, big blonde seas, and resting on the big blonde beaches besides them'. Had she visited his studio she would have seen at least a dozen large canvasses and innumerable drawings of the girl, nearly always lying down, asleep or reading a book, relaxed and inviting.

During the summer of 1929, Marcel toured the whole region between Dinard and Paris, looking for a suitable place to keep this treasure, the model for *Femme Couchée* and other 'rhythmical portraits' (as Françoise Gilot was to call them). The house had to be large enough to accommodate all his legal family, and for there to be a suite of rooms for his studio and a bedroom for illegal encounters with Marie-Thérèse. It had to be near enough to Paris for Olga not to fear that he was suspiciously distant when he left her for a few days, yet not so near that she could take it into her head to drive out there to see what he was up to; Marcel said the car could always be fixed to break down, but Picasso was not taking any chances with a woman who could make a scene in a central Paris street. In the meantime, Montrouge would have to do, though he was to look for a flat near the Seine, near the Gare d'Orsay.

Throughout the autumn and winter, the search went on,

and Picasso went on painting. Françoise Gilot has called Marie-Thérèse 'a sweet, gentle woman, very feminine, and very full formed—all joy, light and peace'. Most of his friends agreed with this description of her but it was Tzara who noticed what he called 'her persistent Christianity'. It was a form of Catholicism superficially different from his mother's, with her collection of rosaries and religious images, and her taste for processions and church affairs. Marie-Thérèse's faith was a more private matter but it was nonetheless fervent, as Picasso soon found out; it showed itself in an insistence on going to Mass on all holy days of obligation, and during Lent, 1930, in a spasm of sexual self-denial. Her lover was furious, but unable to change her mind, and painted a startling and angry *Crucifixion* during his enforced abstinence. It is an interesting version of the story. Christ is alone on His cross—the common thieves crucified with him on his right and left have been taken down and lie dead, ready to be carted away. The distance between their crosses and Our Lord's is so great that the recorded dialogue between them could only have taken place as an exchange of shouts. Much of the remainder of the iconography is familiar, the soldiers dicing for His clothes, for example, but there is a strange figure nailing His right hand to His cross as if it had come loose, and there are various symbols of pagan religions. The faces are not recognizable as such, though there is what seems to be a grinning, Spanish, straw-hatted aficionado and some other bull fight personae. He seems to have done several drawings for a painting of the Three Marys during the previous summer, but all that survives in the *Crucifixion* is an image of Mary Magdalene doing what seems to be an erotic dance.

Marie-Thérèse was always very pleased with and proud of this painting, not only because a work of religious inspiration seldom got beyond the drawing stage with Picasso, but also because she said it showed his soul could be reached. She did not, however, try to reach it in that way again.

To distract attention from the house search in the north, Picasso decided to go south, to Juan les Pins again. His doctor was easily persuaded to advise Olga that Paolo needed the air of the Mediterranean, and the weather in 1929 had not been as warm as the year before, so there were no quarrels over the destination for the summer holidays. Of course, he could not do without Marie-Thérèse for three months, and Paris was too far to be reached, even with Marcel in the Hispano-Suiza on unrestricted roads. The only thing to do was to take her too, and put her in a house nearby. She fell in love with the house and Picasso bought it for her. It was a risky business, but Olga does not seem to have suspected that there was anything different about her husband's absences during the day and occasional night. He came home as he had done before, sometimes with a bundle of drawings, sometimes with a bag full of shells and beachcomber's bric-à-brac. He was always in a good mood and even listened to her ideas about Paolo and an English prep school with a public school to follow (this did not prevent him squashing the ideas at the appropriate time). Marie-Thérèse just enjoyed the place, the chocolates, the cheap novelettes and the regular and efficient sex with her master.

His performance, never less than satisfactory, took most of the sting out of the preparations going on everywhere to celebrate his fiftieth birthday. All the art magazines at home and abroad seemed to be getting ready commemorative special issues, some adopting a tone which implied he was dead. Only the Surrealists suggested that he was eternally young. The two major publications in volume form struck a happy balance. The more important was Vollard's collection of drawings and engravings, which they discussed that summer and well into the autumn. This consisted of woodblock engravings done at Juan les Pins in 1924 and 1926 (the engravings by Subert from Picasso's sketchbook) and nearly eighty drawings and engravings in the Classical style which he had adopted in Rome and during his first years of marriage. The second book was Ovid's *Metamorphoses*, with thirty original etchings in the same Classical style. The news that both these books were to go on sale in 1931 brought sales of Picasso's drawing at the Vollard, Leiris (ex Kahnweiler) and Rosenberg galleries.

As welcome a birthday present was Marcel's discovery of the perfect retreat. Known as the Château de Boisgeloup, it was really a small fortified house which had given its name to the village, not far from Gisors on the road to Rouen from Paris. Marie-Thérèse saw it before Olga did and admired the little Gothic chapel in the courtyard, facing the stables. With her approval, Picasso took a lease with an option to purchase the place and spent a busy springtime moving in his paraphernalia. A huge press for copper engravings, which belonged to Louis Fort (the man who had taught Picasso the limitations of the technique), was brought from Paris; its owner wanted to work less and slowly retire to the South of France. The coachhouse was turned into a sculpture studio, with the help of his old friend the sculptor Gonzalez. Olga furnished the house itself in a *passé* bourgeois style reminiscent of the grand hotels in Moscow and Leningrad during the first Socialist Realist period; as Tzara put it, it looked like an upper servant's dream of how the Family lived. Nevertheless it was comfortable, with a lot of red plush, and Picasso had his own kitchen and 'resting area' in the stables. He was astonished, however, after all the trouble he had taken and the favourable first impression the house had made, to hear Marie-Thérèse say that she did not think she would stay there often. She did not love him any the less and she appreciated all he was doing so that they could be together as often as possible—indeed, that was what she wanted and would try to arrange herself. But all those people coming and going (during the birthday year, both Rue de la Boétie and Boisgeloup were like railway stations), with crowds of friends, well-wishers, journalists and the simply curious present at virtually all times of the day. . . .

Françoise Gilot, who succeeded her over a decade later in his deepest affections, heard from Picasso himself that she was like a very physical ghost. She was interested in his work in a way, but if she were offered a choice between a vernissage and a game of tennis, the courts would always win. This was in her active moments, when she was not curled up with a book and bon-bons. He would often get fits of uncontrollable nostalgia for her while he was at Boisgeloup with his family and Marcel would be ordered to drive him to Paris on some excuse or other 'only to learn that she had bicycled out to Gisors to be near where he was'. Then there would be a mad drive back again to track her down at a small hotel where they often met. 'She haunted his life, just out of reach poetically, but available in the practical sense whenever his dreams were troubled by her absence . . . She had no inconvenient reality.'

He probably saw more of her during that year's summer holiday in Juan les Pins than at the 'Château' he had taken so much trouble to find. However, with her or without her, Boisgeloup was an ideal place in which to work hard to perfect his engraving techniques and, with Gonzalez, on his sculpture. Many drawings which dated back to 'the good old days' at the *Bâteau-Lavoir* were translated into bronze, among them a head of Fernande he had done at Horta del Ebro. The beachcombing rubbish bags were emptied and some of the objects ended as traditional sculpture, others glued to canvasses prepared with sand. Large objects were welded together as Picasso became impatient at the lapse of time necessary for casting in bronze and the 'improvements' craftsmen at the foundries felt themselves entitled to make. He bought all sorts of welding torches, anvils and soldering irons and made a close friend of the local blacksmith. This latter individual was delighted at the new career which seemed to be opening up to him as the tractor and the motor car deprived him inexorably of his traditional sources of income. Peasants' courtyards, goldmines of old iron bars, screws, nuts and bolts and rusting ploughshares were raided and became 'compositions'. Picasso was very enthusiastic about his work, made some macho observations about still being able to use heavy metal working tools at the age of fifty, and complained to Kahnweiler that dealers were slow to find him a market.

Kahnweiler and his sister and brother-in-law, the Leirises, were intrigued but told him he should be patient. The world was not yet ready for Picasso the sculptor. To console him they gave him an enormous St Bernard dog, 'a piece of living sculpture', they said, and urged him to get on with more painting and drawing. There was time for everything, of course, now that the relationship with Marie-Thérèse had settled into its most peaceful and satisfying stage, that of being wholly undemanding. He was, as a man, kinder and more considerate than ever. Braque dragged himself out to Boisgeloup reluctantly during one of Olga's absences and was astonished. He said to Tzara: 'This is the old friend I thought we had lost. Look at all this work. And, see, he has thrown away all those clown's clothes that woman made him wear.' Picasso commented: 'Ha, Braque, he was always the wife who loved me best.'

Among the new paintings are some in the 'Barcelona style', views through the windows. The scenes painted are of his own little chapel, of the house and courtyard, of the village and of his friend the blacksmith, reminiscent of the English at Lamorna at this time. For the first time in his life he tolerated house plants (gifts from Marie-Thérèse) in his studio, which seems to have had the right amount of heat and humidity; a philodendron which had gone mad in Paris, filled a little studio and blocked the drains, was given a stable of its own and its leaves appear in paintings and as designs on the sculpture of the period. During 1931 and 1932 he also painted a number of still lifes, which owe their peculiarity to the stained glass window in the chapel; slabs of colour, vaguely suggesting animate or inanimate objects, are outlined thickly as the coloured panes are held together with strips of lead in the window. Tzara told him of Brancusi's ideas for sculpture parks all over the world, and was rewarded with more enthusiasm 'except that you will not persuade a French *maire*, especially of a small town, that his park is a place for sculpture'. Pieces of sculpture, all large, including some gifts of West African pieces, were tried out in the courtyard and sometimes appear in the still lifes.

For the summer of 1932 there was to be a great retrospective exhibition of his work at the Galerie Georges Petit, and all that winter and spring was spent getting ready what he wanted to show. That, for a retrospective of thirty odd years of work, it was dominated by canvasses inspired by Marie-Thérèse, is evidence of the strength of his feelings for her. Penrose, who met her at this time and did not like her, sneered that 'she had a robust coarseness and an unconventionality about her which formed a complete contrast to Olga'. Nothing could be further from the truth. The set of plaster heads made in the New Year show her with a finely modelled face on a swan-like neck; they are large, but then so was she. In the paintings, she is seen as a sexual cornucopia, the source of all pleasure: her breasts are like ripe melons and all her limbs opulent and inviting: more often than not she is shown asleep, with the features softened and the hands and feet relaxed and tapering gracefully. Tzara said she reminded him, in the flesh and in these portraits, of the huge banner portraits of film stars which were just beginning to decorate the façades of the Paris cinemas. Far from a 'robust coarseness', her profile was so finely modelled and delicate that on one occasion Picasso had tried for hours to capture it and only succeeded by manipulating a cage of fine wires until he could throw the shadow of the profile on the whitewashed wall.

Nearly three hundred works were shown at the Galerie Georges Petit, some of them rushed back from London (the Reid and Lefèvre Gallery), Switzerland, Germany and the United States where 'birthday exhibitions' had been held. He insisted on having the *Crucifixion* and the most recent portraits of Marie-Thérèse, the Boisgeloup still lifes, but also showed many paintings of which he was particularly fond and which were important in his personal portfolio, such as *La Vie* for his mother, the *Burial of Casagemas* as a continuing reproach for Germaine Pichot, and some portraits of Eva. *Cahiers d'Art* published a special issue, collateral with the catalogue, in which his work on show, and his importance as an artist, were commented on by *les Anglais*, Italian, German, Swiss and French artists (including poets and musicians from his past). The funniest bits came from Tzara and the most humourless and incomprehensible from Satie.

It was during this exhibition that Olga 'discovered' Marie-Thérèse. How she had managed to ignore, or not even notice, an intense relationship which was now three years old remained a mystery to her friends if not her enemies; it suggests, however, how far removed from each other were the two ways of life, that of the greedy Society wife living directly off the money and indirectly off the glory of a famous husband, and that of the rather simple man who had done his best to 'smarten himself up' and failed gloriously. There were incandescent scenes of jealousy, carefully chronicled by Tzara who tried to witness them all. On one occasion, Olga discovered what was left of his Bond Street wardrobe, a dozen silk ties, at the bottom of a trunk, made a rope from them and threatened to hang herself from the Boisgeloup chapel roof. On another she kicked the Hispano-Suiza so hard she dented a panel and broke her foot. She threw the head of a hippopotamus at Tzara (it stood in the hall of the 'château') and a silver salver at Marcel ('the accomplice'). She did not, however, do as Picasso had once feared and try to tackle her rival face to face armed only with abuse and her handbag; perhaps she was afraid she would be crushed, 'her skull with its tiny brain cracked between those two huge, perfectly formed thighs like a lemon in a nutcracker' (Tzara). Scene followed scene during the winter of 1932 and the spring of 1933, followed by Picasso's flight either to Marie-Thérèse in Paris or to his studio at Boisgeloup. There is a whole series of etchings, later entitled *The Sculptor's Studio*, which is in a way a newsreel. The sculptor (he has given himself a beard) is hard at work, or at rest with his lovely model, sometimes watching his work come to life like the toys in *Coppélia*, often horrified to see an angry, alien presence determined only to destroy the lovers' idyll and his work.

At the end of the spring, he dumped Olga and her entourage at Cannes and went back to Spain. It is not quite clear whether or not he took Marie-Thérèse with him. Tzara recalls that she went with him, to Barcelona to meet his mother and sister, but his sister always denied this, and his mother pretended not to remember, as if Marie-Thérèse were forgettable. The Hotel Ritz where he stayed offers conflicting accounts of the stay, but from the register it seems clear enough that he was not alone. He summoned all his old friends—Pallares, Manolo, Vidal

Ventosa, the Sotos and the Junyer-Vidals—just the sort of people to whom he would have wanted to introduce her, and Palau i Fabre in *Picasso I els Seus Amics Catalan* notes that 'les relacions de Picasso amb la seva muller Olga havien arribat a un punt impossible'. As it got hotter in the city, the whole gang moved to Manolo's house by the sea where they drank the summer away; then, as the air cooled a little, returned to Barcelona for the *corridas*.

There was more drinking and talking about old times when they were back in town and Picasso promised to return the following year to do a series of bullfight paintings and drawings for two local magazines, and perhaps organize an exhibition. He had shown them the cover design for a new French Surrealist magazine, *Minotaure*, which had just come out, and they were awash with patriotic hope that Spanish themes would re-emerge in his work.

Back in Paris there were endless recriminations from Olga. He was not only wasting his time with this foolish young girl, but making her the laughing stock of her *cercle*; worse, the idea of a fifty-year-old man cavorting with a young whore was ridiculous and people were laughing at him, too. Had he no feelings? What had she done wrong? She had launched him in Society and that was the real reason for his success. There was much more, and he had to find ways of seeing his wife as little as possible if he were to get any work done at all, not to speak of getting old and new canvasses and drawings ready for the promised exhibition in Barcelona. He often referred to that winter as the most tormented of his life. Tzara told him he should leave Olga for good, but it went against all his newly re-aroused Spanish sentiments to abandon the mother of his first-born male child. His paintings and etchings (for a new Vollard collection) reveal something of his sufferings. He became a minotaur as well as the artist in his studio, dying in the ring, sharing orgies, exciting fear and pity from simple fisherman and little girls. Fortunately there were moments of calm with Marie-Thérèse who was always there, calm and devoted, when he wanted her.

In the spring of 1934 Picasso decided to make one last effort at a reconciliation with Olga. He explained to Marie-Thérèse that he was doing it for the sake of the child, and she accepted the explanation without protest. The plan was that he should take Marie-Thérèse to Juan les Pins and relax there with her for a week, with the excuse that he was looking for a house in Cannes for his family. Then he would collect Olga and the household, stay at Cannes for a while, after which he would go with them to Barcelona and see if his mother and sister would be able to bring his wife to reason.

The trip to Spain, which was to be his last, was a great artistic success. Dali set the tone: 'Salvador Dali is pleased to invite all unburied rotting corpses, all painters of crooked trees, in the more or less rural tradition, all the members and patrons of the Catalan Choral Society to visit the Picasso exhibition . . . the extravagant station where we shall see for the first time the arrival in our country of the express train—first class only—of the Iberian intelligentsia and genius, thirty years late. The responsibility for this delay lies mainly with the exquisite corpses of the local intellectuals and artists, exquisitely leaning on the rails of their manorial balconies from which, as we all know, one can see nothing but the overwhelming monotony of our succulent, high class countryside, full of manure, with an occasional cow, perfectly blind, totally famous. . . . Picasso's sensational painting is closer to a rapid fighting bull [than some magnificient bunch of flowers] . . . the symbol, essence and substance of all that is darkest and most turbulent, in the deepest and most delicate roots of the human spirit.'

Carles Capavila in *La Publicitat* was a little more tactful with the authorities and 'official art world'. He wrote: 'Since Picasso and his family are in Barcelona, the directors of the [Barcelona] Museum have invited him to visit the new installations in the National Palace where the municipal holdings have been considerably increased with the acquisition of the Planduria collection. The insipid and banal architecture has been cleverly disguised . . . The whole first floor is devoted to painting and sculpture . . . from the impressive romanesque frescoes to the Catalan eighteenth century. The second floor will be devoted to modern Catalan painting from the early nineteenth century to the present—Picasso will be very well represented here with pre-cubist works . . .'

Capavila had been afraid that Picasso would explode, if not quite as violently as Dali, to discover that the 'official art world' had still not caught up with Cubism after all these years. He was relieved to find him . . . accessible and cordial . . . so ready for friendly discussion that we talked for hours unaware of the time . . . At lunch, using a mixture of Catalan, Spanish and French, which lent an improvisatory tone to the dialogue, Picasso continued his reminiscences of the days when as a young prodigy he made his first friends and admirers. Luckily there was no reference to aesthetic theories or artistic problems . . . In Picasso's calm and assured voice, in his thick-set appearance, in the tone of his words as he described his place in Normandy, one sensed a silent fertile promise. As he left, he told us he was leaving next day. He had taken a month off to tour Spain in his 'Hispano'.' Then he said he had to go home to work.'

The tourist part of the trip, to Madrid and Toledo, was even less successful than the meeting with the 'official art world'— of them all Paolo enjoyed it the most. He was showered with gifts, among them a small Toledo bladed sword (immediately confiscated by *l'Anglaise*) and a mechanical donkey. Olga had no cause to complain about the almost royal welcome they received in the Spanish capital, though she was sometimes alarmed by the insistence that her husband return to live and work in the country of his birth. She need not have worried. His friend, the sculptor Gonzalez, noted that 'everything Catalan is of interest to him. He is 'ours'. A ribbon-sized Catalan flag which he keeps religiously in his pocket will give you some idea of what he feels for Catalonia. So many fond memories . . .' But when it came to giving Picasso a 'mother country', the suggestion met with a shrug of the shoulders whether it came from his biological 'mother country' or others.

It was when Olga and her husband were alone that the recriminations started again. He found it virtually impossible to discuss anything with her. Though she was long past her physical best, becoming scrawny and sometimes forgetting to touch up her hair, she made demands as if she were a young bride in front of a besotted groom. In the end, he sent her back to Cannes with Marcel and returned gloomily to Paris to be consoled, as ever, by Marie-Thérèse.

At that time she was probably the only person who knew that in addition to the painting, the sculpture, the travelling and the everyday chores of a professional artist's life, her lover had been writing poetry. He used the tiny, black-covered sketch books he always carried in his pocket so that when he was scribbling people would think he was drawing, and many of the poems are either illustrated with line drawings (mostly of animals) or blobs of colour which he put in when he could not think of the right word. He had always been treated as a semi-literate who had the good luck to be able to express himself in colour and line; once he even suggested that he would be remembered as a poet who had dabbled in the plastic arts. When, during the winter of 1934–5, he revealed to a few friends that his love had inspired these 'word palettes', there was no difficulty finding a publisher. Breton pre-empted an issue of *Cahiers d'Art* for scribbles such as:

> a river in the empty white in the light blue shadow lilac hand beside the shadow casts a shadow on the hand a very pink grasshopper

As Tzara said: 'He could send a piece of paper on which he had wiped his arse to *Le Journal* and they would photograph it for print, if he signed it Picasso.' Breton in *Cahiers d'Art* tried to give the drivel some substance and Clive Bell tackled the subject courageously in the *New Statesman and Nation* a year later, but as 'literature' it is best forgotten. Its importance, as Tzara saw, was that for the first time his feelings for a woman had gone so deep that they had to be expressed in words—'the hurt was too much to be disguised by decoration'. Perhaps Picasso brought it all out into the open in the excitement when he heard that Marie-Thérèse was pregnant.

Perhaps the only person who was not surprised at the news, which appeared in the Barcelona papers, that her son had written some poetry was Doña Maria. He very seldom wrote to her—perhaps once a year a scribble on a postcard—and always sent messages by friends who were passing through, but as she said: 'Nothing surprises me. They say you are writing poetry now and I dare say you do. If they told me you had become a priest and were celebrating Mass, I would believe that, too.'

Gertrude Stein liked the poems, and gave a party to celebrate his revelation that he, too, wanted to write. They had got into the habit of meeting every February (Paolo had been born on 4 February, the day after Gertrude Stein's birthday, so she said it was an auspicious month) to review the previous year's achievements and disappointments, 'so much more original than making New Year's resolutions'. She was a little taken aback to hear that he was also about to become a father again, but recalled that Hemingway had done it, with regret, so she expected it was all for the best. She wondered what Olga would say and do when she found out. She would be 'surprised'.

'Surprise' was not the word to describe Olga's reaction. She went into hysterics in the Jardins des Tuileries. She threw herself onto a bench and ranted and railed in Russian and French, hitting a *flic* with her umbrella when he tried to calm her down. The friend who had broken the news did not fare much better and was accused first of being a liar then of being am accomplice of the erring husband. Picasso, who was fortunately painting in the Rue de la Boétie, had to be sent for and he rashly arrived with Tzara, who was immediately abused as a Balkan pimp. *L'Anglaise* glared at everybody and said how shocking it was, the whole scene; it could never happen in London. Eventually the combined efforts of all, including her doctor, succeeded in removing Olga from the Jardins to the friend's flat (Tzara said later he thought it was one of her countesses). She refused to go back to the Rue de la Boétie and Françoise Gilot remembered that when she went there with Picasso many years later, in the bedroom 'the two twin beds were made up, one of them in the way one sometimes makes up a bed that is going to be slept in right away, the bedspread pulled back, the sheet and blanket turned down. . . . Beside each bed was a night table and on one of them still lay the remains of the last breakfast . . .' Paolo's room still had its walls covered with pictures of bicycling champions of the Tour de France, there were toy cars scattered about on the floor and in the nearby salon the grand piano, on which the unmusical boy had been forced to practise, was covered with dust.

After some weeks of acrimonious debate, it was agreed that Olga should move the household to the South of France for the summer until it was decided what should be done. Tzara's advice was to get rid of her as fast as possible, but that meant a divorce. This would be difficult because neither Olga nor her husband were French and had to follow the legal requirements of their native countries, which boiled down to permission to dissolve the marriage according to Spanish law. In view of Picasso's fame, this would not have been impossible to arrange, in time, and Marie-Thérèse joined Tzara in urging him to start the necessary proceedings. Instructions were given to a firm of lawyers in Barcelona but they seem to have been in no hurry. Perhaps Picasso, knowing that any settlement after a divorce would involve handing over half of everything he had to his wife, did not press them too hard. In the end, the Spanish Civil War broke out and a Nationalist edict forbade divorce to any Spanish subject who had been married in church, Catholic or not.

During the summer months, Picasso spent his days in Paris. It was the first time for many years that he had not left the capital with the grand exodus in July and he was astonished to discover that there was virtually nobody about to talk to. He enjoyed the birth of his daughter, Maia, and was tender and solicitous towards her mother but he confessed to Vollard that he was not at all sure that even if he had been able to get a divorce, he would want to marry her. As a mistress she had been ideal and undemanding. As a wife and mother he suspected that she could become almost suffocating as she combined devotion with domesticity. However, at the moment she came first and she certainly radiated a light quite different from the blaze he had last seen in Olga's eyes.

The poetry dried up, and he tried to paint. He would have liked to have gone to Boisgeloup but it would have seemed like abandoning Marie-Thérèse, so he slept in his study in the Rue de la Boétie and had the rest of the flat put under dust sheets; he said it was like walking through a morgue every day. At a moment of extreme depression he was more than delighted to hear that his old friend, the poet Sabartés, was back in Barcelona from a mysterious exile in America of which he knew nothing. Though it was an effort for him to write a letter to anybody, he sent off an urgent call to Sabartés, describing his lonely existence, '. . . what has happened and what is to happen', and begged his old friend, if it were possible, to come to Paris, even an empty, hot and dusty Paris, and keep him company.

While he waited for a reply, he went to Boisgeloup. Marie-Thérèse was strong enough to travel so he took her, too, and lodged her in Gisors; neither of them felt inclined to put up together at the 'Château', just in case Olga took it into her head to descend on them and make a scene which would upset the child. As it happens, they had no need to worry. Olga's lawyers, scenting a case which would keep them far from discomfort and fatigue for many years to come, gave her strict orders to keep away from both residences until it was decided which should go to whom; they hinted that should she disobey these strict instructions it might affect her share of the joint property, and her natural greed overcame her urge for hysterical revenge. Until all was signed, she was told, she could stay in a hotel, even with the boy and the governess, and give no thought to the expense, which the 'guilty man' would have to bear.

Nothing ever upset Marie-Thérèse's baby. Perhaps not even Olga would have done more than woken her from a deep sleep if it was an occasion on which she was expected to sleep. Like her mother, she was placid, good-humoured and gave no trouble. Whenever Picasso drove over to see them, mother and daughter looked like some illustration of improbable maternal bliss taken from a woman's magazine. At the end of the first week of November, a reply arrived from Sabartés, and the whole Boisgeloup-Gisors party returned to Paris, Marcel to his flat, Picasso to Rue de la Boétie and Marie-Thérèse to her old flat on the Ile Saint-Louis. Picasso could not wait to see his friend Sabartés, who would not leave his side for five years. Sabartés wrote later:

> '12 November 1935
> Tornó a Paris, aquesta vegada a peticio de Picasso, amb la intencio de viure a casa seva, rue la Boétie, M'aguarda darrera la barrera de la sala de espera de l'estacio d'Orsay. Es la cinquena vegada que vinc de lluny i la tercera que ve a buscarme.' ('I went back to Paris, this time at Picasso's request, with the intention of living with him in the Rue de la Boétie. He was waiting for me at the barrier by the waiting room at Orsay Station. It was the fifth time he had been there since Monday and the third he had been to meet me.')

The days passed, Sabartés remembered, without any counting. They talked endlessly of old friends, dead and alive, exchanged ideas, broke off for meals from time to time or to stroll in Montmartre or Montparnasse. The new baby was admired. Fortunately, Sabartés owned no loyalty to Olga so he could give his devotion immediately to Marie-Thérèse, who thought he was comical but nice. While Picasso was painting, Sabartés caught up with all the correspondence lying about, checked accounts and when he felt in a literary mood translated Picasso's poems (which were mostly in Spanish or Catalan); he wrote a poem of his own to the baby (whose full name was Maria Concepción) and thus earned her mother's high opinion.

While Tzara, who was perhaps jealous, did not like Sabartés and thought him too servile, there is no doubt that he succeeded in calming Picasso down. By the end of the year he was able to face the lawyers and work out the details of the legal separation which was to take the place of a divorce, 'given the situation in Spain'. Olga insisted on having Boisgeloup and all its contents, including the paintings, drawings and sculpture;

her husband kept the Rue de la Boétie. She was also given a choice of two houses in the South of France and a substantial sum of money, plus a yearly allowance for Paolo. It was lucky for Picasso that, as Fernande had noticed years before, he was squirrel-like in his habit of saving. He had pictures, Olga knew nothing about, locked away in two banks, and accounts at three others, in addition to their joint account. He had been a millionaire for many years, but she could not prove it. Nevertheless, what she took away made her a very wealthy woman.

While he was visiting his lawyer's chambers every day, he had the house at Juan les Pins bought and put in Marie-Thérèse's name, and settled a large sum of money on mother and daughter. He remarked to Tzara that he was now as poor as he looked (he had begun wearing baggy woollen trousers and fisherman's sweaters every day); this was not true, of course—his well-dressed days with Olga had been a bore and had attracted many spongers—but a number of the worst hangers-on and beggars, many of them *les Anglais* were discouraged and left him alone.

Friends who visited Rue de la Boétie during the first few months of 1936 said it was like a happy Boy Scout camp. The two friends lived on both floors of the apartment, occasionally moving the dustsheets downstairs to make up temporary beds, or having a meal on one of the tables. The floor Olga had kept so highly polished soon lost its gloss and disappeared under piles of papers; Sabartés had a simple filing system which was to spread letters out by sender, each to its area of carpet—bills were kept under flower vases until paid, then transferred to a cupboard in the kitchen or bathroom. Marie-Thérèse said she did not care to go into another woman's house, or what had been another woman's home, to tidy up—anyway, the child and her own flat took up a lot of time. Paul Rosenberg offered to find a woman to do the daily cleaning but Sabartés refused to move his papers; his only compromise was to suggest that a woman should sweep round them. Once a week, on Saturday afternoon, all the dirty pots would be washed and both men would take a bath. As they talked late into the night, early rising was out of the question and the day would begin about eleven in the morning with Sabartés making coffee and taking his to Picasso, still in bed. The talking then started again; from time to time Picasso would look at Sabartés' watch and say they ought to be getting going, but it was only the thought of missing lunch altogether which got them dressed and in the street by two. They were generally back home by four o'clock, and after a short sleep they would go to work, Sabartés to his translation and secretarial duties and Picasso to his painting, and to some imitations he was doing of Gertrude Stein's pen portraits.

Into this camp, during those months, came Paul Eluard. The poet had also got rid of a nagging Russian wife, Gala, and was about to marry Nusch, an ethereal girl. At a party among the débris, on 8 January, 1936, Eluard agreed to go to Spain to supervise a travelling exhibition of Picasso's works. The uncertain political situation there, and the fighting which was going on, made Picasso, never a warlike man, feel reluctant to go himself, and anyway there were Marie-Thérèse and the baby (growing plumper and more delicious every day) and now Sabartés, not to mention Paul Rosenberg next door, who had agreed to put on an exhibition of his most recent paintings. Eluard, always short of money, said he would cope with the French and Spanish bureaucracy; as a wounded war hero he could cope easily enough with his own ministries and he knew he would have every sort of assistance from the 'old gang' in Barcelona, many of whom had part-time civil service posts. In gratitude, Picasso did a fine line drawing of Eluard (used as a frontispiece for an English translation of some of his poems) and promised to illustrate a collection that their mutual friend Christian Xervos was about to publish.

Eluard left for Spain in March and sent back enthusiastic reports of the exhibition, his part in organizing it (he gave innumerable interviews to the press and on the radio) and its reception in Barcelona, Madrid and Bilbao. The critics were enthusiastic—'the supreme example . . . of an inventive spirit'— perhaps because the painter himself was not there to remind them of their natural preference for bucolic scenes in the Academy manner. There were readings of Picasso's poems, which were received politely and then just as politely ignored.

In Paris the Rosenberg exhibition, and a show of his sculpture (Xervos) and drawings (at the Renou and Colle Gallery) were even more successful and Sabartés was pleased to see the money rolling—innured to a lifetime of poverty, he had never seen so much, nor believed that Art could produce it. Marie-Thérèse, often present with the baby in her arms, was ecstatic, as well she might be. More than half the paintings at Rosenberg's were of her, at her voluptuous best, though she did notice that many of them showed her asleep. She was complimented by everybody, even by some of those doyens of Society who had been Olga's friends and now seemed ready to drop her if that was the way to get back into Picasso's good books. Tzara, who acted as Marie-Thérèse's escort, made diplomatic noises. The weather was beautiful.

At the end of March, Picasso decided that as things were going so well he would leave Paris in the hands of Sabartés and Tzara and take Marie-Thérèse to Juan les Pins. They could have a 'little honeymoon' together and she could furnish the house he had just put in her name; their privacy was to be strictly preserved and letters were to be sent to him care of the post office as M. Paul Ruiz. After a week of silence Sabartés was astonished to receive a whole series of letters, longer and chattier all the time. Tzara, too, who had never had a letter from him in years of friendship, found gossipy missives waiting for him almost every day. It was apparently a very happy 'little honeymoon', with days spent in bed, a little painting and drawing and crooning to the baby—'I am giving up painting . . . so as to consecrate myself entirely to singing' (to Sabartés on 23 April). The novelty, as Sabartés said, lay in the cultivation of the art of correspondence under Marie-Thérèse's guidance and it came out that she was a compulsive letter writer, had been so all her life (and was to be to the end). Both Picasso and Tzara began to worry about his work, and were relieved when he came back in mid-May, alone, with two portfolios of drawings of himself as minotaur carrying out household tasks, moving furniture (though a cart seems to be a disembowelled Olga) or playing the fool to naked young girls.

Eluard returned at the end of May, to be congratulated, and with more poems to be illustrated, Picasso engraved the first, *Grand Air*, on 4 June, but then excused himself and said that he had taken over a studio in Montmartre—Marie-Thérèse would spend the whole summer in the South—and wanted to get to work on a commission from Vollard, a new edition of Buffon's *Natural History*. He would do the other illustrations when he had time. He was soon lost in the company of the technicians and printers at the engraver's, enjoying the smell and the expertise of craftsmen; he even forgot that he was supposed to design a drop curtain for Romain Rolland for Quatorze Juillet at the Alhambra, and in the end had to ask Sabartés to choose something suitable that was lying about in the Rue de la Boétie.

It was good to be back in Montmartre and to be able to spend idle hours in the cafés and bars. He had to keep a clear head for the fine work he had to do preparing drawings which had to be approved not only by artists but also by high school teachers, so he often drank only Perrier water between meals. Lunch was always taken with the workmen. Dinner was open for friends and acquaintances, including some *Anglais* who were trying to persuade him to loan them some canvasses for the first International Surrealist Exhibition in London that summer. Xervos, always trying to wring more work out of him for his gallery and various publications, often paid the bill and his wife and Nusch Eluard provided the not-so-discreet feminine background; both women were suspected of 'adventures' among the acquaintances, *maris complaisants*.

It was probably Nusch Eluard, who had taken an unreasoning dislike to Marie-Thérèse, who suggested to her husband that this would be a good moment to get Picasso interested in another woman, 'one of them', who could keep him on the straight and narrow artistic path, perhaps even detach him from 'that awful woman' and 'those awful men' (Tzara and Sabartés). As it happened, she had a girl in mind, talented, a member of their Surrealist circle, highly intelligent and 'not just a dumb cow'. She spoke Spanish—Picasso was always complaining that he had nobody to talk intelligently to in his own language, and he seldom read in any other language. She had jet black hair and dark flashing eyes just like a Spanish girl. Her name was Dora Marcovitch, known as Dora Maar and they would be well advised to bring her along for inspection before the bird flew off after another worm.

Dora

'Marcovitch! That's a Serb name. I wouldn't trust a Serb, not even to murder a Croat.'

(Tzara, to the author)

To Dora Maar's great chagrin, and to Eluard's disappointment, Picasso did not notice her in Paris. It was Paolo who first drew his father's attention to the 'black girl' who seemed to be always hanging around, watching carefully until the right chair was empty so she could see and be seen. At first, Picasso, who was trying to find, with Tzara's help, 'just the right girl' to take away his son's virginity, said there were always girls hoping to be noticed. Anyway, he was busy and anxious to finish the work he had set himself to do before going to the South of France to join Marie-Thérèse at Juan les Pins; Paolo should mind his own business.

However, when the time came to go South, the plot, as it were, thickened. Eluard convinced Picasso that it would be safer not to stay with Marie-Thérèse, just in case Olga decided to make a scene. By chance, he had been offered a flat in Mougins, a small town inland from Cannes which combined medieval charm with marvellous views of the 'côte'. Not far away there was a rambling old hotel called Le Vaste Horizon at which Picasso could put up—Paul Rosenberg and Man Ray would be along later to stay there. This seemed to be a good idea, and on 30 July Marcel drove them through the night to Mougins, arriving on the hillcrest overlooking the town at dawn. 'This is the place,' said Picasso, 'where I shall live some day.'

His initial enthusiasm was not dimmed when he found that the 'black girl' was staying at the same hotel. Unfortunately for her, the following morning when the whole party went down to the sea to bathe, a large blonde girl emerged from the waves, naked to the waist. Tzara, who had come over from Juan les Pins, was struck dumb for five minutes but soon recovered to strike up an acquaintance. The girl, Rosemarie, had heard of Picasso and was demurely excited at the prospect of meeting him. The whole morning was spent in not-so-innocent flirtation and 'the black girl' was virtually ignored. The situation was saved by Tzara, who told Picasso that this was the big blonde he had dreamed of all his life. Her rising from the waves was a mystical, even religious experience; more concrete were those huge, firm breasts. He could see himself now, pillowed on them, or tying them round his neck during a moment of passion. Think what each one would weigh! And yet so solid you could kill flies with them. Tzara's passionate pleas had their effect and at the end of the day he was allowed to take her away to do his worst.

The incident, apart from generating a lot of obscene laughter, solved a minor problem, that of the continual bickering between Eluard and Tzara; the Surrealists, reluctant to acknowledge that their 'Movement' was anything other than French, and angry at Tzara's refusal to concede parentage of their idea, were always jealous of Picasso's attachment to his Romanian friend. Now the coast was clear for Dora. Some years later Picasso said: 'It wasn't that I was all that attracted by Dora but I felt that at last I had found somebody to talk to.' He was always astonished by the breadth and depth of her knowledge. She was certainly the best educated of any of the women he knew. She had studied painting in Paris at the Julien and Passy Academies, and at the Ecole d'Art Décoratif. She had been one of a handful of women students at the Paris School of Photography and had been taken up by Brassai in 1930; a recent biographical note in a museum catalogue says coyly that she shared a darkroom with him. She was an early devotee of Surrealism and shared Eluard's dislike for Tzara, a dislike compounded by her feelings of contempt for all Romanians. It came out during her first conversations with Picasso that her name at birth had been Marcovitch; her father, an architect, had fled from Serbia after some plot or other in Belgrade and had worked in Argentina for many years—half her life had been spent there. She spoke fluent French, Spanish and Serbo-Croat. What also attracted Picasso was the fact that she was a good enough photographer to earn her living at it, and yet she had made 'artistic' pictures good enough to be included in that year's International Surrrealist Exhibition in London.

It was obvious that this was going to be quite a different relationship from any other he had had. His friends first noticed it when he began to get up early in the morning to go out for walks along the beach, with Dora. They would talk endlessly, about everything and anything. Things he had wanted to say in Spanish for years now found their audience. He explained that on his rare visits to Barcelona he had spent most of his time joking or whoring and had never had a chance to talk seriously, and Sabartés had already become a sort of butler; anyway, talking to a woman was easier. He told her that for years he had been interested in photography and hoped she would teach him some of the skills he knew he lacked. Tzara being now absent, there is no reliable or unreliable record of when their sexual relationship began, but a drawing dated 1 August suggests that the first hurdle had been leaped by then; it is a rather touching work, showing an old man (and a dog) and a young girl about to set out on a journey together. What is certain is that he lost interest in Nusch Eluard, who had been hopping from his bed to her husband's, and also in one of the daughters of the hotel proprietor, Inès (who was, however, taken back to Paris with him the next year).

Everybody, except presumably Nusch and Inès, were pleased to see the new lively Picasso, eyes sparkling, full of jokes and jollity, doing imitations of Hitler, Mussolini and

Franco at lunch, painting portraits in mustard, wine and vegetable juice on the tableclothes. Roland Penrose, who turned up in mid-August in a new Ford tourer, enjoyed the scene— and another of the hotel proprietor's daughters; his mistress, Lee Miller, Man Ray's favourite model, seems to have been away modelling. He was anxious to show off his new car and took everybody for drives, except Dora Maar who said she had no confidence in his skill at the wheel. Dora was proved right. Towards the end of August, Penrose gave Picasso a lift to Juan les Pins, to make one of his regular visits to Marie-Thérèse and their daughter, and lunched alone while waiting for his friend to do his pleasant duty. On the way back to Mougins from Cannes, Penrose misjudged a bend and collided with a car coming from the other direction, in the hands of a similarly inexpert driver. The car was badly damaged, and so was Picasso, who pretended gallantly that he was unhurt. Penrose went back to England sulking and apologizing, but threatening to return. After a few days Dora noticed that Picasso was very stiff and moved painfully. When she saw the bruises on his side, she took him off for an X-ray immediately, but there was nothing broken.

Apart from the incident 'with an Englishman in his car', the summer passed pleasantly enough, and there were even other drives, chauffeured by Marcel, into the countryside and down to St Tropez (a friend, Lise Deharme, the writer, had a converted farmhouse there and eventually put Dora Maar up when she had to leave the hotel in Mougins). Little or no painting was done, and none after the accident, but Man Ray, who reappeared with Lee Miller, and Dora showed Picasso a lot of interesting new techniques in photography. Picasso was able to impress his new mistress with sheafs of articles about himself, including a prophetic *Open Letter to Picasso* from Eugeni d'Ors, an old Catalan friend, calling for a great masterpiece from the Spaniard at this time of trial and suffering: 'Old Duran, when he became a teacher at the French Academy in Rome, used to say to every new student: "Make a masterpiece" . . . It was a sort of joke, of course . . . but in the tradition of *Els Quatre Gats* it is better than the most solemn advice. Gravely, then, I shall tell you—Pablo Picasso, produce a masterpiece . . . like those time-honoured ones now in the best galleries of the best museums.'

Pleasant idyll or not, the arrival of Dora Maar produced some administrative problems which had to be faced as soon as he got back to Paris. Tzara did not like Dora Maar (Romanians feel the same way about Slavs as Slavs about Romanians), but during their first conversations realized that she had come to stay. Picasso put it to him: 'Where do we house Marie-Thérèse in the winter?' It was back to 1929 again, though at least she had the flat on Ile Saint–Louis in Paris as a stable home for all seasons. He needed a place big enough for him to live there with all his paraphernalia. Sabartés was beginning to become a bore and the prospect of winter with him in the chaos and confusion of Rue de la Boétie was daunting. There was an urgent need to find somewhere which could be a real home— he was tired of hotel life.

It was Vollard who came to the rescue this time. He had bought an old farmhouse at Le Tremblay sur Mauldre, with the intention of turning it into a sort of residential studio complex for painters on his books. It was near Versailles, and so handy for Paris; they would stay there for a few weeks or months at his expense and he would have the guarantee that what work they produced would pass through his gallery. It was a scheme which ought to have succeeded, as similar schemes later succeeded in Italy, Great Britain and America, but did not. He was turned down by the last of his protégés, Rouault, in late September, and did not know what to do with the place. It was large and could be made comfortable, and there was a splendid barn which could be made into a sculpture studio, but it was one of those places which had to be lived in, otherwise it would deteriorate rapidly. Tzara, who knew everything, heard of the scheme and Vollard's failure to get it going and told Picasso. He also told Vollard that Picasso was looking for just such a place, and over lunch the deal was done. Almost immediately, a *camion* was sent to Boisgeloup for Fort's presses, and Marie-Thérèse was brought from Juan les Pins. She was entranced. It was, Tzara said, the only time she ever gave me a big kiss, though his mind was still on Rosemarie ('When she was on top of me I had to tell her to sit up straight otherwise she could have knocked me out with one swing of those big tits.')

Dora Maar was not pleased at this turn of events. She already had a flat of her own, in the Rue de Savoie (where she was still living at the time of writing), but it was anything but spacious. It was too small for Picasso to move in with her and she had hoped that they would soon come to an arrangement to share a larger establishment; a proud woman, she never raised the subject again. She blamed 'that dirty gypsy' Tzara and told Picasso she did not want to see him around, in summer or winter. He could play gigolo to Marie-Thérèse, if he was so devoted to her (and indeed they were devoted to each other in a platonic way, notwithstanding Marie-Thérèse's public pretence to be shocked by his Rabelaisian wit). Dora had to be content with an occasional visit to Paris by Picasso, knowing that once he was there her intelligence and brilliant conversation would hold him for at least a week.

Marie-Thérèse, of course, knew all about Dora but for a time did nothing about it and never mentioned her. Life at Le Tremblay was very pleasant, and she overlooked his occasional absences. The painting he did at this time shows the depth of his domestic contentment. There are drawings of his daughter, dandled on Tzara's knee or on her mother's, drawings and paintings of Marie-Thérèse in her usual poses, and a whole series of bright works full of sunshine, pots and pans, fruit and flowers, bottles of wine and glasses. So as not to offend Dora, he did not send all this to Rosenberg or Vollard for several years.

Picasso had never been interested in politics. Fernande thought of *la politique* as a way of getting to know ministers and important people; Eva thought politicians less interesting than pimps; Olga associated politics with the Russian Revolution and would have none of it; Marie-Thérèse was more familar with Groucho Marx than with Karl. Dora Maar was the first really politicized person Picasso had ever met, man or woman. The Surrealists, like all artists and intellectuals in the 'Thirties, were vaguely left-wing, but not really interested in Marxism, Communism or any other complicated political formula; this made them easy meat for skilled Communist recruiters, who turned many of them, especially in England among the homosexual undergraduates at Cambridge University, into traitors. Tzara, in his Byzantine way, tried to see good and bad in every party.

Dora knew her politics and was extremely well informed. She was rather upset when she found Picasso very angry with the Communist Republicans in Spain one day: his mother had written to say that local Communists and Anarchists had set fire to a convent near their flat in Barcelona and had committed many atrocities; Lola, just recovering from the death of her husband and desperate to know how to bring up five children alone, was in a state of shock. For a week in January, 1937, he was given a series of short, sharp lectures by Dora to concentrate his mind. It is difficult to say how deep all this went, but it certainly produced a set of prints to be sold for war victims, which bore the title *The Dream and Lie of Franco*.

The news from Spain became more and more upsetting, and under Dora's tuition his painting became more explicitly political. He had agreed to contribute a canvas to the Spanish Pavilion at the International Exposition, partly out of nostalgia for his emergence on the scene at the 1901 Exposition, and partly with the prospect of selling it later for the benefit of refugees from the Civil War. He had only a vague idea at first of the subject he should choose, but his mind was focussed sharply by the German blitzkrieg attack on Guernica, on 29 April. He knew the town well, and it had a special historical significance for the Basque minority, so it was not necessary for Dora to steer him towards a commemorative mural. The immediate problem was where to paint it. Marie-Thérèse did not like 'violent' painting, and the atmosphere she created at Le Tremblay was not conducive to it. Dora realized that this was the moment she had been waiting for, and told him that out of the back windows of her flat she could look out at the old Savoy Palace in the Rue des Grands Augustins, a stone's throw from the Seine; all his life he liked to be able to walk along the river and look at the involuntary models going about their business there. The next day he arrived with Sabartés and they climbed the crooked stair to the two vacant floors at the far end of the courtyard. The lower floor had been used by a weaver, and bits of an old loom were still lying about; above it was a suite of rooms which had been used by the actor Barrault. Dora had been into this part of the Palace before to meetings of Bataille's short-lived Counter Attack group, later merged with the Surrealists, and she remembered the large room Barrault had used for rehearsals. Three days later the move from Rue de la Boétie began and by the end of the week an enormous canvas, about eight metres by three, was stretched across the rehearsal room; it was so big that it was higher than the roof (that floor had been the servants' attic) and so sloped outwards, making it very dangerous to paint the top part from the ladder, even with a paintbrush attached to a broom handle.

Work on *Guernica* began immediately, while Sabartés fitted up a kitchen downstairs. Dora set up her cameras and began to photograph the work at every stage. Inevitably, Marie-Thérèse was told of the new studio and on her next trip to Paris walked in, past a protesting Sabartés, and found her lover painting and Dora clicking the shutter. She stood for a time, looking at them both with immense dignity, then introduced herself as the mother of Picasso's daughter. Dora, as dignified, acknowledged the introduction as if she were talking to the person who repaired his car or soled his shoes. This infuriated the normally calm Marie-Thérèse, who turned to Picasso and asked him which woman he proposed to choose. To Dora she said: 'I am the mother of his child.' Dora replied: 'I am not yet the mother of his child', which was the last straw. Seconds later the two women were wrestling on the floor among the pots and paintbrushes, to Sabartés' alarm and Picasso's great satisfaction. In the end, Dora broke off the fight because she was afraid her cameras would be damaged, deliberately or accidentally, and her rival walked out.

That weekend Picasso went home to Le Tremblay, expecting a scene. He was relieved to find that Tzara had convinced Marie-Thérèse that she need not feel insecure. Picasso would not leave her, and she was safe with her daughter in the beautiful old farmhouse. What her lover did in Paris was none of her business. He might go to brothels, if he were promised something really unusual. He might spend his time with Dora, might even amuse himself with her on the dirty floorboards—could that compare with the relaxed, luxorious man she saw playing with Maia and enjoying his blonde in bed? Anyway, he said, Slav women were no good in bed—that was why Picasso had been disappointed with Olga. They only liked to be ridden by big Cossacks and then get a taste of the whip.

And so for years Picasso kept up two establishments (not counting Olga's, and the education of Paolo), which were essentially non-competing. His paintings, always a mirror to his mind if not his heart, showed that Picasso was living a life, or rather two lives, in tandem. During the week, he was in Paris, sleeping at the Rue de la Boétie and working in the Rue des Grands Augustins, occasionally being entertained by Dora in the Rue de Savoie. On Friday evenings he was collected by Marcel and driven to Le Tremblay: there he lived the life of a *pater familias* and produced scores of paintings and drawings of Marie-Thérèse and their daughter, completely different in mood from the *Guernica* which was evolving in Paris. Each establishment had its major-domo, Tzara in the country and Sabartés in town, and each had its circle of visitors and friends. Paris was Surrealist, Le Tremblay was the more amusing with a variety of Tzara's friends, including two other Romanian poets, Ilarie Voronca and Benjamin Fundoianu, who both became great favourites. Life at Le Tremblay was comfortable and amusing, in Paris intense and intellectual. There was never any doubt about which relationship would last the longer.

Dora kept up the political pressure throughout the spring and early summer of 1937, offering suggestions and suitable symbols. Sometimes Picasso would give her a brush and say: "It's no use telling me these things. Painting has nothing to do with words. Show me what you mean". Some of her ideas remain, as she translated them into paint. In the background, as he worked on the painting and she photographed it, there were always left-wing intellectuals including Henry Moore, Penrose and sundry homosexual English poets, off, as Tzara said acidly, 'to fondle the poor boys on the stretchers'. Before it was finished, *Guernica* had been appropriated as a major Communist, anti-Fascist work, slightly deviant from orthodox Socialist Realism but with its heart in the right place thanks to the stimulus of the comrades around him. The artist himself said nothing at the time and let them go on blathering about the symbolism of the Fascist bull goring the [working class] horse, the house [of democracy] in flames, the dead child [liberty], the sun and the sheaves of corn the future [Communism] round the corner. It was only years later, in 1945, that he told Seckler that this interpretation was all nonsense, that the bull 'is not Fascism but any sort of brutality, the horse is all the common people . . . *Guernica* is allegoric'. Of the stimulus of the comrades he said baldly: 'Towards the end I had the feeling I was working all by myself'. Only once, in 1937, did he show his contempt for his 'interpreters'. Penrose was going on about 'clarifying the symbols' so that people could get the political message. Picasso got down from his ladder, took a long strip of toilet paper from a roll he kept on the floor to wipe his hands on, and stuck it on the bare bottom of the woman running on the right of the picture. 'There,' said Picasso, 'she was having a shit when the bombs started to fall. Here she is with her arse bare. You couldn't get anything clearer than that, but I'll work the paper into the thing if you like.'

In the middle of June, *Guernica* was finished ('for the moment', Picasso said) and delivered to the Spanish Pavilion. It was time to move the two establishments South; again, after seeing Marie-Thérèse safely to Juan les Pins, he set off, with Dora and the Eluards, for Mougins and the Hotel Vaste Horizon. He was touched by the gift of a dog, an Afghan hound called Kasbec, by Dora, who hated dogs, and he repaid her thoughtfulness, or tact, by cutting down on his visits to Juan les Pins and devoting most of the summer to her. He began the long series of portraits of her which are really (much more than *Guernica*) the most important legacy of the seven or eight years of genuine intimacy between them. She appears in various 'disguises', sometimes as herself, recognizably so in spite of the erratic use of colour; sometimes she is part of another minotaur scene, being gored, or rescued, or hovering like a bird over some familiar house or beach. She criticized him for having an aristocratic, distant attitude to life and people (he had taken the only room with a large balcony and looked down on them all as he painted), and of neglecting the political events of the day—Mussolini had chased the Communists out of the Balearic Islands, and Hitler and the Communists vied with each other in committing atrocities. He never replied to this criticism and went on painting. In the end, she received so many compliments that she wilted politically in the heat of the immortality she was getting. She was, she thought, the only subject he took seriously—Eluard was painted several times as a woman, Nusch and Lee Miller as fish, and several *Anglais* as pigs. Once he painted Tzara as a ringmaster and once as a headwaiter in quite a different style. When he slipped over to Juan les Pins he painted Marie-Thérèse and Maia. Neither Dora nor Marie-Thérèse ever saw the work done in the company of or inspired by the other.

Picasso was in a very good mood when he went back North. At the end of his stay at Mougins he had gone off to Berne where a curious *comédie* was taking place. A local business man had bought a couple of Picassos when they were cheap, before the First World War, and had decided to cash in and take his (huge) profit. The local press seethed with righteous indignation and said it was a scandal to deprive the city of these works of art which had been on permanent loan to the municipal gallery. The businessman had suggested that, as the city had enjoyed the pictures, free, for many years, it should buy them itself, if it really cared so much. With a rare demonstration of civic pride, the good citizens had been out on the streets for weeks collecting from passers by and wheedling cash out of bankers. In the end they had collected enough to match the market price and 'their' Picassos were saved. Picasso was so pleased he gave them two more paintings as a reward for their efforts. He was still talking about this when Penrose turned up at the Rue des Grands Augustins and was 'astonished at the captivating power of a small, newly painted canvas placed on an easel as if he were still at work on it'. It was a portrait of Dora, in red, blue, green and yellow, dressed for a party but for some reason weeping. Penrose, seeing Picasso so euphoric, immediately offered him £250 for *The Woman Weeping* and to his astonishment had the offer accepted. He took the painting off the easel ('the paint was scarcely dry') and hurried away before the deal could be called off.

Dora was not pleased when Picasso remarked to Eluard that she was always for him the woman weeping. Later that year she saw some canvasses and drawings, probably done at Le Tremblay, in which both the women in his life appeared. She did not show up very well, she said. Marie-Thérèse was always shown in glamorous, even provocative postures, even when she was asleep; Dora was always either watching over this creature, as if protecting her, or standing by, looking miserable. Not even her tears were worth much, apparently—£250 for the painting Penrose bought was very little and Picasso's reassurance that the price was low to make up for the *Guernica* toilet paper incident did not make things any better. Even his playfulness seemed to have an undesirable undertone—why had he brought home a monkey during the holidays? It had nearly killed the dog she had given him and it had served him right when it had bitten his finger.

As Tzara said, it was impossible for her to reconcile her desire to be thought of as an intellectual, the equal of men, and her feminine instincts which drove her to emotional dependence. She was not as good at being feminine as Marie-Thérèse and her undoubted intellectual qualities were tiring; when Picasso got home at weekends he always complained that she had made his head swell like a balloon. Marie-Thérèse, on the other hand, made him feel superior; he did not know much, but she did not even know there was anything to know.

The winter passed and the turbulence died down. He was at the centre of attention as an intellectual debate raged on where men and women should stand *vis-à-vis* the Spanish Civil War, and Dora was always called upon to comment and even to draft his letters to foreign newspapers; the bombing of the Prado so outraged him that he was edged slowly towards an unqualified condemnation of the Nationalists, though he continued to hear from friends in Barcelona of Communist atrocities. He was glad to get away in early summer to the South of France, taking Marie-Thérèse as usual to Juan les Pins and moving back into his old room at the hotel in Mougins. There was a *frisson* of scandal over the pregnancy of Inès (who was taken back to Paris at the end of the holiday) but he denied the paternity of the child and a husband was found for her. He painted and drew portraits, many of them of Dora, but this time more flattering. She had turned thirty, so he gave her what he called a mature gamine look and concentrated on the strong lines of her face softened by her long, unruly black hair. At Juan les Pins he painted Marie-Thérèse on the beach, in the sea, with the amazing child who never irritated and never complained. He also did some interesting drawings and many sketches of peasants at Mougins. These did not please Dora who thought it was patronizing to show stupid men eating a sort of toffee apple, playing boules and talking (their heads blown up to suggest that there was nothing in them).

Guernica was in Scandinavia during the holiday, being used as a rallying point for anti-Franco intellectuals, and a steady stream of them came south to see him and make their obeisances. This he found rather boring, but in September it became obvious that Hitler intended to dismember Czechoslovakia and nudge the world in the direction of war or submission. As they all got back to Paris and Versailles, the British Prime Minister's abortive visit to Munich and unjustified optimism (Picasso thought Chamberlain looked like Charlie Chaplin, but not so funny) infuriated Dora and she insisted that they do something. The something turned out to be a showing of *Guernica* in London (organized by Penrose), together with her photographs of the creative process and sixty odd sketches and ideas for the finished work; the exhibition opened in the West End, then moved to the left-wing Whitechapel Art Gallery (where it was opened by Attlee, the leader of the Labour Party). Picasso refused to go himself because he knew it would be a very political occasion, and he was relieved when Herbert Read (*London Bulletin*, October 1938) echoed his own thoughts about the undesirability of apportioning blame absolutely: 'When it is given out that a great Christian hero (Franco) is leading a new crusade for the faith, even his followers are not deceived. A Christian crusade is not fought with the aid of infidel Moors, nor with Fascist bombs and tanks. And when a Republic announces that it is fighting to defend liberty and equality, we are compelled to doubt whether these values will survive the autocratic methods adopted to establish them.' Read was the first person to comment truthfully (difficult in that hysterical anti-Nationalist environment) that 'Picasso's great fresco is a monument to destruction, a cry of outrage and horror amplified by the spirit of genius.'

Reassured that somebody realized just where he stood, he gave Paul Rosenberg permission to organize a major exhibition at his gallery in January 1939. At first he intended to do a new series of portraits and still lifes, but just before Christmas 1938 he had his first serious illness, variously diagnosed as arthritis and sciatica. Marie-Thérèse blamed the rigid temperatures of the studio in the Rue des Grands Augustins (heated only by a pot-bellied stove), and Dora said it was the well-known damp of the whole Versailles area. However, once the recriminations had ceased, they compromised. Whatever Olga had or had not done, the two floors of her former home at Rue de La Boétie were draughtproof and could be heated efficiently. Sabartés, delighted to be at the centre of things, took off the dust covers and turned the lower floor into a sort of hospital, hiring a nurse and a cook; the cook did not last for long (Inès took her place) but the ambience was ideal. Dora and Marie-Thérèse came to an understanding about which days they should visit and add a little tenderness to the efficient nursing and from then on never quarrelled. By the end of January, 1939, the patient was up and about.

Deprived of brand new work, Rosenberg put together a retrospective of the most famous paintings (except *Guernica* and *Demoiselles d'Avignon*, both in the USA) and the catalogue was a retrospective of critical esteem. This annoyed some people, whose spokesman was André Llote (*La Nouvelle Revue Française*, 1 March 1939). He took issue with Gertrude Stein's 'amazingly pretentious statement that, if world painting in the nineteenth century was the work of Frenchmen in France, in the twentieth it is the work, in France, of the Spaniard Picasso . . . I prefer to this kind of criticism the remark made to me by a talented young painter who was much excited by the exhibition: "Picasso is a toreador—brilliant, alert, skilful; he kills a new bull with every stroke. It is a wonderful performance, but if a Frenchman tried to do it, he would fall flat on his face." ' But Picasso approved the conclusion that he was 'the true portrayer of the absurd and fabulous times in which we live'.

The exhibition launched, he spent the spring and early summer painting his menagerie, especially his cat and birds. When he was well enough to walk, he would spend a day or two in Montmartre working at engravings, especially of illustrations of poems by Eluard and others. When this proved very tiring, he had Fort's press moved from Le Tremblay to the Rue des Grands Augustins, so that his weekends could be devoted solely to rest and to the enjoyment of family life. Dora helped him with the press, and brought Man Ray, Eluard, Michel Leiris and André Breton round to cheer him up, but she herself was not the best of company; she was obsessed by the tragedy of Europe, more than ever with a 'face like a Madonna without the smile' as Pierre Cabanne put it, and liable to blow up and attack her in the studio, breaking the breakable.

When summer came, he was quite well again and left for the South of France, this time with Sabartés. It was a reward for looking after him so well, and for transferring (on a fish porter's barrow) a lot of moveable essentials from the Rue de la Boétie (once again under dust covers). Marcel drove them all down the Côte d'Azur, slowly exploring Roquebrun, Nice, Monte Carlo and Cannes, ending the Grand Tour at Mougins. Sabartés, who had been cast by fate into the Dora Maar camp, was charmed by his reception at Juan les Pins and was thereafter an unreliable ally for Dora. He noticed that this year his friend and master was not staying at Mougins but had taken an apartment in Antibes, and before returning to Paris he helped to rearrange the furniture. Dora was not pleased at the change of holiday venue, even though the breath of scandal about Inès had diminished the appeal of 'the place where we met', but she soon adapted to life in a rather smarter place full of left-wing *Anglais*. She felt she had a counterweight to Maia when Fin and Xavier, the sons of Picasso's sister Lola, escaped from Barcelona (which had surrendered to Franco) and needed 'mothering'. It was a very hot summer and impossible to be out of doors after ten o'clock in the morning. Dora and Picasso got into the habit of dining late and spending most of the night walking about, especially on the beach and in the harbour, watching the whores and fishermen at work. After breakfast and an early morning bath, Picasso would then retreat to the denuded studio room of the flat and work on what was to become *Fisherman at Night, Antibes*, a colourful painting of the locals using bright lights to stun the fish and then spearing them; the lights showed up the marine life under water and the painting is full of odd representations of fish and insects looking like some of the illustrations for Buffon.

While Picasso was busy for the day with his paints, patent medicines (a glass of wine at meals only) and cooling fans, Dora spent her time with Penrose and other Left-wing *Anglais* and Spaniards, listening to horror stories from refugees and to debataes about the Republican defeat. She was worried about the implications of Franco's victory. Hitler and Mussolini might be encouraged to think they could gobble up the rest of Europe, with the the Iberian flank now secure. If they moved East

(Poland) or West (France), there would be another World War. What would happen to her mother country, Yugoslavia, as artificial a creation as Czechoslovakia. Though fortifications were going up along the seafront at Antibes, enraging the fishermen and setting in motion a wave of racism (the soldiers at work were West African). Picasso seemed unflurried and it was only when the Foreign Legion began to take over the pensions, bars and brothels that he decided something should be done.

On September 1st, 1939, Hitler invaded Poland. This was the signal for a general exodus from the Cote. Major Dodds, the Consul at Nice had told the Anglais to try to get back to England before Sunday 3rd. Penrose left on the 2nd and noted that Picasso was still at work painting fisherman, but late that same day Marcel was told to load the car and call for Marie-Thérèse and Maia to take them back to Le Tremblay. Picasso himself left with Dora by *wagon-lit* from Nice.

The following week there were lengthy discussions in the menage. At first Marie-Thérèse refused to leave and said, quite rightly, that he would miss his weekends there; food and fuel would be easier to find than in Paris. However she was told by the local gendarme that the house would almost certainly be requisitioned by the Government for billetting troops. She decided to move back to the old flat on the Ile St Louis while negotiations went on for the purchase of 1, Boulevard Henri Quatare, not far away on the Right Bank. Dora refused any suggestion that she should 'go home' to Yugoslavia. She said Argentina was more her 'home', but she had lived all her adult life in France and that is where she would stay. She also said she thought Picasso might need her to 'arrange things.' Spain might stay neutral (this was more likely than Yugoslavia keeping out of the war) but if Franco did come in on the side of the Axis and Hitler or Mussolini conquered Yugoslavia they would both be harassed to say the least of it.

Picasso was very worried at the prospect of France being invaded. Tzara tried to cheer him up, saying he would stay in Paris with Voronca and Fundoianu. Romania had been invaded regularly for two thousand years; the Daco-Romanians would survive. However, his advice to Picasso was to remove himself to somewhere on the Atlantic coast from where he could escape to England or America – he was not short of pounds or dollars.

In the middle of September, Picasso, Dora and Sabartés (with his wife) left suddenly for Royan, a little port only an hour away from Bordeaux but on the direct route to Paris. They found rooms in the Station Hotel and ransacked the town for paper, paints and canvasses. He had no easel, so he painted sitting on the floor as he had done thirty years before. He used an assortment of chair seats as palettes; when he ran out of canvasses he pulled up floorboards and painted on them.

When she heard of the move from Tzara, Marie Thérèse panicked for the first time in her life. She left immediately for Royan, followed by her grandmother Mémé (Emilie Marguerite Walter) and later by her parents. They set up a rival establishment to watch over her interests. Picasso was pleased, flattered and intrigued.

In October, the bureaucracy caught up with them. In the days before the computer, all the *fiches* filled in by foreigners and held in central and Departmental offices had to be shuffled by hand. The existence of two rival police forces, the Police Nationale and the Gendarmerie complicated matters. Some foreigners lived in the country (Gendarmerie), and some in towns (Police Nationale); other lived in hotels which often 'forgot' to register cleints. There were foreigners like Picasso who rented or owned several properties and so were listed as resident by several municipalities. By the middle of the month the Interior Ministry had discovered that Picasso was 'in an irregular situation' and called him to Paris to 'regularise' himself. He was told that Marie-Thérèse, Dora and his wife were all 'irregular'. Marie-Thérèse had the flat in Paris and the house in Juan les Pins; his wife had Boisgeloup, was living in a hotel in Paris and was listed as the joint owner of Rue de la Boétie; Dora had her flat in the Rue de Savoie but was listed, like Marie-Thérèse, as cohabiting with Picasso, who appeared as having an interest in Boisgeloup, Juan les Pins, the Rue des Grands Augustins and Rue de la Boétie, to say nothing of sundry rooms where he stored paintings and sculpture. Everybody had to opt for one place of permanent residence and not more than one alternative residence.

It took a long time and many friends in high places to sort it all out. Picasso, Dora and Sabartés were given the right to stay for up to a year in Royan, provided they returned regularly to Paris and called at their local police station, his 'storehouses', and locked away the paintings and drawings, and small sculpture, in the vaults of the Banque Nationale pour le Commerce et l'Industrie in Paris, at a fortress-like branch near the Seine; the building was so intimidating that he seldom dared to go there and when asked by a cataloguer for this or that work, he replied that it was easier to do the whole thing all over again.

In spite of all this turmoil, he managed to do some painting, some more portraits of Dora, ironic paintings of nude men and women waiting in police stations to be documented, one of Sabartés as a sixteenth-century Spanish courtier, and a number of still lifes. At least he had been able to bring from Paris a huge stock of canvasses, paper, brushes and pencils—the Ripolin paint they could buy at the local hardware store. For the winter they moved into an empty holiday home, the *Villa Les Voiliers*, where there was plenty of space and a good view over the harbour. Apart from regular visits to Marie-Thérèse and the police in Paris (Marcel was having the first difficulties with petrol), he stayed in Royan with Dora Sabartés and Marie Thérèse until the end of January, 1940. In February he returned to Paris for a month and reported that all was gloom and despondency. The French Government was afraid and incompetent and the French Army "seems to be commanded by art school teachers" (he could not have said anything more damning). There would be difficulties in publishing some books he had illustrated (including Eluard's *Fleurs d'Obéisance*), there was just a chance of an exhibition of watercolours at the *Mai* in April, Xervos' new art magazine seemed doomed (it died after three issues) and most of his friends, except the Americans, had been called up. After a couple of weeks in Royan explaining this to his friends, he returned to Paris at the end of March and lived a desperate life alone in the Rue de la Boétie until mid-May.

On 10 May, Hitler's troops invaded the Benelux countries without meeting much resistance, and on the 15 May defeated the French at Sedan. It was obvious that his adopted country was going to follow Republican Spain as booty of the new European Right. On 17 May he was back in Royan and decided he could do nothing better than to get on with his work until the 'art school teachers' had lost everything and the dust had settled. His painting and drawing reflect this state of mind. Women disintegrate, skulls and bones proliferate as the Germans marched into Royan and took over the port, restricting his late night walks. It was a miserable summer, and his only consolation was the thought that a touring exhibition in the United States was making him a lot of money and that things could not get much worse.

In August, after the capitulation of France and the division of the country into Occupied and Unoccupied Zones, Picasso had to choose where he would take up his wartime residence. He chose Paris. He turned down an offer from Dora to live with her in the Rue de Savoie (it would make his other life with Marie-Thérèse impossible), and at first tried to live at the Rue de la Boétie and work in the Rue des Grands Augustins. He was always being stopped by police as he walked from one to the other and this got on his nerves to such an extent that he decided to move everything to the Rue des Grands Augustins; at least Dora was a neighbour, as it were, and could look after him, and cheer him up.

Life was neither cheerful nor easy and if it had not been for Dora, it is difficult to see how he would have survived the war. She was a born scrounger, for one thing, and always knew someone who knew where the meat, bread, and so on, were when officially there was none. There was no fuel for the enormous old-fashioned stove but somehow fuel was found. Linen was carefully repaired, shoes soled with expedients (she was one of the first women to wear wooden soles) and a broken window replaced with bottles. She was also very skilful in dealing with the Germans, playing off the Gestapo against the Wehrmacht; she was lucky in that the German Governor, Otto Abetz, had been an art teacher and knew very well that Picasso was an important painter—harassing him would be extremely bad propaganda at a time when the Reich was still trying to make a few friends. She had to try to control Picasso's tongue when the Gestapo made their regular visits to the Rue des Grands Augustins, lecturing him on the degenerate nature of his art. He would hand out postcards reproducing *Guernica* and shout: 'You did that, not me!' He boasted of his friendship with Jews—those like Paul Rosenberg who had escaped to the United States—and complained about the shortage of everything.

He was consoled by Matisse, who was also being harassed by the Gestapo and some collaborationist critics who urged that his paintings should be dumped on the garbage heaps outside the city. Some informer suggested that as Matisse was widely travelled, especially in North Africa and Polynesia, he was probably a spy and his 'unintelligible scrawls' were really messages in code; this really frightened the Abwehr and neither Picasso nor Matisse were allowed to have public shows during the whole of the Occupation. Both men were accused of being Jews, but the Archbishop of Paris went in person to Abetz to tell of the absurdity of the accusation.

Dora herself somehow managed to play down her nationality. Maar had a German flavour to it, like Saar, and for some reason she was allowed to have this surname on her documents instead of Marcovitch (after the German invasion of the Soviet Union even the sight of it would have got her sent to a concentration camp). The fact that she had her own flat and was not living with Picasso helped to take the spotlight off her, though she was with him most days, haranguing and feeding him. He was very depressed during the winter of 1940–41 and for a time could not paint or draw. As many of the cafés were forced by the Germans to close at the time he usually went out to them, he had to spend lonely evenings at home. He even wrote a play called *Desire By the Tail*, and did a drawing of himself, wearing spectacles and holding a pen, to be used as frontispiece when the text was published. In the play he recreates himself as Bigfoot, the Poet, and Tzara as Onion. His dogs were written in, too, and a composite whore with relatives and friends. There is no plot of any kind, merely a sequence of absurd incidents and complaints about life, the cold, the lack of food, the bombs, Dora's electric cooker. The play ends with everybody being suffocated by the smell of potatoes chipping in oil. This 'masterpiece' is dated 17 January, 1941. The only interesting parts of the play are the Rabelaisian dialogues of which Tzara's parentage is clear, and the echoes of Voronca's *Ulysses 5*.

He partially solved the problem of keeping warm, when this literary effort was over, by tackling some sculpture. He said he did not know how writers managed to survive without the excuse to hit and chip, throw clay about and warm themselves up on a blowtorch. During 1941 and 1942 he made more pieces, in plaster, metal and clay, than at any other period in his life; Dora got so tired of this frenetic activity that she retired to paint at home, and was punished by being modelled in plaster in an enormous bust (this later became Apollinaire's monument at the St German des Prés cemetery). Many of the works are interesting and ingenious. He took a piece of clay, made a head out of a lemon squeezer and called it *The Reaper*; a piece broken off a child's scooter welded onto what looks like a metal hat rack becomes a heron; bottle tops, burnt paper, wire and old bottles are everywhere. After being without during the summer of 1941 he was given a huge slab of clay to keep him going for a few months. There was raw material there for any number of normal sized pieces but he was so impressed by this 'little clay mountain' that he decided to turn it into one monumental piece (*L'Homme Avec Mouton*). This portrait of the Good Shepherd (with *Crucifixion*) is his most important religious work. Unfortunately at the beginning he did not have enough metal rods to make a skeleton to hold the weight of the clay, modelled into a shepherd with a lamb or sheep in his arms, and it kept falling to pieces; this drove him into a frenzy until, helped by Dora and Eluard, he managed to stiffen the statue with old umbrella ribs and baling wire. To make sure it would not disintegrate and be lost, they all went foraging for plaster and managed to find enough to make the cast.

Better known now than the sculpture are the portraits of Dora. There were many of them. Some of them are almost 'realistic'; the features are recognisably hers even though the colours reflect his mood and not nature. Others are 'distorted'; there are portraits with more than one profile, like some early Cubist work he had done many years before; some are so twisted that not even Dora could say for sure that they were of her; sometimes she appears mixed up with some animal, half woman and half dog or horse. In her studio in the Rue de Savoie he turned paint splashes on the white walls into insects, some of them with her features (others were so lifelike that well-meaning visitors tried to squash them).

On 9 October, 1942, he was delighted to get a copy of the Buffon *Natural History* he had illustrated and which had been waiting for five years for an imprint. He took a copy round to the Rue de Savoie, and while he was waiting for Dora to get ready for lunch at *El Catalan* (a sort of imitation *Els Quatre Gats* in the Rue des Grands Augustins, now a Vietnamese takeaway), he drew her as if she were an illustration from the book—she is a bird with taloned feet gripping a branch in the approved manner.

Harriet and Sidney Janis (*Picasso, the Recent Years*) comment on the portraits and say they 'show how the artist alters his approach to his subject, retaining the essential resemblance to the original model, but also conveying in varying degrees of subtlety and penetration a representation of the qualities of outer composure and inner intensity which are so characteristic of Miss Maar as a person'. Penrose explained away the horrible distortion of many of the portraits by saying he had done the same for Eva and Olga, and that 'the face of his closest and dearest woman friend was liable to suffer the same violence'.

Tzara was wiser. When he was sure that Dora was safely at work in the Rue de Savoie (he had bribed the concierge with some sausages) he would go round to the studio in Grands Augustins, check with Sabartés to make sure that Eluard was not there, and go in to amuse his old friend. He also brought with him the time and place for the next meeting with Marie-Thérèse, who had a German officer billetted on her and was not always available. When he saw portrait after portrait come off the easel in 1941 and 1942, he said shrewdly: 'By next year, you will have said all there is to say about this.' He knew that Picasso was painting Dora out of his life.

Françoise

'When feminism triumphs, yes on that day and without further procrastination, the origin of humanity's profound evils will be discovered to rest in the mute war between thin women and fat women'

(Ezra Pound)

It was common knowledge on the Left Bank that Picasso's relations with Dora Maar were getting rather strained, and that he was on the lookout for a replacement. His friends were already supplying him with attractive stopgaps; Paul Eluard had sent him a blonde with 'the biggest tits in Paris', but she apparently has no brains at all. It was perhaps by chance, and perhaps not, that Alain Cuny took Françoise and Geneviève to dinner one Wednesday evening in May, 1943, to the one restaurant where he could be almost certain to find Picasso; *El Catalan* was the natural haunt of French and Spanish 'Catalans' who exchanged gossip and smuggled food into the capital from the unoccupied South of France.

Everything went according to plan. Picasso was there, dining with the Vicomtesse de Noailles, a Romanian-French literary hostess, and Dora Maar. The two girls were strikingly dressed; Geneviève had on a long pleated tunic and had her hair scraped back to look like a portrait on a Grecian vase; Françoise had a mysterious air, in a green turban which came down to her eyebrows. They made an agreeable contrast to the ethereal Noailles and Dora Maar in a square shouldered fur coat and clogs with high heels. Picasso noticed the girls immediately, launched a few quips in their direction, and profited by his acquaintance with Cuny to introduce himself; he came over bearing a bowl of cherries.

There was the usual probing conversation, necessary in the circumstances. It had to be established which girl was available, and why. The girls were introduced as 'the beautiful one' (Geneviève) and 'the intelligent one' (Françoise). Cuny added that they were both painters, Geneviève that Françoise was 'a Florentine virgin'. Picasso did not know much about medieval Italian politics, and had never read Boccaccio, but the message was clear. The two painters were invited to visit the master's studio in the Rue des Grands Augustins (the restaurant was in the same street) whenever they liked. No time was wasted. The appointment was fixed for the next Monday morning.

As a matter of form, Geneviève went with Françoise on the first occasion. Cuny had done his homework well, and had told them to be careful with Sabartés, who would receive them, and not to take too much notice of the crowd of sycophants who could be hanging about upstairs.

Pretending not to notice Sabartés' chilly reception, the two girls followed him through the three rooms on the first floor, rashly admiring a Matisse on the way, and up the spiral staircase to another studio where Picasso was entertaining. He left his guests, and with a smile showed them all over his apartments. He stressed that unlike most establishments in Paris at the time, he had constant hot water, and they could take a bath there whenever they wanted to. That first visit ended at lunchtime, with an invitation to come again. Encouraged by the fact that Picasso took the trouble to visit the gallery in the Rue Boissy d'Anglais where the two girls were having an exhibition, they went back to the Rue des Grands Augustins a few days later bearing a potted plant as a gift. On this occasion he did not mention the hot water, but showed them a lot of his paintings. He also made it quite clear that he preferred the Florentine virgin to the Attic vase.

Geneviève went back to Montpellier and the field was left free for Françoise. She used the rest of the months of May and

June to consolidate her position. One day she arrived with her hair wet in a sudden shower, and he dried it tenderly. There was a first kiss, almost casual, as he showed her his sculpture; he was rather shocked, or pretended to be, to find that she offered no resistance. Towards the end of June, there were the first caresses. The most serious of these involved Picasso placing his cupped hands over her breasts as though they were 'two peaches whose form and colour had attracted him.' He satisfied himself that they were ripe, but Françoise noted that 'apparently it was not yet time for lunch.'

At the end of July, she sent to report progress to Geneviève. By the end of the summer, she had made up her mind to have Picasso, and to give up her other studies for life as a painter. When her father heard the news, he was furious. He had her brought back to Paris, and on the top floor of the grand estab-lishment near the Bois de Boulogne, out of sight and sound of the servants, he beat her up. When her black eye had become less swollen and the other bruises had faded he tried to have her declared insane, and put away in a 'nice asylum' in which a business friend had a wayward son. Of all the psychiatrists who saw her, only a woman took M. Gilot's part, and Françoise escaped to the grandmother's house, much less grand but at least safe from psychiatrists.

Picasso, who had tired of the girl with the 'biggest tits in Paris', and a Spanish offering who used to bite his arms and interfere with his work, was glad to see Françoise again in November. He found the tale of her father's violence incredible, but to her chagrin was more interested in another item of information she dropped, that her father, 'fundamentally a gentle man', had invented a floating soap for the bath.

Having lost her allowance from her father, Françoise had to earn a living somehow (she could only depend on board and lodging from her grandmother), and took a job giving riding lessons at a stable outside Paris. However, as she no longer went through the charade of attending lectures at the Sorbonne, she could spend three days a week at the Rue des Grands Augustins, and the affair progressed. She was introduced to many of Picasso's friends, André Malraux (illegally in Paris on Resistance business), Jean Cocteau, the actor Jean Marais, and Brassai, the photographer who had been Dora Maar's 'dear colleague'. She was taken more and more into his confidence that winter, to the point of helping him in the vaults of the Banque Nationale pour le Commerce et Industrie where he and Braque stored their paintings; the Germans, about to remove anything valuable from Paris as they prepared for their inevitable retreat, had asked for a 'valuation'.

It was one afternoon in February when he decided that the time was as ripe as her breasts. He took her upstairs to his bedroom and undressed her, 'moving his hand lightly over my body like a sculptor', and talking all the time. Then he made love to her very gently, and she had arrived.

With the liberation of Paris (24 August, 1944), life became easier. The Americans were the first to come back, and Françoise was struck by the numbers (first of all the artists and writers, then GIs as tourists), who placed a call on Picasso at the top of their list of priorities. Sabartés and the concierge thought this was a good opportunity to stock the larder and the *cave*, and began to hint that a 'little gift' for M. Picasso would be appropriate. Hemingway put an end to all that when he left a case of hand grenades with a note to say he hoped Pablo would know what to do with them. Before long, the expected invitation came from Gertrude Stein. With her morale reinfored by a good, sentimental meal at *El Catalan*, Françoise set off with Picasso for the Rue Christine. The afternoon was rather unnerving. Gertrude was intrigued by the new mademoiselle, and interrogated her briefly, while Alice B Toklas supplied the cakes and little sandwiches. Françoise did not like Gertrude Stein and her boast that every American writer of any importance had been influenced by her (Hemingway, Scott Fitzgerald, Dos Pasos, Erskine Caldwell, even Faulkner and Steinbeck were on her list), and she was put off by Alice B Toklas' moustache; anyway, she always felt uncomfortable in the presence of lesbians. There was much to see, of course, in the flat, many paintings to admire including Picasso's portrait of Gertrude under which she sat and held court, but the atmosphere was tense. Even Picasso seemed ill at ease, and resented the implication that he was an acolyte, too. The visit with Françoise seems to mark the beginning of the end of a long and warm acquaintance; perhaps this was the first change the 'mademoiselle' made in Picasso's life.

In later life, Françoise often wondered if she would have been able to prevent Picasso joining the French Communist Party that autumn. It was, of course, a very stupid decision on the part of her lover. Picasso's works had been collected by the rich and powerful, landowners and capitalists, all his life. They were the people with the money and the curiosity about modern art. They had paid the high prices asked by Kahnweiler and other dealers and it was to them that Picasso owed his several establishments in Paris and the South of France, the secretary, housemaid and chauffeur, the meals nearly always eaten in restaurants, the Hispano-Suiza, the women, and the freedom to do as he pleased. The Communist Party had not done much for his friends Eluard and Aragon, who had to write their poetry in the intervals between spewing out propaganda. Françoise was not mature enough or close enough to Picasso to do more than accept the explanation that 'Communists had done so much in the Resistance'; there was no talk of the Stalin-Ribbentrop Pact at the time of France's fall. She realized, however, how incredible the decision seemed to thousands of people, when there were riots at the Picasso pavilion at the Salon d'Automne.

The political fuss died down, as all political fuss does, and the winter of 1944–45 was a pleasant one. She was allowed to see how he treated dealers (Carre, Kahnweiler and the Americans) and literary visitors like John Pudney and Jerome Seckler. Dealers were encouraged to come in pairs, but were received singly and made to watch each other's elation or dejection as they went to and fro from the room in which Picasso was doing the haggling. He would play with them for hours, and told Françoise it was the least he could do to make up for the years during which they had exploited him. He treated journalists and writers more kindly, and urged Françoise to watch the English very closely. 'Look at the labels on their hats and gloves,' he used to say,' and you will know how seriously to take them. The Lock bowler hat! The Lock bowler hat! That is the thing.' He also told her that, contrary to what they thought, the English had very little sense of humour; she heard him tell John Pudney that he painted pictures of sailors because he always wore blue striped underwear.

During that winter the topic of Françoise's move to permanent residence at the Rue des Grands Augustins came up with great regularity. On the one hand she had nothing to lose; her virginity and what her father would have called her reputation had gone, and her grandmother was losing patience with her non-paying guest. She had a considerate and famous lover, who treated her seriously as a painter and gave her invaluable advice. He seemed to want her to share his life, even his past life; one afternoon, he had Marcel drive her to Montmartre and showed her all the scenes of his early years, the *Bâteau-Lavoir* in the Rue Ravignan, his studio (occupied by an unknown), even the living shell of Germaine Pichot who had driven Casagemas to suicide (he sent her money from time to time, remembering the meals she had given him when he was starving). And his devotion seemed to be increasing to the point that when she joked that all Spanish men dreamt of the day which would begin with Mass, then go on to a bullfight in the afternoon and a brothel at night, he replied that since he had met her he no longer felt any desire to go to his favourite brothels, even for a drink.

Françoise's problem was Dora Maar. Of course, there was Picasso's wife, Olga, living in a hotel nearby and writing abusive letters daily, but she was obviously deranged. Marie-Thérèse lived not far away on the Boulevard Henri IV (Ile Saint-Louis) with her daughter Maia, but she seemed a rather pathetic figure. And there were some women who eyed Picasso on the street in a way which suggested that they had once known him well, and not from a distance. Dora Maar, however, a very talented photographer, an intellectual and respected painter, was the real challenge.

During the late winter and spring of 1945, Françoise stopped seeing Picasso regularly, to give herself time to think what to do. Inevitably she was drawn to a major exhibition of Maar's paintings at Bucher in Montparnasse, and was frightened by the sombre colours of the (mostly) still lifes on show. They were very well done, but seemed bloodless, as sharply drawn as the features of a corpse after a visitation by a vampire. Dora Maar herself was there, dressed in black, her strong oval face white below her black hair. In her colourful striped cotton print dress, Françoise felt out of place and rushed out of the gallery, brushing past Picasso on his way in. For two months she never even saw him, then one day decided to go to the Rue des Grands Augustins and have it out with him. It was high summer, two months after the exhibition, and they sat on the bed for three hours as he reassured her. Yes, he had found his years with Dora stimulating – 'she made my brain work, it was sometimes very tiring'. Yes, she was a marvellous artist, as painter or photographer. And, yes, he was still seeing her – but not as a lover. She was apparently going mad, having hallucinations. She made up stories about having been attacked by men in the street; this was a common menopausal delusion, but she was not yet forty. He and his friends found excuses to see her often just to make sure she did herself no harm. He had even asked a psychiatrist, a Dr Lacan, to see her and he had advised sending her to a mental hopsital where she could be cared for properly (she went for three weeks and seemed to improve). Picasso swore that not only did he not love Dora Maar any more – she did not love him. He had made one last effort to help her, and had promised to go with her to the Midi for a couple of months.

Françoise did not know what to make of this last, and decided to spend her holidays in Brittany. She left Picasso her address but ignored letters which reached her begging her to join him at Golfe-Juan, in an apartment had he rented for her. The months in Brittany made up her mind. On her birthday, 26 November 1956, she went to the Rue des Grands Augustins and restarted the affair.

It was a blissful winter. As she went to and fro with him

to Mourlot's to make his prints she saw more and more evidence that she had crept into his work; one print pleased her more than the others, a portrait of Dora Maar sleeping, while she, Françoise sat and smiled.

Paradoxically, it was a minor disaster which precipitated her deep into his life. The wiring of most French buildings, especially on the Left Bank, looks even now as if it were done by odd-job men; wires wander over the exterior of flats, shops and offices in such profusion that they look like unfinished nets. Electricity still fails in the 'Eighties. Just after the war it was a regular occurrence. On one such occasion, Françoise fell down the stairs at her grandmother's house, and was rushed to hospital where she spent ten days (she broke her arm and elbow). Picasso was frantic, even sent flowers (something he was usually too mean to do), and when she came out of hospital arranged for her to stay with the old engraver, Louis Fort, near the harbour on Golfe-Juan. She made the mistake of asking Geneviève to join her (Picasso, when he came down, frightened the girl away by pretending he was going to rape her), but by the middle of March the whole Picasso establishment was in the Midi dancing attendance on her. She was taken to see Matisse, who flattered her (she was wearing mauve and green, his favourite colours) and said he would paint her portrait.

When they returned to Paris, Picasso was shrewd enough to realize that only a public confrontation with Dora Maar would remove any lingering doubts in Françoise's mind, and he arranged three – one at a restaurant, *Chez Francis* in the Place d'Alma where they lunched together, and twice at the *Flore*. Dora knew what was expected of her and gave him his *congé*, not without a barb worthy of a woman's magazine: 'You don't know how to love anybody.'

By Easter 1946, Françoise was installed as mistress of the Rue des Grands Augustins and even Sabartés became slightly more friendly. Picasso himself was very excited, and set to work to paint the famous portrait of Françoise known as *La Femme Fleur*. After he had made a series of drawings and eleven lithographs, he asked her to sit and talk to him while he worked

– she did not have to pose. As he painted or sat in his high-backed wicker chair, he explained his approach. He began with a recognizable portrait, of a woman sitting on a stool. Then he decided to paint that out and show her standing, with her hair like stylised leaves on a tree, her breasts flowing out of the trunk. Using cut-outs of blue paper, he said he would develop her face, making it a wide oval, continuing the lines already there and making it 'like a little blue moon'. Then he slimmed down the body and the left arm, and moved the right arm until it branched out from the middle of the trunk, ending in an orb: 'a woman holds the whole world, heaven and earth'. There is an account, almost brush stroke by brush stroke, in her memoirs. For two more years he painted her always in more or less the same way, almost like a Lowry figure, with green hair. She was so pleased with the first portrait that she went with him, without a qualm, to see Dora Maar's exhibition at Pierre Loeb's.

At first, she faced with equanimity the prospect of a summer at Menerbes, in the house he had given to Dora. The house itself was delightful, built against a hillside so that the fourth floor was the ground floor at the back; it was furnished in a rather grand style as befitted the retirement home of one of Napoleon's defeated generals. The mornings were spent in idle talk. At noon there was lunch at a local bistro, then an afternoon siesta and dinner at the *Café de l'Union*. It all culminated in a Quatorze Juillet with the local buglers (Picasso was an enthusiastic amateur bugler) blowing the night away.

After three weeks or so, Menerbes seemed less attractive. There were the daily contests with the scorpions which found their way even into their bedroom. Then letters began to arrive from Marie-Thérèse, patient, mute complaints disguised as news about Maia. These made Françoise aware that she was living, after all, in another woman's house. This fact, and the steady streams of billets doux, got on her nerves to such an extent that she told Picasso she was leaving him to take a job as an art teacher in Tunisia (she had had a vague offer of a job there). Picasso was furious. There were rows, in private and public, then a passionate reconciliation. They left Menerbes for the Cap d'Antibes and, a few weeks later, she realized that she was pregnant.

When he heard the news, Picasso was ecstatic. He told her that now she would be a real woman, his woman. He was sure the child would be a boy. He celebrated by offering to paint the Musée d'Antibes, a former château of the Grimaldis which had been turned, half-heartedly, into a museum in 1928; it was looked after, in his spare time, by the Classics master at the Lyçée Carnot in Cannes. Picasso's offer to the curator (who had adopted the forenames Julius Caesar) was to decorate the old castle as some painters had decorated churches – he would be the Michelangelo of the Cap d'Antibes. He swore to dedicate it to Françoise, and they swore eternal fealty in a nearby church.

The news of the 'old goat's latest proof of potency' soon spread throughout the Midi. It was the talk of the Cannes Film Festival. Paul Eluard left the Festival, with his wife Nusch, to see if it were true, and came away with a bookplate he could sell; his poetry and hack work for the Communist Party had always kept him hungry and it was only by clever dealing in fine old books and memorabilia that he was able to live well. André Breton came back from exile in the United States to see if it were true that (a) Pablo had joined the Communist Party, and (b) he was about to become a father again; when he heard that both were true he shouted 'Betrayal!' from the street in Golfe Juan and never saw them again. Women, envious, curious, gushing, were much in evidence offering congratulations. Braque received them cordially, but refused to give them lunch (Picasso stayed until four in the afternoon and burnt the lamb). Tristan Tzara turned up with a Romanian gypsy girl, and enlivened the ménage all day; he alternated between extravagant Byzantine courtesy and loud vulgarity (slapping the gypsy's rump and shouting 'you don't get a good, cheap, clean fuck like this every day'. Picasso said Tzara was still a genius, but bisexual; he believed that Tzara had made queers of his turtledoves in Paris.

On their return to Paris in the autumn, there was a German

comic interlude. Picasso went periodically to the bank, where he had two vaults, one for his own work and one for his collection of Renoirs, Cézannes, Matisses and other masters; he took Françoise with him on this occasion, 'to choose a present for the baby'. Somehow, Françoise got herself locked in one of the vaults, but instead of being worried, Picasso accused her of having done it deliberately, 'to aggravate my stomach pains'. He insisted that she see Dr Lacan the psychiatrist. Lacan, seeing that she was pregnant (and, of course, quite normal), asked who was her obstetrician. She said she did not have one and Picasso that she did not need one – 'all doctors can deliver babies'.

Fortunately, in February, her grandmother wrote asking her to take her to the Midi for the rest of the winter. Picasso raised no objection, even saw them off at the Gare de Lyon. For a week or two, flowers and letters arrived from Paris, then dried up. After a fortnight's silence, Françoise had a phone call from a girl friend who said Picasso was putting it about that he was being ruined by the cost of the pregnancy – teams of doctors had been called in, a clinic taken over and so on. On her brisk return to Paris, Françoise found that the truth was slightly less dramatic. Picasso could have afforded to take over several clinics – in fact, Lacan had engaged an obstetrician, Dr Lamaze, a nurse and a midwife, and had taken a room for her at the clinic in Boulogne.

The baby was born, without problems, and at little expense, on 15 May 1947, and was baptized Claude Pierre-Paul. There were flowers again, but a complaining note was not lacking. Picasso remarked that he had just found his favourite old grey flannel trousers again – out of shape: Françoise had been using them? She said she had, because he had bought her no maternity clothes and the old bags were the only things in the house she could get into. It was time he gave her some money, if only so that she could look after his child decently.

The birth of Claude upset Picasso's court, especially the Spanish and most jealous members of it. Sabartés had grown steadily more friendly, but now saw the baby as a threat to

Picasso's affection for him and as evidence that Françoise had been well and truly installed. Inès and her sister had been cook and chambermaid for several years, and were so much a part of the 'family' that they had appeared in several prints and paintings; Inès, who had a year-old baby of her own, resented the new arrival and neglected it.

When Picasso's wife Olga began to follow Françoise in the street as she took the baby out in his pram, it became obvious that two establishments would be necessary in the future. Françoise confided in her friend that she was determined to spend as little time as possible in Paris and was looking for a way to make Picasso more or less abandon the capital.

The 'way' became a turning point in Picasso's career. One day, as he was complaining of being frustrated in his plan to decorate the old Grimaldi castle, the Ramies accosted him on the beach. They reminded him that a year before he had casually decorated some plates at their pottery – would he like to see the results? He said he would, and began months of hectic activity which made of him one of the most interesting potters of the century, and shifted the centre of his interests away from Paris.

During the previous visit to the Ramies' pottery in Vallauris, Picasso had been more interested in the couple, fugitives from the declining silk industry in Lyon; he had been a weaver, then a works manager, and she a designer, the sort of craftsmen Picasso always found congenial. The two or three plates he had decorated had been done more to please them than for any other reason. When he saw them finished, fired and glazed, he was almost ashamed, certainly dissatisfied, and swore to Françoise that he would make a potter of himself if that was the last thing he did. On their return to Golfe-Juan he went to see the Englishman in charge of a chemical factory there and had himself briefed on the use and limitations of the different enamels. Then he found a potter who taught him how to use the wheel, and worked for a time decorating the objects he threw before they were fired; in a couple of months he was amazing his tutor by taking half-dried clay amphora and twisting them into marvellous shapes, translating some of the ideas he had worked out in sculpture into the new medium. Then he set to work on fired clay or 'biscuit', using the enamels (powdered glass in a holding paste) he had prepared in Golfe-Juan. Françoise went with him to the pottery every day they were in Vallauris and even made one suggestion (to polish the pottery with milk) which proved successful; she was determined to keep his interest alive during the six weeks which passed between the end of the artist's input and the appearance of the finished product.

The Ramies, who saw their fortune being made, were delighted, and Françoise was grateful; she did not know that Madame Ramie was to be as great a 'mistake' as Marcelle Humbert had been for Fernande Olivier.

Picasso was eventually so delighted with what was coming out of the kilns that he scarcely left the South of France that winter: the only other work he did was to complete an edition of twenty poems by Gongora for a publisher in nearby Monte Carlo.

During two of their occasional trips to Paris, Françoise had two other 'warnings' which she did not heed. On a visit to Matisse who was in the capital on business, she heard the story of the arrival of Lydia, his 'secretary', in 1932. At first an unwanted and unpaid secretary, she gradually became an integral part of Matisse's life until one day Mme Matisse rashly gave her husband an ultimatum – 'that girl or me!' Matisse had replied, after a minute's reflection: 'I'll keep her. She saved me a lot of income tax.' Françoise also met a sweet Swiss girl called Annette who wanted to be Picasso's secretary; she was directed to Giacometti who took her on and later married her. But Françoise just laughed at these two incidents, enjoying Matisse's compliments and those of Miró who came to see them several times that winter.

A more immediate threat was Olga, Picasso's wife, who also showed up during those brief visits to Paris, and established herself in Golfe-Juan when she saw that the centre of gravity of Pablo's life had shifted in more than one sense. A stringy figure, with sandy hair and a crinkled face, she bore no resemblance to the ballerina Picasso had painted twenty years and more before. Embittered beyond belief, she would follow Françoise in the street as she pushed Claude in the pram, shouting threats and abuse. Whenever she saw Picasso she would scream that she needed his attention, that they had to talk about their son, a ne'er-do-well like his father, who did not want to work (Picasso had never worked harder in his life). She even forced her way into the house of their friends the Forts and virtually settled herself there every afternoon, announcing to visitors that she was living with her husband again. In the end, Picasso bought a house for Françoise, *La Galloise*, in a large garden; it was far up the hill, at the end of a mile of stone steps, there was no road, and it was well walled and protected.

Unable to reach Françoise in the streets of Vallauris, Olga turned her attention to the young mother as she sat with her child on Golfe-Juan beach, walking over Françoise's hands in her high heels; Françoise dealt with that one by grabbing Olga's ankles and bringing her down flat on her face on the sand.

This constant persecution, and the periodical arrival of a sheaf of letters from Marie-Thérèse, did not improve Françoise's temper, and three months after the move to *La Galloise*, the announcement of Picasso's departure for Poland and a Communist Peace Congress was not welcome either. However, of fortunately for both their sakes, just before Picasso left on his trip, Françoise discovered she was pregnant again.

Françoise had never been so well, physically and psychologically, as when she was pregnant with Claude, and the prospect of another child delighted her. She did not relish the long separation from its father, but she had her own establishment at last and so much could be done without any interference from his staff. Sabartés was pleased to be able to spend more time in Paris, in the tiny flat he lived in with his seldom-seen wife. Inès had time to look after her own child. Marcel had gone to Poland. Apart from the concerns of any housewife, Françoise had some particular problems; she had to try to prevent the gradual transfer of the Paris menageries to *La*

Galloise. There was a brisk winnowing of the birds – parrots, pigeons, a thrush, some turtledoves and other winged gifts. A billy goat which had arrived and was stinking out the house was given away to a passing gypsy tribe. Having de-animalised and disinfected it, she soon had a home to which even her father might have come.

At first Françoise was worried about Picasso's reactions when he returned, but he played into her hands by not living up to his promise to write every day. His excuse was that he had spent too much time quarrelling with the Soviet delegation which abused his work, but this was only part of the truth. In any event, Marcel was given the job of sending a daily postcard signed with the French equivalent of 'wish you were here', or 'Having a wonderful time', not the sort of greeting a pregnant mistress expects from a lover famous for his imagination and creativity. To make matters worse, Marcel, an unashamedly ignorant man, misspelt her name when writing the address.

Pressing home her advantage when the lover did return, stifling his protests about the goat, she drew his attention to the fact that they had agreed to have the baby born at the fashionable Belvedere Clinic in Paris. He would, she hoped, visit her there. Unfortunately he had no clothes other than his working rags and the shabby jackets and trousers (his one English sports coat was twenty-three years old) he wore to discourage borrowers. It was only when he split the seam of his favourite pair of trousers, and it became too hot to hide his bare bottom under a trenchcoat, that he agreed to go to a tailor. To punish her, he made her draw in a painting (*La Cuisine*) of the kitchen in the Rue des Grands Augustins stripped of every-thing except a few birds ('those who escaped the massacre').

Not overstrong on subtlety, he left drawings of the vanished birds and animals everywhere during the months which led up to the birth of their daughter, Paloma, and painted portraits of her as an aggressive flower stalk with a green flocked ball for a head. The day she was due to leave for the clinic, 19 April 1949, was the opening day of the Communist Peace Congress in Paris; she was delivered to the Belvedere after he had been safely installed as the star of the Congress.

The thing which struck Picasso most about the Congress, apart from a lack of the Soviet-set hectoring tone he had heard in Poland, was the ubiquity of what had been baptized his 'Peace Dove'. He had forgotten that the French Communist Party, on one of the many preparatory visits to him at *La Galloise* and in Paris, had asked him for a drawing to use as a symbol for the Congress. He had rummaged among the bird drawings displayed to punish Françoise and handed over an old one of Matisse's favourite pigeon. now the pigeon was everywhere and had become a dove. He was showered with congratulations and when he heard at eight o'clock that evening that Françoise had given birth to a daughter, he rushed to the clinic and announced that she would be named Paloma, the Spanish word for dove. Nobody ever mentioned the bird's parentage again.

It was a pleasant summer, nursing Paloma at *La Galloise*, and Françoise enjoyed some new relationships with women. When they had bought the house, they had had to take over as a sitting tenant in the garage flat an eccentric 'artist' known always as Madame Boissière; the agent had said encouragingly: 'Don't worry. She's very old and half mad. She'll die soon or they will put her away.' She showed no signs of dying, however, and the presence of Françoise with two young children seemed to rejuvenate her. Though she did not like Picasso – 'a bad painter' – she thought Françoise 'promising' and though she moved with difficulty, often appeared in a bizarre Gay Young Thing's outfit to wave at the family in the big house. She refused flatly to be moved into town (so that Marcel could be put in her rooms instead of a hotel in Golfe-Juan) and became an amusing fixture.

Françoise got to know Marie-Thérèse, too, that summer. She always spent the holidays at Juan les Pins nearby and Picasso was a regular visitor. Feeling that it was time she organized these meetings, Françoise suggested that Marie-Thérèse come over so that she could meet her daughter's half-brother and sister. Picasso was not very keen at first, but Marie-Thérèse did not hesitate. She had been in some difficulty recently with thirteen-year-old Maia, who had asked pointedly why her father could spend every day of the week on the beach with his new family and yet was 'too busy' to see her. The meeting of the children was a great success (Maia could 'mother' the two babies) and they remained good friends for years, even adding the first born Paolo to the 'gang'. Françoise and Marie-Thérèse never became friends in the accepted sense of the word, but they came to understand their respective roles in Picasso's life, and animosity vanished; they even took turns to try to keep another woman's child, Paolo, out of trouble with the police as he commuted on his racing motorcycle, with or without a whore on the pillion, between their two summer homes.

In addition to these major encounters, there were long and confidential discussions between Mme Ramie and Picasso about Picasso's pottery. They seemed to be very friendly indeed. Mme Ramie, in spite of her boast that her husband was 'the one who decides everything', had taken over the role of manager as well as designer. She saw very clearly what 'Picasso the potter' really meant and explained it with many a hint and a nod. For the Ramies, the interest he had found in the possibilities and limitations of clay had been the making of their fortunes. Quite apart from what they did for Picasso they were inundated with requests for firings from hundreds of potters, good and bad (mostly bad), who had arrived in Vallauris. They were also making the old Roman town's fortune (the mayor smirked to think that Vallauris meant Valley of Gold), as the streets became lined with 'potteries' and crowded with tourists, creating a spectacle to rival that of Deruta in Italy, another magnet for brightly coloured and glazed rubbish. Mme Ramie knew that Picasso's interest was fading, could not be kept alive in the circumstances, and had correctly assessed the importance of what he had done in terms of 'shape'. As she said shrewdly, he had changed the shape of plates for ever (his predominant form was an irregular oval, rather like Indian *nan* produced by hand in a tandoori oven).

While the women talked, and Mme Françoise became a respected customer at the most enterprising shops (a vogue for all things Spanish had been created), the men found it ever easier to enjoy the most masculine and macho of all pastimes, the bullfight. Perhaps even the word pastime is offensive to the *aficionado*, but time was what the passion consumed, or so the women complained. Françoise learnt that there was more to the business than one or two bulls and a matador. She was not interested in the finer points of working the cape, and all the balletic moves involved, but she was fascinated by the protocol and superstition. Apparently, trimming the nails or the hair on the eve of a *corrida* was ill-advised; Picasso was so obsessed by the need to deprive witches of the raw materials of their spells that he even had his own Spanish barber, Arias, who could guarantee the safe disposal of hair. All the usual indiscretions (opening an umbrella in the house, putting a hat on a bed, sitting down at table in a topcoat) were avoided and a pretence kept up that he did not want to go to the bullfight, that he was being dragged there against his will; this was awkward because tickets for the best places had to be ordered in advance but, fortunately, this superstition was known to the box office and seats were booked in fictitious names for the regulars. Again, the size of the party had to be kept a secret from the evil spirits; this problem was solved by inviting the first person they met on the street on their way to the bullfight to accompany them. Leaving for Nimes (the nearest good arena) had to be done early enough to collect the 'uninvited', inspect the bulls on arrival and (in the case of distinguished guests) discuss their fine points with the bull breeders. Lastly, there was the *paella* lunch, the mountain of yellow rice full of kitchen scraps washed down with enormous quantities of equally indifferent wine.

The only interesting person Françoise met at the *corridas* was a woman bullfighter, Conchita Cintron, who fought on horseback. She resembled Françoise closely, and Françoise was asked for her autograph several times – not as a painter or Picasso's mistress, but as the latest *rejoneadora*.

The only domestic fly in the ointment that summer of 1949

was Picasso's refusal to modernize *La Galloise*. In fact, Françoise made a real mistake by suggesting that he would work
better if he had a studio large enough for him to 'spread himself
out' in a way which was impossible in a house now run as a
home for a family with two children. They settled on a disused
perfume factory. It was ideal. There was enough space to store
the pieces of sculpture, many of them not yet cast, which were
scattered about Paris, and there was one large room which
could be turned into a workroom for both painting and sculpture; Picasso's interest in pottery was waning and could not last
for much longer. But there was no central heating, just the
French equivalent of an early English Aga wood burning stove.
As autumn approached, this meant that Françoise, after the
usual late night, had to bicycle to the new studio and light the
stoves; being old, they did not always catch first time, and then
there was the ash to be disposed of and a bit of tidying up to
do. Back on the bicycle and to a still sleeping household she
went, to light the stoves there, equally primitive Agas. The
children had to be fed and dressed, and Claude sent to the
nursery school, after which it was breakfast for Pablo,
answering his letters and thinking about what to do for lunch.
There were often guests, who might be local notables like the
police chief (who had to be kept on a string to keep Paolo out
of gaol), or friends like André Gide, Tristan Tzara, even Nicole
Vedrès who was trying to persuade Picasso to make a film with
Gide.

When Françoise asked for new heating at home, and maybe
more domestic help, Picasso would complain that she was
bleeding him of all his hard earned money, though he kept a
red leather trunk in the house which never contained less than
five million francs, and he had been for years a millionaire in
dollars. Anyway, he pointed out that when they had had,
briefly, a nanny in addition to their daily Marcelle, the two of
them had come to blows in the kitchen.

It was a hard winter, filming and stoking, even doing a little
painting of her own, but there were compensations. Mean and
eccentric though he was, Picasso was devoted to her and the

children. He took her seriously as an artist, notwithstanding his reputation as a harsh critic even of his friends. She lacked for none of the essentials in life and she had an acquaintance in the French World of art and letters envied by men as well as women. Apart from the eighty-year-old Gide, with whom she got on like a lifetime friend, she now saw a lot of Matisse and Tzara. Tzara amused her, with his apparently endless chain of gossip and ideas. He seemed to have forgotten nothing, especially if it were scandalous, which had occurred since he had left Romania in 1916. Picasso was rather a prude in public, disapproved of women dancing even on Bastille Day, and liked 'proper' dress and behaviour in restaurants ('no bad language, please'), no matter how scruffy and obscene he often was in private. Tzara was maliciously witty and really depraved. Fortunately for the *petit bourgeois*, he spoke so eruditely that his famous description of how the Romanian beauty, Lupescu, had discovered that she had a *caisse noisette*, a 'cunt like a nutcracker', and had trained it on walnuts in Cluj, sounded to the uncomprehending like an American freshman class in rhetoric. And, as Françoise knew, he understood better than most people, the real nature and importance of Picasso's work.

Matisse was Françoise's wise counsellor and father confessor during that winter of 1949–50. He appealed to her in many ways, not least because he was so good at 'managing' Picasso , who hated to be contradicted or even take part in an argument if he thought he might lose. Matisse's long illness had left him semi-paralysed, but he had not stopped work. He was involved (and had been since 1943) in the design and decoration of a Dominican chapel at Vence, though he was not a Christian; he had agreed to make some stained glass windows (the only natural source of light) for the chapel, because his former nurse had become a Dominican nun. Françoise, who had spent some years in a Dominican convent as a schoolgirl, had mixed feelings about the Order. Picasso thought Matisse was 'crazy to get mixed up with such people'. It says a lot for Matisse and Father Coutourier that they overcame the hostility of *La Galloise*, and kept them interested in the project – though when it was finished Picasso said the light was all wrong and made the chapel look like a whore's bedroom. Matisse was not only convincing and a natural peacemaker, he gave confidence to Françoise who had taken up painting seriously again (she had been concentrating on her drawing) to such good effect that Kahnweiler gave her a contract to buy all her work (he had refused to take on Dora Maar). Picasso always pretended to be jealous when Matisse offered to paint her portrait, but at the same time thought it was 'scandalous' that a cripple should surround himself with so many beautiful girls – a woman was safer with a bullfighter, he said.

But Picasso's real or pretended jealousy was a danger signal for their relationship which Françoise did not see. Another warning light should have gone on when he began to show signs of an obsession with female flesh, the quantity and quality of it. The first public showing was at a bullfight, at which a Spanish painter turned up with the Vicomtesse de Noailles. Marie-Laure had put on a lot of weight but had not changed her wardrobe to cope with it; several extra kilos were protruding from above and below her chemise. 'Ah,' said Picasso, 'there is a woman who can give you comfort and excitement.' Then there were letters from Chagall, announcing a visit, perhaps a return to France, from the United States. The painter's arrival was preceded by an enormous lunch prepared by Chagall's daughter (by his first wife Bella), Ida. Françoise remembered later that she had curves everywhere, and practically draped them round her guest like an opulent Russian eiderdown. Like all Spaniards, Picasso thought with affection of even his mother's middle-aged spread, and Ida's breast and thigh overwhelmed him. By contrast, when Chagall did arrive in the South of France he brought with him his second wife, an Englishwoman, Virginia, who was extremely tall and thin and had a skinny teenage daughter, too. Françoise put on a lunch for them and tried to rival Ida's groaning table, without success. The two gaunt Chagalls, who towered over Picasso and Marc, were also food cranks and gave their host a long lecture on how to eat sensibly and glow with health. In the end, Virginia left

Chagall, and Picasso gave Françoise many a wink and nudge, hammering home the point that you could never expect satisfaction or fidelity from a thin woman.

During the winter of 1950–51, there were various references to this timeless topic, immemorialized by Ezra Pound. Françoise was accused of never walking about the house and garden nude, yet 'all painters need to see nudes'; the real reason, as Picasso knew well, why Françoise had to keep her slender body covered for most of the time was that their 'daily', Madame Michel and her husband, were prudes and always complaining even if they saw her in a bikini. In February 1951 came the news that Eluard was to marry again, a girl who served in Madame Ramie's pottery shop, Dominique, who had literary pretensions and had followed him to Mexico after his first wife's death. The wedding took place in June at St Tropez, Picasso and Françoise as witnesses. Dominique was a substantial woman, still young enough to have most of the flesh under control, and she fascinated Picasso; when, soon afterwards, she was taken ill at *La Galloise*, he used to make excuses to visit her in the sick room and eulogize everything he could see, which was quite a lot. Another guest at the wedding was Lee Penrose, wife of Sir Roland, for years his mistress and a model for Man Ray (as Lee Miller she became a Condé Nast photographer). Picasso observed: 'That woman, now, she is the wife of an English milord who bought paintings of mine for nothing. Under that English dress there are breasts like aubergines. I have seen them. They used to drive Man Ray mad, but I don't know if he ever got hold of them.'

Relevant to the old argument of flesh *v.* fire were several visits by members of the French Communist Party hierarchy. Picasso's relationship with the Party was rather strained, since he had done a drawing (from a photograph) of Stalin for one of its back journals, but he enjoyed the company of Casanova and Aragon. He did not enjoy having to entertain the Politburo, whose members usually came *en bloc* so they could spy on each other; they said they would prefer to eat in a restaurant but the workers would not like that, the more so since it would certainly be a good and expensive restaurant. Françoise did what she could to compete with the *Colombe d'Or* and they certainly did her table honour – everything went, washed down by litres of good red wine. Picasso, who ate very little at the best of times, used to look astonished as walking skeletons like Cachin put away kilos of stuff. He theorized that because such men never got fat, the food was metabolized in some mysterious way as part of an attack on capitalism, but like Caesar he said he would rather have around him men (not to mention women) who slept at night.

It was during 1952, in November that he suddenly turned on Françoise and said, as she records in her memoirs: 'You were a Venus when I met you, now you're a Christ – and a Romanesque Christ at that, with all the ribs sticking out to be counted. I hope you realize you don't interest me like that'.

A rather more brutal, if indirect, threat came with the dismissal of Marcel. To anyone with even the slightest acquaintance with the *ménage*, this was an event of dramatic proportions. Marcel had been chauffeur and confident for a quarter of a century. He had seen Picasso through Olga, Marie-Thérèse and Dora Maar to Françoise, and had hurried dozens of young girls to much briefer appointments with fame. He had become a family friend, a trusted servant with even the licence to speak sharply to his master when he thought the occasion deserved it. His master also grumbled at him, of course, accused him of stealing money intended for petrol, even of selling his old uniforms so that he could always have new ones (in fact, Marcel looked as shiny and shabby as his master). Living as he did with another Marcel in town, at Vallauris, he got into the habit of drinking all day when he was not needed at *La Galloise*. One day coming back from a bullfight he scratched the side of the white Oldsmobile during a piece of rash overtaking at 90 miles an hour. It was a portent. A few days later, while Picasso was in Paris, he took his wife out for a drive and smashed up the car against a tree. He was instantly dismissed. When Françoise protested that this was rather harsh treatment for an old friend, Picasso was furious. He reminded her that during a period of harsh foreign currency control he had traded in a painting, now worth $200,000, for that car. Now he would have to buy another, or even take the Hispano-Suiza out of storage and have it put back on the road. In the end, he bought a Hotchkiss and suggested to Françoise that she help him save money by becoming his chauffeur.

It was interfering bureaucracy which put a foolish idea into her head. She made the mistake that millions of women have made, of assuming that if she absented herself her lover's heart would grow fonder, in spite of the fact that Picasso had been hovering about Brigitte Bardot's visible assets at Cannes and was rumoured to be thinking of taking a new interest in the girl with 'the biggest tits in Paris'.

The French Government, trying to cope with a serious housing shortage, had told Picasso several times that he must give up some of his establishments in Paris; the Paris municipality, which seemed to have lost him to the South of France, was offering no resistance, and when André Baylot, a fanatical anti-Communist, became Prefect of Police, that was the end. Françoise offered to help Sabartés remove everything from the apartment in Rue de la Boétie and rearrange it at the Rue des Grands Augustins. Her offer was accepted, and she stayed away for several weeks. It was certainly a relief to be back in Paris and to meet men and women of her own generation, to visit galleries and friends she had neglected for years to look after the father of her two children. She relaxed, and went back to Vallauris at peace with herself.

Her absence, however, did not have the desired effect. When she suggested that she go with Picasso to Paris to do the Christmas shopping, he refused. She was hurt, but they were very busy preparing major exhibitions in Milan and Rome and he showed that at least he valued her cooperation; it was certainly true that nobody knew how to choose from hundreds of works only those which would have the greatest appeal, either as an anthology or as paintings representative of a particular period. There were a few jibes, of course. He had never made much of his Italian ancestry, but suddenly his mother's Ligurian blood became very important. Genoese women, how beautiful they all were (he had never been to Genoa), how kind, how generous, and all beautifully formed. He hinted that he knew a few of them in France, that Charlie Chaplin (they had met in October 1952 in Paris) had recommended them as a cure for impotence in old age. She tried to ignore the jibes and get on with exhibitions.

By the summer of 1953, life at *La Galloise* was only made bearable because of Picasso's repeated absences and infidelities, chronicled by a delighted press. Françoise took advantage of these absences to vent her feelings on the innumerable chairs he had commissioned from Sylvette David and her English fiancé in the hope of getting Sylvette into bed; however Sylvette was virtuous, or her fiancé watchful, and Picasso was left only with a large collection of odd iron frames round which were wrapped felt and rope, not very good for sitting in but good for throwing about to sublimate rage and frustration. The only friend Françoise seemed to have was Maia Walter, who stayed for six weeks that summer and acted as a confidante. There was, in fact, something to confide. On a trip to Paris in the spring to do the sets and costumes for a Janine Charrat ballet, she had met a Greek translator called Kostas who had paid court to her, told her she was wasting herself on that old man, who had never appreciated all she had done for him. A Greek woman poet, Matsie Hadjilazaros, a friend of Picasso's nephew Xavier, played the matchmaker to such good effect that Françoise had promised to think seriously about opening her heart to another man. During Maia's stay, letters from Kostas arrived regularly, urging her to be strong, to make a new life with him for her and the children's sake. Maia did not know what to say. The truth was that after so many years of living with a famous man (not to speak of his talents) it would have been hard for any woman to go to live with a nobody, and an impoverished one to boot (Kostas lived by translating, though he was writing an interminable history of literature). In the end, she told Françoise she must make up her own mind, but be sure she knew she was doing the right thing: her father was not the sort of man ever to forgive.

It was physical rather than psychological weakness which decided the issue. Since the birth of Paloma, Françoise had had a succession of internal bleedings. There was something wrong with her womb and ovaries, and in September she was told by her doctor that she ought to have an operation as soon as possible. When Picasso returned she broke the news to him and instead of being sympathetic (he was, after all, in a sense responsible), he ranted and raved about women always being ill, about the expense of operations in private clinics, and, more important, about his need for her at this precise moment.

There was no point in arguing. She told Picasso that on 30 September she would be leaving for Paris, would be moving into one of the apartments in the Rue Guy-Lusac which he had bought with the proceeds of his forced sales of property, and that she would write when she was better. The children would go with her and start school at the Ecole Alsacienne. She would send them to him for Christmas. He took the news without surprise, and, though she hoped he would relent, said nothing until the cab came to take them to the station. He did not say goodbye to her or to their children. He just stood at the door, shouted 'Merde!' ('Shit!'), and quickly disappeared back into the house.

Ten days later, she heard that she had been replaced.

Jacqueline

'I didn't tell her to go to hell. I told her to go to Sheffield'
(Picasso to Tzara)

Madame Ramie seemed to have taken up procuring for the famous, as a distraction from the rather boring life at her pottery. After her success with Eluard, marrying him off to her salesgirl, Dominique, it is not surprising that she had had her eye on Picasso. She knew that for more than a year before Françoise left, Picasso had been in and out of women's beds in Paris, Perpignan and the Côte; she had passed on the news of this or that escapade to Françoise with malicious glee. Now she had a girl ready to take Françoise's place, her cousin Jacqueline, a divorcée with a six-year-old daughter who had been working in Dominique's place since 1952. By the end of October, 1953, Jacqueline was visiting *La Galloise* every day, never staing too long; as she knew virtually nothing about art, she had to learn as she went along.

At first, Picasso does not seem to have noticed that a siege had begun. He missed Françoise and their children, and anyway he was very busy. He was doing a bit of writing, revising his second play, *The Four Little Girls*, which brought Claude and Paloma nearer to him. He was busy painting panels with which to decorate a small chapel in the town; before they were finally mounted they had to be shown in Milan and Rome. And most important, he started a series of drawings (which grew in number to 180) to be published by Zwemmer in London in 1954, under the title *Picasso and the Human Comedy*. And

Jacqueline was not the only woman at *La Galloise* – Manolo's widow and her daughter had come for an extended stay.

The arrangement between Picasso and Françoise was that the children should spend the school holidays with him, and that they should meet when they felt like it – 'the reward for love is friendship', as he put it. At Christmas 1953, Françoise took the children by train to Cannes, but instead of being met by Paolo (who had taken over from Marcel as chauffeur protem), she found La Ramie at the station; Jacqueline had intercepted her telegram. Madame Ramie seemed to be distraught, begging Françoise not to go to Vallauris to 'upset the poor old man' – she herself would accompany the children and return them to Cannes whenever their mother saw fit to collect them. There was nothing to be done. Françoise went back to Paris, to a painter who was courting her, and returned in the New Year to take the children back from Cannes.

In retrospect, it is easy to see that Françoise made a great mistake. Jacqueline, who saw no way of getting into Picasso's? while Manolo's widow was in residence, was still in a weak position. The 'poor old man' was missing his children and a woman he had lived with for years, a woman who, as a painter, he could talk to (when he wanted to) as intelligently as to Dora Maar. During the three months between the Christmas holidays and Easter, La Ramie and her protégée had time to poison this relationship and, after Manolo's widow went back to Spain, to establish another. Their technique seems to have been simple and direct. They reminded him that Raynal, Léger and Matisse were dead or dying. All the *Bâteau-Lavoir* and *Els Quatre Gats* men were dead, though some of their women lingered on (some, like Pixtot, maintained by Picasso). The time had come for a 'new beginning'. The relicts of the past were all treacherous and unfaithful.

When Françoise went to *La Galloise* with the children at Easter 1954 she found evidence of at least some 'penetration' – the hooks and eyes of some of her dresses were broken, as the plumper Jacqueline had tried to force herself into them to please the 'poor old man'. However, Picasso seemed genuinely glad to see her and she stayed for two weeks, much to *La Ramie*'s chagrin.

When Francoise left at the end of the Easter holidays, another strategem was brought into play. The local blonde, Sylvette Jellinek, with the British boyfriend, was paraded before him again he was again attracted by her, painting a whole series of portraits of what he called his *Anglaise*. Unfortunately the British boyfriend was not prepared to pimp, and the interest faded fast. When Françoise reappeared in July with the children, Picasso was delighted and said, uncharacteristically: 'Now we shall have some fun.' What he meant by this was an endless round of nightclubs after dinner, to bed at dawn and *toujours gai*. He had never been a nightclubber, had never taken his women anywhere, except to restaurants and bullfights, on his own initiative; Eva had taken him to the theatre and he had been compelled to keep this up with Olga; Marie-Thérèse had dragged him to some romantic films and Dora to some worthy Socialist Realist efforts by Communist directors; Françoise had never even asked to go anywhere. It turned out that this sudden taste for the *vie mondaine* had been created, unwittingly, by Tzara who had explained Françoise's departure as the consequence of neglect – 'You never took her anywhere'. By the end of July, Françoise was exhausted, and made an excuse that she had to return to Paris.

Picasso was astonished, but agreed, with one proviso – she must open the first *corrida* to be held in Vallauris. She was a fine horsewoman and anyway she had followed all the negotiations with the authorities to overcome the legal ban on killing bulls in a ring in France. Jacqueline became hysterical. Madame Ramie hurriedly hired a local riding instructor, but the new pupil turned out to have no feeling for equine manoeuvres (those at a bullfight inauguration are quite complicated) and even fell off twice while doing a simple turn. Tears and impassioned pleas were of no avail, and on the day Françoise enjoyed a double triumph.

At that point she could have suppressed her rival, but she seems to have decided that her life with Picasso was over, and left. Jacqueline stepped in quickly and proposed that they should all (Claude, Paloma, her daughter Cathy and the two adults) go to Perpignan. They had been invited by the Comte de Lazerme, or rather his wife, an old flame of Picasso. There would be the seaside at Collioure for the children, and Manolo's widow at Ceret was hoping to see them; Maia, who had been at the *corrida*, would go that far with them before proceeding to Spain.

Jacqueline seems to have consolidated her hold on the 'poor old man' that summer. In the autumn, Françoise had to have another operation, but this time there were no flowers or messages. When she came out of hospital, she was invited by Kahnweiler to spend a day with him at St Hilaire (on the way to Orleans). Picasso would be there so she should bring the children. The day, which may have been Kahnweiler's attempt to bring about a reconciliation, was a complete disaster. After an hour, Picasso took to his bed and accused Françoise of making him ill. He never wanted to see her again, he said. Years later, when somebody reproved him for having told her to go to hell, he commented: 'I didn't tell her to go to hell. I told her to go to Sheffield' (referring to a Communist Peace Congress he had to go to briefly, alone, in 1950).

The sulk lasted for a long time. When his son Paolo had to go into hospital (for a hernia operation, which had serious complications), he was not visited either, and his father haggled over the bill. His excuse was that he had started a new series of variations on the theme of Delacroix's *Les Femmes d'Alger*; Jacqueline's arrival in his life is commemorated by her portrait as one of the plump, bejewelled women in the harem. From all reports, he was unmoved by the news that his wife, Olga, had died of cancer in Cannes, and refused to fulfil a promise he had made to have her buried in the Russian Orthodox cemetery in Paris. His temper was not improved by a meeting with Françoise in Paris at which she told him she had decided to marry a young painter, Lue Simon; his reaction was to throw at her a wristwatch she had given him in happier times. He returned to the South of France, muttering threats.

For Madame Ramie all these were very healthy developments and good for her protégée. Not only was Picasso hooked on Jacqueline, and otherwise fancy-free (Marie-Thérèse had faded out of his life and Dora Maar had propelled herself out of it), he was now unmarried. He had to be brought ashore, landed and gutted so that his enormous wealth would find its proper home. Vallauris, with its associations, was obviously an unsuitable place, and anyway lawyers had found it impossible to invalidate Françoise's legal ownership of *La Galloise*. While the two women looked around, they loaded the drawings and large canvas of *Les Femmes d'Alger* into a van in February 1955 and drove it and its author to the studio in Rue des Grands Augustins where he could be left to get on with it. There were exhibitions to plan as well, and complications with the Communist Party to enjoy with Tzara; the Soviet Union had had to hurriedly cancel their entry in the show at the Maison de la Pensée Française because Shchukin's daughter, in exile, threatened to have them legally sequestered.

In the late spring, *La Ramie* and Jacqueline went to Collioure again to have a look at the castle there; the mayor and local businessmen would have liked to have given it to Picasso in the hope that he would fill it with his work, as he had done with the old Grimaldi castle at Antibes. Jacqueline liked the idea of being a chatelaine, and she liked Collioure – the castle was large enough to store the 'works' safely, too. Unfortunately, the place was in such a state of disrepair that the offer had to be refused. As Olga was now dead, there was no objection to Cannes which, as La Ramie said, was so convenient and full of wealthy art connoisseurs who could keep the francs flowing into the new housekeeping budget. Looking round at that part of town where the hills began to rise sharply, they found a large, Edwardian villa which they knew would suit them perfectly. The rooms were large, well lit, and had high ceilings. It was 'tastefully furnished' and needed very little decoration. There was an iron fence and a little porter's lodge, any unwelcome visitors could be kept away. Picasso was brought down to see it and approved of everything except the 'tasteful furniture'. His new mistress had to bite her lips and fight back her tears as he ordered workmen to take away the solid Edwardian furniture, three grand pianos and some 'elegant' bedroom pieces. Out of store in Paris came all his favourite bric-à-brac, some dating back to the *Bâteau-Lavoir*, and including his English chairs. The floors were covered in ceramic pieces, statues, packing cases full of junk. Millions of francs worth of paintings and drawings were stacked against the walls or hung indiscriminately wherever a nail could be driven into the plaster. A kitchen and a bathroom were turned into litho and engraving rooms. Easels were set up everywhere. When it was time to eat, the dining room table was partially cleared and they ate.

A part of the explanation for this (even for Picasso) chaos was that Jacqueline had demanded a reduction in the size of the menagerie. She had decided to have a kitten and hoped he would choose a few caged birds; he settled for his three dogs and his new goat. The chaos was a warning. They had barely moved in and unpacked when lawyers began to arrive. Maybe unbeknown to Picasso, maybe not (according to Tzara), Jacqueline had stripped *La Galloise* of everything, furniture, paintings, pots and pans, and had given away Françoise's clothes to the local charities. The first Françoise knew of this was when she came back from her honeymoon in Venice that summer to find her home bare (although La Ramie had forgotten the attic where the correspondence was stored). Her husband was not rich and they had planned to spend the winter in Vallauris, having heard that Picasso had gone. They had not been prepared to see everything else go, too, and it was some time before a settlement was reached; in general this was to Françoise's advantage, but she could not prove that Picasso had given her some of the paintings she claimed.

After this unpleasantness, life at *La Californie*, as the new home in Cannes was called, settled down and the stream of visitors, all admiring, did much to calm Jacqueline's fears about the disorder. Knowing there was nothing she could do about it for the moment, she accepted it as 'quaint' and 'interesting'.

She was thrilled to entertain Clouzot, who proposed to make a long colour film about Picasso for next year's Cannes Film Festival, and she found herself the subject of innumerable portraits, always a sign of reassuring semi-permanence for Picasso's women. In a foolish attempt to rival Dora Maar she took up photography, but in the main she was very shrewd in adapting herself to his whims, learning when he needed to be entertained and when to be left alone. She was not very interested in sex – that had been the principal reason for the failure of her marriage – so she did not expect more from a seventy-four-year-old man in her bed than she had any right to. She was a good cook, and like many sexless women, voluptuously attractive. Tzara always felt that she had strong lesbian tendencies, maybe she had been active with La Ramie, but there was no gossip for him to work on: now that Marie-Thérèse did not need his 'protection' he was a frequent visitor, tolerated by Jacqueline because he always left her man in a good humour. He was quite sure that Picasso had her pose erotically, and some of the nude paintings done about this time tend to confirm this.

Inevitably, La Ramie saw to it that he kept her supplied with ceramics to sell in Vallauris. He used some masks and other Polynesian objects left him by Matisse, and his goat, as subjects for his new pots and plates and Jacqueline appears often in profile, rather like a Deruta piece done for the tourist trade. More interesting were pieces of sculpture derived from the beach combing he had taken up again, which came out as dragon's teeth and other wartime repellents for landing craft. Perhaps the most interesting new departure was work in silver and gold (the best pieces are now in the Hakone Picasso Museum in Japan). The silver pieces were mainly massive items of tableware (plates and chafing dishes) and were made in answer to Jacqueline's complaints that they ought to have 'a decent service' – it was bad enough having to struggle to make a place to eat when they had guests. She ought to have been pleased to have a more than 'decent' service, but Picasso missed the point that half the satisfaction is in the possession and half in actually buying expensive things, ideally at a shop one's best friend cannot afford. Writers' wives, she said to La Ramie, when they say they have nothing to read, do not get the reply: 'Hang on, I'll write you something.'

In a way she was also responsible for the excursion into goldsmithing. Perhaps her most important contribution to their association was the care she took of Picasso's health; despite his grumbling she insisted that he have regular check-ups and visit the dentist every three months. He hated dentists and dentistry, the medical airs and graces, the unnecessarily complicated machinery and the soothing chair-side nurses, and he was always afraid of pain. However, he had no alternative but to go, and his powers of observation had not diminished. His child-like curiosity, which Tzara said was more than half his appeal, led him to ask his dentist to show him how the various drills operated and how the gold was worked. He was so intrigued he ordered a set of drills for his own use and, using them, fashioned work which even Dali, no mean jeweller himself, said was exquisite. Jacqueline was given most of the silver and gold, though Maia had several pieces promised for a wedding present.

1956 was to be an eventful year. Clouzot finished the film of the life and work of Picasso and it was shown at the Cannes Film Festival to universal applause; it was noticed by many people who had known him for years that at seventy-five, he was still spry and looked better than he had done for years. Jacqueline enjoyed the receptions and compliments and rashly began to hint that they should marry. He had in fact been thinking of proposing to her, but when she raised the topic he changed his mind and told Tzara she would have to wait another five years, just for asking.

His relations with the Communist Party became strained after the Soviet invasion of Hungary; workers in Warsaw carried his painting, *Massacre in Korea*, through the streets to point the moral that the United States did not enjoy a monopoly of imperialism. With nine other intellectuals and artists he signed a letter of protest to the Central Committee asking that a special

Party Congress be held to explain the brutality of the brotherly Soviet Union, and had his knuckles rapped smartly in *L'Humanité* for 'anti-Party attitudes'. An American newspaperman who had helped Fernande Olivier write her memoirs of Picasso and his friends asked him if he intended to resign from the Party; he got the reply that he was not a 'Political Communist' but supported the party to whom most of his friends and fellow craftsmen belonged, rightly or wrongly, and would keep his card.

Penrose, who was a frequent visitor at this time, describes Picasso as 'the little white-haired man whose black eyes have stirred . . . emotions like a redhot poker sizzling in a pot of mulled wine.' Other visitors thought he had gone 'gaga'. New acquaintances, including some humourless officials from UNESCO trying to persuade him to do a mural for the headquarters building in Paris, were likely to find him in a Stetson, waving a pair of revolvers (gift from Gary Cooper), or a false nose and clown's whiskers (gift from an Italian circus). At the slightest provocation he would show off his non-existent musical skills by blowing a trumpet or beating an African drum. Often strangers and friends alike would have to sit patiently through several performances before they could talk or even eat; Graham Sutherland once had to wait three hours for lunch while the charade was played out. Jacqueline's explanation was that it was Picasso's way of discouraging the unwanted and uninvited, and pointed out that one sure way of putting a stop to the show was to talk of money.

Tzara and Kahnweiler have reported some extraordinary conversations about the 'business point of view' in producing works of art; customers 'don't buy pictures out of pocket money . . . and a picture with plenty of finish will command a higher price'. He said once that he bought Cézanne's *L'Estaque* because it had a good finish and 'would always fetch the highest prices'. He was multiplying *Les Femmes d'Alger* series and putting on a lot of paint because 'that is the way things are going now'. He announced early in 1957 that after Delacroix he was going to tackle Velazquez and 're-do' *Las Menimas*, which he thought would go well: Maia, more or less settled in Spain, was asked to send some coloured postcards of the masterpiece for him to think about.

Tzara believed that the obsession with money was innate but had been encouraged by Jacqueline and her tutor, La Ramie. At the New Year celebrations they talked about nothing else. There was to be a great exhibition in New York which she said 'will bring us enough to buy a chateau' – disappointed at Collioure, she had in mind an establishment in the Loire. He was obviously by now very dependent on her, flattering her when with friends and using almost Tzara-esque language to describe her ample figure, but even these gross compliments had echoes of the counting house. He told some English guests they should fatten up their wives to see them through the Northern winter, but added: 'I know you won't. You English pretend you like thin women, but it is only because it costs less to feed them.'

The UNESCO project was approved, if only because it would, as it were, give him a hoarding ten metres square in a building through which the world's 'official culture' and its representatives would pass. He told Kahnweiler he should set up a stall nearby to take advantage of the publicity. The final effort certainly attracted publicity. It had been done in separate panels like the Vallauris chapel murals but no key to the jigsaw was ever given to Georges Salles (who received on behalf of the organization) and there are still people who think it has been put together wrongly. One of his friends said he thought it was inspired by some photographs of a bridge at Hiroshima, on which the atomic explosion left visible only the shadow of a woman who was passing at the time, and this seems a convincing explanation. At UNESCO, the shadow, with a hint of a skeleton, has been put up so that it hangs head downwards. The 'sky', which should probably be the ground, is white hot as it would be after the blast and the sky above the mushroom cloud has become a blue wave. Picasso refused to answer any questions about it or give it a title, so Salles called it *The Fall of Icarus*. Picasso was probably wise to keep his mouth shut. His lack of any formal education in his youth, and his pathetic attempts at self-improvement often showed embarrassing gaps in his knowledge, even of art, and he had almost certainly never heard of the legend of Icarus.

Jacqueline, whose ever-increasing confidence was reinforced knowing she had taken up with a genius who was not much less culturally backward than she was, returned to the subject of 'a suitable castle'. Apart from her *folie de grandeur* there were sound reasons why they should have a large establishment. It would be a good idea to close down the last establishments in Paris, including the Rue des Grands Augustins, and transport everything to one place large enough for it to be set out and catalogued; the fact was that Picasso no longer knew what he had done all these years, had forgotten many works and even occasionally thought he had painted things which had remained in his sketchbooks. As far as Jacqueline was concerned, she was anticipating the day when the 'poor old man' would die and there would be a battle royal among the women and children to see who could get the largest and most valuable share; the French Government, too, would want an almost astronomical amount of money in death duties, but would take the works of art instead. The matter was really brought to a head that summer in August when, after the bullfight at Vallauris over which he had presided, he announced that he was very tired, that the bullfight would be his last, and that he had decided to stop celebrating his birthday.

Immediately, the search was on. Two of Jacqueline's friends combed the Côte but most of the desirable properties had been bought by the British and Americans; they had even started to build highrise apartments at the back of *La Californie*, which gave her an extra weapon (the need to protect his privacy) in her armoury when the moment came to make the right decision. It was a friend of the Ramies who discovered the old Château de Vauvenargues, with its two thousand acres of land on the slopes of Mont Sainte Victoire, often painted by Cézanne. Picasso was taken there in October, 1958, baited by the name of the painter he admired most, and it was all done in a week. Jacqueline was at last a chatelaine, and told everybody that in happier times her predecessor had been a Marchioness; Picasso was cajoled into doing a portrait with the subscription Jacqueline de Vauvenargues. He was at first quite happy with the place, paid for with his American dollars, and mobilized his friends to get the last of his stuff from Paris, even some of the Cézannes, Gaugins and Matisses which had been in the vaults of the bank. The packing cases at *La Californie* were nailed up again and most things transported to the Château. Jacqueline prevented its transformation into another junk shop by insisting that everything was to be unpacked in the outhouses; the sculpture was left in the driveway or dumped on the terrace, later to be arranged by Henry Moore, where water could splash about them from the fountains. The château had been abandoned for years and had to be completely redecorated, armorial bearings refurbished, the walls whitewashed; this entailed commuting from Cannes, but the weather on the Mont was so bad that it was just as well the new owner was not exposed to the rain, snow and mistral. More furniture had to be bought and Jacqueline spent millions of francs in antique shops nearby, and in Chambéry and Grenoble, in many cases buying back pieces stolen by the caretaking staff and sold there. Tzara had never seen Jacqueline so radiant.

As Picasso began to count the cost of this, Tzara noted that 'his digestion came under pressure'. He tried to work it off by painting furiously during the Spring of 1959, muttering that he had to double the number of exhibits at the forthcoming show in Marseilles if he were to have a crust of bread to eat; he always worked best under pressure, and many of the still lifes and portraits are full of splendid light. By the middle of May he felt he had done his bit and as the catalogue of an exhibition of unsold paintings from Vauvenargues noted in 1962, did only four more works before his departure for the Côte on 24 June, 1959, and only five more in 1960 and 1961. More exhibitions at the Galeries Leiris, in New York and in London, soon replenished the bank accounts and paid for lengthy stays on the Côte and ever shorter periods 'at home' in the Château. His mind was kept off the expenses by a stream of visitors from

Spain. Like Jacqueline they were worried that he might die without making provision for a major, permanent show of his work at least in Barcelona – they knew he would never give his permission to establish a museum in the capital. Picasso himself suggested the old house of the Pixtot family at 20 Calle Montcada, but for some reason the authorities preferred the Aguilar house in the same street, where the Museu Picasso was eventually established. In Málaga the miserly local authorities took a year to debate the advisability of a plaque on the wall of the building in Plaza de la Merced where he was born, and a small collection of *objets d'art* and memorabilia donated by Sabartés.

It was the beginning of a new Spanish period, heralded by the dismissal of most of the French staff of the Château and their replacement by indigent, highly recommended Spaniards. As it was very tedious for a foreign visitor to get up to the Château it became urgent to find a new home; *La Californie*, half emptied of furniture, could not put them up and anyway speculative builders were accelerating the pace at which they were surrounding the house with high-rise flats. Jacqueline was also afraid that more time spent at Vauvenargues would increase the size of the menagerie; a Dalmatian had joined the other dogs, cats, owl and caged birds which seemed to appear mysteriously whenever she was absent, consulting the Ramies on her next move.

The Marseilles and Tate Gallery exhibitions (1959 and 1960) and some large sales at the Leiris provided some unexpected funds and an estate agent in Cannes thought he had found a buyer for *La Californie*. On a drive in January, 1961, Jacqueline and Picasso stopped for lunch at the Hotel Vaste Horizon in Mougins, where he was given a warm welcome. The landlord, in casual conversation, said that an old farmhouse on the top of the hill was for sale: its only neighbours were occasional visiting priests at the nearby chapel, Notre Dame de Vie, which had given its name to the farm and the olive groves around it. After lunch, a large party drove down from Mougins and up the hill to the property, which, Picasso said, was just what he had been looking for; before they left he gave instructions for negotiations to begin about price and guarantees that the mayor would discourage all invasive building. Euphoric, perhaps because he had found what really is a beautiful house, perhaps because he had had more wine than usual, he said to Jacqueline, abruptly: 'I suppose we ought to celebrate by getting married.'

This was really the high point of Jacqueline's career, and next day she rushed over to Vallauris to give the Ramies the good news. Realizing that Picasso could change his mind without giving any reason, they went in a body to see the Communist mayor and give notice of the marriage. Part of the deal, which involved overlooking some bureaucratic formalities, was that Picasso's eightieth birthday should be celebrated in his town, Vallauris, and once he had been assured of this the mayor gave his approval and promised absolute discretion. Armed with an official invitation from his 'Comrade', Jacqueline sped back to *La Californie* to get Picasso's signature; he could not refuse. On 2 March, 1963, the marriage took place and somehow was kept secret for fourteen days.

Having taken the decision to mark his eightieth birthday year with a memorable event, he threw himself wholeheartedly into the preparations for his party. There were more bureaucratic complications when he insisted on a *corrida* as the centre-piece for the celebrations, with his friends the matadors Domingwin and Ortega killing and dedicating bulls to him – this is still illegal in France – but the mayor said he would overcome them somehow (Picasso was pleased to be able to embarrass Paris, since 1958 in the grip of De Gaulle, whom he disliked intensely). Invitations were sent out to friends, and a long list of suggestions flowed from them as to who should perform – singers, dancers and musicians from all over the world. Derigon, the Mayor of Vallauris, did virtually nothing for six months except organize the show, and put pressure on the Party (successfully) to have Picasso awarded the Lenin Prize in the 1 May list.

The curtain-raiser to the party was a Music Festival in Nice on the Saturday. Though he had been up until the early hours,

Picasso with Jacqueline (in a mock Spanish costume) was ready for a ceremonial drive to Vallauris, arriving just after eleven; he enjoyed the motor cycle police escort as much as anything. After a civic reception, the couple went arm-in-arm to see an exhibition of some fifty of his paintings put together by friends; for Jacqueline it was the first time she had seen most of the works on show, and for her husband it was often a revelation, too, as he had forgotten many of them. Then it was down to the seaside for lunch and back up to Vallauris for the illegal *corrida*, at which four bulls were killed and dedicated to him. In the evening, the whole party of several hundred guests moved down to the Palm Beach Casino in Cannes, where another reception, fireworks and general drinking and conviviality went on until Monday morning. Picasso seemed to be as fresh at the end of it all as he had been at the beginning; as soon as he was back at *La Californie*, he kissed his bride and disappeared into his studio for two days.

In addition to his 'imitations' – after Velazquez came Monet and Raphael – he found a new enthusiasm for sculpture. There were two external stimuli for this. Nearby there was a small ironworks, making tubes and sheet-iron and rods for reinforced concrete. The owner, Lionel Prejger, a cultured man who was intrigued by his famous neighbour, once asked him to define Cubism. He was shown a sheet of paper with what seemed a confusion of lines on it. Picasso said: 'That is a chair, or rather what a chair would look like if a steamroller ran over it. Cubism always looks for what things might be or are invisibly. Watch this.' Then he took a pair of scissors, made some quick cuts and folded along the lines to produce a chair. Prejger said that if he could do that with paper, he could do it with sheets of iron, and the casual meeting led to sheet-iron transformations of old and new drawings and models. As the iron would rust in its natural environment, out of doors, Picasso painted the new sculptures and gave them an extra life. The other stimulus was a meeting with a young Norwegian, Karl Nesjar. This meeting took place in 1962, when Picasso drew a sequence of Catalan dances as a frieze for the new Barcelona College of

Architecture. The group of young Spanish architects who had begged him to do the drawings were faced with the problem of getting the drawings cut into the band of concrete left for them on the façade of the building; to chisel them out would take years, even if they could find the craftsmen. Suddenly the Norwegian appeared with a new sandblasting tool and did the job in record time. When he saw the photographs of the inauguration in April, 1962, Picasso insisted on meeting Nesjar, who became a family friend (he was doted on by Jacqueline and La Ramie, which was no hindrance to his rise). Kahnweiler was also impressed and commissioned a version of the *Woman with Arms Outstretched* for his garden at St Hilaire. The original sheet-iron sculpture by Prejger was done this time in reinforced concrete with a shirt of pebbles inside the smooth surface. Nesjar blasted this surface concrete off as he drew out Picasso's original project and this became the first of many 'Nesjar-Prejger' couples of interpretations of their friend's ideas. Henry Moore, who had persuaded the authorities in London to show Picasso's sculpture in the Battersea Pleasure Gardens, hoped to get commissions for a series of these for the capital, but no money was forthcoming from les *Anglais*.

By the Spring of 1963, word of this new, almost totally absorbing, interest in sculpture had spread. New York commissioned an enormous head (it turned out to be Sylvette) for the Columbia University environs, and the Swedish Government a large figure for the entrance to Kristinehann Harbour to rival the Danish mermaid. In May, Penrose was approached by a group of architects in Chicago who wanted a statue by Picasso for the new civic centre piazza. They brought with them when they arrived, uninvited, in Mougins, a portfolio of photographs and 'artists' impressions', including details of the height of the surrounding buildings. Picasso enjoyed playing with these, and making little models of the civic centre in clay, but he would say neither yes nor no to the project. He had also been in touch with representatives of the cities of Marseilles and London, and had been as noncommittal with them. Jacqueline said his sulks were due to a feeling he had that he was being taken for granted. Anyway, he had no new ideas and was going through a crisis of identity, gripped by the fear that he was now copying himself.

All new projects were suspended in 1964, a year Jacqueline described as his worst for 'disasters': 'He was unspeakably saddened by the death of Tristan Tzara, even more than I had seen him saddened by the deaths of Matisse and Leger. For months afterwards, he often did not speak to me from one day to the next.' Jacqueline herself, one of the most chauvinistic of all Frenchwomen, had not liked Tzara very much, but she had put up with him, even welcomed him, because he was the only person who could be relied upon to put Picasso in a good mood in any circumstances. Marie-Thérèse wrote a series of long letters to her former lover, saying how distressed she was at Tzara's death, and how she understood his feelings. She could no longer think of living in Paris at the flat on Boulevard Henri IV Tzara had helped to decorate, and was moving South for good. Jacqueline was not particularly pleased to hear this, but her husband seemed relieved to hear that somebody from the past was not too far away (Marie-Thérèse went, in fact, to Menton and not to Juan Les Pins). In 1964, another ghost from the past came to haunt the house. One of the Chicago architects brought with him, on another uninvited visit, a copy of a book Françoise Gilot had written with the American journalist, Carlton Lake. The ten years of stormy life together, remembered vividly by Françoise (helped by the letters and diaries she had saved at *La Galloise*), made *Life with Picasso* a best-selling and controversial book. Picasso was not pleased, especially with the dedication 'To Pablo' (removed when the French translation appeared), but all the members of the Ramie clique were furious. *Paris Match* thought it was an exciting book and published long extracts. Penrose thought it was 'in bad taste'. Pignon said: 'Picasso never talked the way he is reported to have done . . . it is grotesque.' Unwisely, Picasso was urged by Jacqueline and the Ramies to take action to stop the publication of the French edition, and try to mobilize public opinion in Britain and America to suppress the original in English. The action failed.

The controversy about *Life With Picasso* was to drag on for years, which is perhaps surprising. The book is no more malicious than could be expected from a woman who bore a man two children only to see him marry someone else, and it is bright, lively and full of anecdote. As an account of the daily life of a great artist it has some historical value; the words create an atmosphere, as Dora Maar's photochronicles do. Perhaps Picasso had become an institution, and therefore 'ought to be immune from the slightest criticism'.

The only bright spot that year was the unforeseen success of an exhibition of 160 paintings in Japan, in the old and new capitals Kyoto and Tokyo, and in Nagoya (it was even visited and praised by Mikoyan). Photographs of the crowds, and of the splendid settings of the exhibitions, intrigued Picasso to such an extent that he wrote to the Japanese Embassy and asked for everything they could send him on Japanese art – an odd letter in the tone of a schoolboy asking for a statesman's autograph. He recalled that he had been given some Japanese paper (*washi*) during the war, which had excited him so much he had not dared to use it. When an immense quantity of books of reproductions of paintings, statues and calligraphy arrived, it kept him busy for weeks. He was very taken by the calligraphy and bought some brushes to try for himself some of the techniques which were explained to him. It was this exhibition which sparked a continuing interest in Picasso's work and eventually led to the establishment of the Hakone Picasso Museum.

By the Spring of 1965 he had recovered his good humour sufficiently to welcome the delegation of architects from Chicago (they had been coming and going in relays since 1963 but had not got past the door). One fine, warm day in May he produced his model (maquette) for the piazza sculpture. It was a head composed of a central strip of metal (the profile) and rods connecting it to other sheets of metal suggesting a complicated hairstyle. The spaces were as eloquent as the metal strips and rods. Picasso seemed to be experimenting with the siting of the head as he sent for Prejger's foreman, Thiola, and had him make some arms to attach to the head, arms which were supposed to dangle in a pool in the new piazza; everybody had to view this from upstairs, from all sides, and lying prone on the gravel. Then he tired of the joke and said the head was to be set on a low pedestal, almost on the ground itself (it was magnified many times and eventually unveiled in 1967). He was offered $100,000 as a fee, but refused it, saying it was a gift. He had enjoyed making the head, and enjoyed even more keeping them waiting. London and Marseilles never got their statues because they sent nobody to be teased; some time later Marseilles got a small sandblasted statue for a school playground because he said it was not right that one of the world's great gangster capitals should have a statue and the other one remain without.

The year ended with a bout of bad health, and an operation on his gall bladder in December, 1965. The American Hospital insisted on doing the operation in return for his generosity to Chicago and it was a success (he was booked in as Mr Ruiz). However, it left him very tired and for the next three years he was a semi-recluse. Jacqueline kept all visitors away, except for a restricted number of old friends who were allowed an hour or two once a month, at most, and he pottered about, mumbling and playing with the animals. Perhaps the most important work he did at this time was a series of engravings (twelve on copper plate) to illustrate a play, *The Burial of the Count Orgaz*, which he had written ten years before. The text and the engravings were published by Gilli in Barcelona, and it was while he was correcting the proofs in 1969 that another arrow from Françoise's bow struck him – his son Claude started an action in the French courts to decide exactly on what basis his share of his father's wealth should be apportioned. 'Just as if I'm dead already,' he said to Jacqueline. 'We must show them. We will have a great exhibition and I will help to set it up.'

The idea of a major exhibition with the old man directing it excited the whole art world, and many cities offered to stage it. Barcelona and Avignon were the favourites, and eventually

Avignon won, for the simple reason that it was nearer. Christian and Yvonne Xervos came to see him and offered him the Palais des Papes; Yvonne died shortly afterwards, but Picasso and her husband set to work to plan the show, in the Saint Clémentine chapel and the rooms which give off it. Somehow he completed over 150 canvasses (many of them had been half finished for years) in time for the exhibition and added fifty drawings – 'We must show new work, or Claude will convince them that I am dead or paralysed'.

This spasm of work may have been prompted by displeasure, but it was a great relief to Jacqueline to have her husband cheerful and hospitable again. All the old gang, including *les Anglais*, were soon at the door, offering to help to transport the canvasses to Avignon, to hang them, to photograph them (Douglas Cooper and Mario Atzinger). Picasso decided not to frame the paintings, but just to attach them to the bare walls in a rough chronological order (as far as he could remember it) as if he were opening the pages of his diary for the public to read.

The exhibition was a great success ('magnificently obsessed with sex', said Emily Genauer in the *New York Post*), though saddened by the death of Christian Xervos. It is a pity Tzara was not alive to sum up the colourful display of hundreds of big, ripe breasts, open, welcoming thighs and hairy slits, not to mention the painter slapping colour on his model with his penis. It was a better proof of the old man's mental vitality than the huge tapestry, from a collage made in 1937, which was delivered that summer (in June 1970) with apologies for the delay. He celebrated this extraordinary year by giving to the new Museu Picasso in Barcelona all the artifacts his dead mother and sister had kept about them, a priceless collection of paintings, drawings, early ceramics and personal memorabilia, which still forms the heart of the Barcelona collection.

He decided to make his ninetieth birthday last for the whole of 1971. At first he planned to open up the Château and hold the festivities there, but his doctor forebade it – for most of the year Vauvenargues would be cold and damp, and the plan was as near to suicide as made no matter. Mougins was redecorated, the cellar restocked, and the word sent out that old friends would be welcome; in spite of his pleading this did not include Marie-Thérèse or Dora Maar, and he, reluctantly, decided not to see his children. All sorts of people drifted out to Mougins, stayed for a few days, and moved on. Publishers like Skira, Brassai and his wife, painters, *Anglais*, greedy gallery proprietors and museum curators, all crunched across the court-yard and were royally entertained. The old man was on good form, though he said to Brassai, 'I have had to give up fucking and smoking since I turned ninety, but I still think about them'. Skira said he was going to reissue the *Metamorphoses* and call it *The Metamorphoses of Picasso*, and Brassai brought a copy of a new edition of his *Conversations With Picasso*. Jacqueline resented the latter because part of the case against Françoise had been that the old man never made long monologues but spoke only in one-liners (not, of course, true), but she put a brave face on it and set the new book on a shelf with the other homages.

What little remained of Picasso's life was in a way an anti-climax. The Mayor of Avignon had exacted a promise that there would be a new exhibition in 1973, and over two hundred works were completed in time for that. Drawings and engravings for Leiris multiplied, but there was nothing of great importance in all this. For the last six months in his life, Picasso was deaf, and angry because he was unable to hear his birds sing. On 8 April, 1973, the great heart reluctantly stopped beating.

Paolo staged the funeral. Jacqueline wanted a great State occasion like the funeral of Braque, but as her stepson explained, Braque was a war hero and a Frenchman – her husband had fought in no wars, and was still a foreigner in France. In any event, his father had wanted a peaceful retreat to Vauvenargues. Having closed up the chapel of Saint Séverin, the dead man's wish was that he should be buried at the foot of the steps in front of the house. He had not calculated that the steps were set into solid rocks, and the day before the burial, men with pneumatic drills broke the silence, in a snowstorm, as they struggled to make a hole for the coffin. In a rare moment of acute observation, Marie-Thérèse said that it was a scene which could be easily fitted into *Parade*.

Epilogue

'Picasso? I've known him for years. I think he's great, a phenomenon apart, but you can't say he's a great painter. Even if there's something weird and mysterious about everything he does, there is something about him which is very attractive. It is as if he had the key to a room full of things only he ever saw, then throw away that key, and that's it. The only thing he never really tried is painting. Being outside painting altogether, he could never be the leader of a 'school', and so the so-called Picassians make me fall about laughing, because how on earth can you copy something which, in a way, never existed?'

(de Chirico)

History and literature sometimes offer strange analogies and parallels. I read once about a fishing port, a left-wing rotten borough, a place without art or aristocracy, on the periphery of national life, which had had one moment of glory in the past, during a siege centuries ago: ' . . . the nineteenth century in its miserable aspect, where the buildings are all peeling, the communal watertaps drip, the paintings are rotting in the gloomy churches.' (Mary McCarthy). It might have been Hull. But it was not Hull. It was Chioggia.

Similarly, Antonia Fraser writes of a man dominated by his wife ('The only thing that worries their friends is if she should die before him'), a man of uncertain temper, adolescent in senility, who 'never outgrew the habits and expectations of his youth, and to everyone but his wife could be formidable.' She

217

is writing of the Duke of Windsor, but the portrait could well be of Picasso seen through the kitchen window, especially when she adds that in age his face was wistful, and that he never accepted advice.

In his last years, Picasso (like the Duke of Windsor) often seemed to be a living caricature of undeserved fame. He snapped at Penrose, who was grovelling before him trying to get endorsement for an 'official' biography: 'If you ask me the wrong questions, I will give you the wrong answers.' In Picasso's case, as de Chirico suggests, he deserved fame, but for reasons other than those usually given. He was probably not a great painter, sculptor or potter, but he was certainly a great innovator, always bubbling over with ideas even if they were not his own, like ones of those amiable eccentrics Aubrey seemed to meet at every street corner. This seems to me to be his most outstanding characteristic, more endearing even than his ability to make a fortune out of art, or to keep cheerfully churning out the stuff ten hours a day.

Picasso's women were responsible for keeping the ideas bubbling. His mother, it seems to me on reflection, probably had the idea of his becoming an artist, notwithstanding his father's lack of commercial success. Of course, she did not want him to become a 'dirty' artist, with a messy studio and controversial attitudes. Probably, she hoped he would settle down, after sowing a few wild oats, to being a member of the Art Establishment, with a stiff white collar and an Iberian billycock hat, like one of the innumerable *professori delle belle arti* to be seen hanging round the Venetian Biennials. His obvious talent as a draughtsman would be no great disadvantage; he could always have done respectable street scenes and interiors, to be collected later in the sumptuous volumes handed out, free, by Latin local authorities and savings banks to past and future *clientes*. There was always something of the 'well known local artist' about him, though he enjoyed the mess in his studios, not to mention controversy. Maria's insistence that he should settle down as soon as possible with a local girl drove him to the passionate friendship with Casagemas, and, after

Casagemas, to the morbid introspection of the Blue Period, with its typically Spanish preoccupation with death and disease. In some ways, the work he did at this time was his best. He accepted his poverty as only Spaniards and Italians can, as the natural condition of man and not something to be ashamed of; later on, as he became rich and fell under the influence of the worst sort of *Anglais*, he fleshed out all the skeletons.

Like Peter Sellers' mother, Maria Picasso did not give her son an identity, but merely made him realize that he was without one, and had better take or borrow one. Fernande Olivier, when she met him, noted his clumsiness, but also his hands, 'the hands of a woman, beautiful hands but neglected'. He was 'part-Bohemian, part common working man in his dress', and had restless, staring eyes. There were, however, touches of 'respectability', the carefully brushed hair over the shabby jacket, to say nothing of the matching underwear, like the foremen at a Neapolitan municipal dog kennel hinting at a Dongiovannesque past.

Fernande really went to work on him. By pandering to his feeling of inadequacy and analysing his talent, she very nearly turned him into the *professori delle belle arti* of his mother's dreams. She cleaned up his studio and tidied his mind. The basic education he had neglected in Spain she gave him at the *Bâteau-Lavoir*. His pride was not hurt because he got it in French, and like the devoted schoolma'am she was, she convinced him that he had the makings of an intellectual. She was responsible for the saleable charm of the Rose Period, and her careful choice of acquaintances assured them of solvency, even prosperity, by the end of her regime. One interesting consequence of this rapid advance was that he was able to ignore critics; he did not need those who would have used him to make money and reputations for themselves, though unfortunately he was unable to understand those who might have helped him to be more coherent. The money coming in regularly made it possible for him to experiment with what came to be known as Cubism, and secured his future fame and fortune. Unfortunately, Fernande did not know when to stop. He tired of the schoolroom and used her two weaknesses, for hats and perfume, to accuse her of extravagance.

Eva never tried to teach him anything. She was undemanding and economical. Though she introduced him to the theatre, she seldom paid for the tickets; these were supplied gratefully by the Futurists and other avant-garde playwrights, desperate to fill the empty seats. She put away his money in the warm, dark vaults of banks and helped him to avoid paying taxes. He owed to her his brief career as a costume and scenic designer (after her death) and his introduction to the Classical Art of Greece and Rome. Had he not met Cocteau and gone to Rome, he would never have met his first wife.

It is difficult to see what Picasso gained by his reluctant marriage to Olga, or even why he married her. perhaps it was because she was the first woman who had ever suggested it. Perhaps she reawakened in him his mother's desire that he should become a *professore delle belle arti*, with a *vie mondaine*. Tzara, who liked to try to find some good in everyone, once observed to me that at least she had put an end to his unsuitable flirtation with Classical Art, and in the late 'Twenties 'inspired' some of his most horrendous works, some of them rivalling in nastiness those of Hiëronymus Bosch. This seems to be a high price to pay for the unhappiness (while they were living together) and the harassment (after they had separated). She hung around his neck like a millstone for over thirty years, and, in the person of their unsatisfactory son Paolo, he was never really rid of her.

Perhaps Picasso's life in an émigré Russian hell prepared him for the most important relationship in his life. At first he took Marie-Thérèse at Tzara's valuation. She was a safety valve through which to release his frustration, but, of course, as he soon realized, no ordinary safety valve. He could never get her out of his system. He hated to write letters, and even boasted, of being a bad correspondent, but until the last week of his life, as his daughter Maia told me, he took time to write a few lines in answer to the pages of love, '*Readers Digest*' philosophy and drivel which she sent him. Very few people ever wrote to him, except on business. She never asked for anything, which is perhaps why she was not seen as a threat by greedier companions.

What did Marie-Thérèse give to him, other than, for a few years, some sexual satisfaction? The visible impact on his painting was tremendous. Frank Elgar notes that 'the straight lines gave way to long, supple curves, abbreviated artifacts were filled out in arabesques and the colours on the palette became lustrous and heavy with sensuality' (*Picasso*, F. Hazoo, Paris 1974). This super woman, archetypal Venus, overflowed into every angle of his life, occupying them all. He was still sthinking about the miracle of it as death approached and it was not by chance that he settled on a sculpture of this period to surmount his tomb.

Tzara, at first dazzled by her beauty, came to respect Marie-Thérèse and marvelled that everybody liked her. He rated her greatest achievement that of introducing religion into the Picasso *pensée*. Like Madame de Pompadour, Picasso was essentially irreligious. As Nancy Mitford put it, 'not one of those who, believing in God, are kept away by some weakness of the flesh . . . [he] simply did not grasp the meaning of religion'. Somehow Marie-Thérèse, who had every weakness of the flesh, exhaled a comfortable Faith and we owe to her Picasso's few, but remarkable, Catholic perhaps more than Christian paintings.

Dora Maar was undoubtedly a positive, though minor, influence on the oeuvre. She woke up his mind for a while, but he soon tired of intelligent conversation. She certainly revived his interest in photography and a recent publication by the San Francisco Museum of Modern Art is a salutary reminder of her importance in the history of this craft. She came too late into Picasso's life to take the place of Gertrude Stein as a literary mentor, though she tried to revive his interest in Surrealism. She made her presence felt physically, and we owe to her startling appearance and immense vitality the most arresting portraits he ever did. Tzara recorded only one memorable saying from Dora, and that was a quotation from Rimbaud;

after a particularly sloppy performance by Picasso (he did not say which), she observed: 'So much for the wood when it discovers that it is a violin.'

The relationship between Picasso and Françoise Gilot always puzzled those who knew them well. At times he seemed to be extremely irritable and dissatisfied with life at the side of an attractive, well-educated young girl with a real talent for painting; some people said unkindly that she had too much talent, that she was a better painter than her lover. At other times he was full of tender solicitude, and there is no doubt about his feelings at the birth of their son Claude (1947) and their daughter Paloma (1949); his portraits of the children with their mother are exquisitely tender. It was said they often quarrelled about money, and certainly he became even meaner than ever: Tom Keating tells of an incident at a café in Vallauris when Picasso sold a tablecloth he had been doodling on to two Americans for three thousand pounds, although Françoise never had a wardrobe of decent clothes. However, something kept them together for ten years. Perhaps it was because they seemed to outsiders to have turned life itself into a work of art; she spread his energies widely over painting, etching, sculpture and photography, interested him in pottery, gold and silver smithing. Their home in Vallauris was always bustling with artistic activity, as if it were all being staged for a visiting film or television company. Keeping him moving seemed to be the objective Françoise had set herself, and in her 1987 Retrospective at the Picasso Museum in Antibes her own paintings of the period are full of this restless creativity. It is a pity she did not hang on a little longer and collect her reward – the legal status of a wife and the legitimization of their children.

Even after Françoise had walked out on him, Picasso kept on the move. He had tried almost everything, Naturalism, Expressionism, Classicism, Romanticism, Realism, Abstraction, and back again to Naturalism; as Frank Elgar says, 'Grace alternating with horror, elegance with monstrosity'. Jacqueline presided over the last spasms of this frenetic activity, pandering to his deviousness, rudeness and senility. Tzara, who was once attacked by the goat Esméralda at *La Californie*, said that the menagerie was typical of a man in his dotage, and admired Jacqueline's patience. Sometimes that patience wore thin, and as the years passed her tongue and facial features became sharper. He took his revenge by painting her into his reworked Spanish Masterworks as a bilious nanny, but he could not do without her.

Indeed, the same could be said about all the women with whom he had lasting relationships – he could not do without them. Far from offering the world of art a strong, dynamic leadership, he was a rather weak man who liked to have his private life ordered for him; sometimes he rebelled, violently or sulkily, but he always either came to heel, or changed his woman for another. Compromise was not in his nature. One thing he shared with women in general – he was a born actor. He played the role of the artist to the end, eyes blazing, gestures violent, and even tried to play the role of the genial host and man about the house. But he died in the arms of the wife he called Mother. Maria Thérèse survived him for only a year, but his portrait of her still watches over him on his tomb.

BIBLIOGRAPHY

Apollinaire, Guillaume. *The Cubist Painters*, New York, Wittenborn Schultz

Blunt, Anthony. *Picasso: The Formative Years: a study of his sources* London. Studio Books, 1962

Brassai (trans. Francis Price), *Picasso and Company*, New York, Doubleday, 1966

Breunig, L. C. (ed). *Apollinaire on Art*, New York, The Viking Press

Cirlot, Juan Eduardo. *Picasso: el nacimento de un genic*, Barcelona, Gili, 1972.

Daix, Pierre, *La vie de Peintre de Pablo Picasso*, Paris, Seuil, 1977

Daix, Pierre, Boudaille, G. and Rossellet, J. *Picasso: the Blue and Rose periods*, Neuchatel, Catalogue Raisonée Idées and Calandes

Daix, Pierre, *Picasso*

Daix, Pierre and Boudaille Georges. *Picasso: 1900, 1906.* Catalogu Razo Nado, Barcelona, Blume, 1967

Fry, E, *Cubism*, NY OUP

Fioux, C, *Maiakovski Par Lui-Même*, Paris, Seuil

Gilot, Françoise. *Life with Picasso*, McGraw-Hill, Nelson, Penguin 1964

Janis, Harriet and Sidney. *Picasso, the recent years*, Garden City NY Doubleday, 1946

Jung, C. G. *Collected Works*, Routledge and Kegan Paul

Kahnweiler, D. H. *The Rise of Cubism*, trans. Aaronson, New York Wittenborn Shultz

Lindsay, J. *Four Poets*

Museu Picasso, *Picasso: catalogo de pintura y dibujo*, Barcelona juntament de Barcelona, 1985 ed. en Catalan

McGully, M. *A Picasso Anthology*, London, Thames and Hudson, (Arts Co)

Olivier, Fernande. *Picasso and his friends*, Paris 1933, Heinemann 1964

Otero, Roberto. *Forever Picasso*, New York, Harry Abrams 1974

Palau I Fabre, Josep. *Picasso I Els Seue Amics Catalans*, Barcelona, 1971

Palau I Fabre, Josep. *Picasso Vivent*, Ediciones Poligrafa, Barcelona 1980

Parmelin, Helene. *Picasso Plain*, London Secker and Warburg, 1963

Penrose, R. *Picasso, his Life and Work*, London 1958

Penrose, R. *Scrapecok*, Thames and Hudson

Sabartés, J. *Picasso*, NJ Prentice Hall 1948

Sabartés, J. *Picasso* Documentes Iconographiques Geneva

Severeni, Carra, Prampolini ecc. *Cinquanto Disegni di Pablo Picasso* Novara 1943

Tzara, Tristan, *Picasso Colmes de Picasso*, Paris 1935

Tzara, Tristan, *Picasso et la Connaissance de L'Espace*, Paris 1947/1948

Tzara, Tristan, *Picasso et la Peinture de Circonstance*, Paris 1952

Tzara, Tristan, *Picasso et la Poésie*, Paris 1953

Tzara, Tristan, *La Rose et le Chien*, Paris 1938

Tzara, Tristan, *A Haute Flamme*, Paris 1955

Tzara, Tristan, *Oevres Completes/Presentation et Annotation par Henry Bear*, Paris 1980

Tzara, Tristan, *Picasso et les Chemins de la Connaissance*, Paris 1948

Tzara, Tristan, letters and notes, interviews in the possession of the author.

Abetz, Otto, 9, 165
Addington Symonds, John, 12
Apollinaire, Guillaume, 47-8, 55, 56, 57, 60,
    67, 70, 76, 79, 81, 89, 94, 96, 97, 98, 103,
    109, 120, 166
Atzinger, Mario, 2, 3

Bakst, 87, 88
Bardot, Brigitte, 192
Barzini, 39
Bataille, Georges, 124
Bell, Clive, 98, 99, 135
Bellini, Jacobo, 52
Berdyaev, Nikolai, 76
Blasco, Carmen, 23
Bloch, Jeanne, 34
Boisgeloup, Château de, 127, 128, 129, 130,
    131, 138, 139, 149, 162
Braque, Georges, 3, 11, 56, 57-8, 60, 64, 69,
    72-3, 80, 83, 98, 100, 102, 103, 106, 107,
    114, 129, 215
Brassai, 9, 172, 215
Breton, André, 9, 11, 99, 103, 105, 107,
    108, 135, 159
Bridgman, Joan Olivia, 28
Brissen, Adolphe, 29

Cabanne, Pierre, 159
Cadone, 26
Cahiers d'Art, 114-15, 130, 135
Canals, 47
Capavila, Carles, 133, 134
Casagemas, Carlo, 27, 28, 29, 30, 31, 32, 36,
    37, 40, 108, 218
Casas, Ramon, 27
Cézanne, Paul, 2, 47, 52, 62, 82, 89, 205
Chagall, Marc, 2, 189
Chaplin, Charlie, 193
Clouzot, 201, 202
Cocola, Manuel Rodriguez, 27
Cocteau, Jean, 7, 85, 87, 88, 91, 93, 94, 109,
    111, 112, 172, 220
Collen, Ludwig, 76
Cone, Dr. Claribel, 79
Cone, Etta, 79
Coquiot, Gustave, 33, 45
Cortado, 32
Corot, Jean-Baptiste, 60, 62
Costales, Ramon Perez, 19, 20
Cuny, Alain, 169-70

Dali, Salvador, 2, 110, 133, 134, 202
David, Sylvette, 193
Degrain, Antonio Munoz, 15
Deharme, Lise, 148
Derain, 55, 59, 80, 99
Diaghilev, 7, 86, 87, 89, 93, 98, 101

Duran, Rouel, 146
Durio, Paul, 46, 47

Eluard, Paul, 9, 10, 78, 103, 105, 141, 143,
    145, 147, 154, 155, 156, 159, 167, 178,
    190, 195
Errazuria, Mme, 97

Franco, Francisco, 19
Fry, Roger, 62, 74, 75, 98, 99

Gauguin, Paul, 29, 76
Germaine, 30, 31, 32, 40, 54, 55, 56, 57, 68,
    70, 72, 108, 130, 174
Giacometti, Alberto, 109
Giacometti, Diego, 109
Gide, Andre, 187, 188
Gilot, Françoise, 3; and Picasso, 10-11, 124,
    125, 127, 136, 169 passim, and "life with
    Picasso", 211-12, 215; assessment of
    influence, 222
Gonzales, Sra Jesapha, 20, 21, 127, 128, 134
Gouel, Eva, 6-7, 68, 70-95, 130, 150, 181,
    197, 220
Gremnitz, 56, 57
Grigoriev, 93

Havill, Frank, 64
Hind, Lewis, 65
Hoeber, Arthur, 53
Hugnet, Georges, 120, 121
Hugue, Manolo, 47, 64, 131, 132, 196, 198
Humbert, Marcelle, *see* Gouel, Eva
Huntley, Carter, 65

Ignato, Marques de, 15
Iturrino, 37

Jacob, Max, 34, 36, 40, 43, 47, 50, 51, 52,
    54, 55, 56, 62, 64, 66, 67, 70, 71, 78, 79,
    82-3, 84, 85, 94, 102
Jarry, Alfred, 47
Jellinek, Sylvette, 197
Juner, Vidal, Carl, ??
Jung, Carl, 38
Junoy, Josep, 75

Kahnweiler, Daniel-Henry, 11, 51, 52, 57,
    62, 79, 80, 93, 100, 101, 128, 173, 189,
    198, 203, 204, 210
Keating, Tom, 222
Keynes, Maynard, 75, 99
Koklova, Olga, 7, 11, 93, 94; married to
    Picasso, 96-138; legal separation, 139,
    145, 174, 180, 181, 191, 197; death, 198

Laurincin, Marie, 56, 57, 60, 67, 71, 72, 78,
    86
Lazerme, Comtesse de, 198
Lindsay, Jack, 117
Llote, André, 159

ACKNOWLEDGEMENTS

Grateful acknowledgements are due to David Higham Associates for permission to reproduce some of Gertrude Stein's inimitable prose. Where it has proved impossible to contact other authors, newspapers and magazines (most of them deceased) acknowledgement is made in the text of the provenance of various comments.

Photographs in this book, and on its jacket, are reproduced courtesy of The Keystone Collection; The Lee Miller Archive; The Musée Picasso, Paris; The Museu Picasso, Barcelona.